Replays, Rivalries, and Rumbles

Replays, Rivalries, and Rumbles

The Most Iconic Moments in American Sports

EDITED BY STEVEN GIETSCHIER

**UNIVERSITY OF
ILLINOIS PRESS**
Urbana, Chicago, and Springfield

Cataloging data available from the Library of Congress
ISBN 978-0-252-04152-5 (cloth : alk.)
ISBN 978-0-252-08313-6 (paper : alk.)
ISBN 978-0-252-05014-5 (ebook)

Contents

Foreword

I am old enough that I saw the Brooklyn Dodgers play in Ebbets Field. My memory of these games is vivid. There were three of them, and the Dodgers won them all. Two were afternoon games, and one was a Friday night. Journeying to Ebbets Field was a big deal for our family, probably a once-a-year outing, so logic tells me that the games occurred in 1955, 1956, and 1957, after which season the Dodgers left town. Truth be told, the two afternoon games converge in my mind. What I remember beyond the hot dogs and soda is the Cincinnati Reds, 2–0, Sandy Koufax, and some sort of strikeout record. But were there two games like that? The night game is much clearer. The visiting team was the Milwaukee Braves. Hank Aaron hit a home run, but the Dodgers prevailed when Carl Furillo drove in the winning run in the bottom of the ninth. Of these things, I am sure. There's one problem, though. Some of what I remember—and some of what you've just read—is not true.

Individual memories of sporting events are, not surprisingly, no more reliable than any other memories. Some of what we remember is so, and some is not. But there's an additional problem with sporting events. They are overlaid with our desire to see something significant, to have been present at a "great moment." If we can say, "It was the first" or "the last" or "the biggest" or "the best," then our memory is made richer. Then, too, the temptation is great to embellish, to inflate our memories, to remember what really didn't happen just because we were there. Sandy Koufax? Strikeout record? Walk-off win? Maybe.

Collective memory, that is, what the universe of sports fans remembers, behaves in much the same way. We remember, but we exaggerate, and we simplify, and in the process, we distort. British historian Stephen Wagg explored this phenomenon. He argued, first of all, that the great events, the ones we collectively define as important, are often complex, much more intricate than we want to remember them. Our memory tells us black and white, but reality displays shades of gray. Did Abner Doubleday "invent" baseball? It's complicated. Have American Olympians always refused to dip the "Stars and Stripes" during the Parade of Nations? Likewise.

Wagg argued further that key events in sports history have become mythic, that is, made untouchable in some way and placed beyond critical discussion. Was Walter O'Malley the villain in the Dodgers' move to Los Angeles? Of course. Was the 1958 National Football League championship game the greatest ever played? Certainly. In other words, "Don't confuse me. My mind is already made up." Finally, Wagg argued that iconic moments in sports history often involve athletes and coaches who themselves are generally revered as great. Did Babe Ruth call his shot? Well, he was Babe Ruth, wasn't he? Did the 1979 NCAA championship game matching Magic versus Bird redefine college basketball? Without a doubt. But maybe not.

To all of the myths and the overstatements and the downright distortions, this book offers a gentle corrective. In it, twenty-three historians, all of whom write and teach about sports at American colleges and universities, scrape away the barnacles that have attached themselves to some of America's most famous athletes and sporting events. Each author has devoted years of research to the topics at hand. Each is intimately familiar with the crust that has encumbered our ability to understand what really happened. And each author believes that truth is more fascinating than fiction!

Think of the tales examined here as the zombies of American sport history, always ready to spring back to life. We hope you will enjoy our authors' attempts to use their scholarly knowledge as the ultimate weapon and to render these mythic corpses motionless—and truly dead—once and for all.

Now about those games at Ebbets Field. Modern research tools sometimes allow us to check our memories, and it appears I saw two games at Ebbets, but maybe not three. Koufax really did beat the Reds. The date was August 27, 1955. The score was 7–0, not 2–0. Koufax gave up only two hits and struck out fourteen, but it was no record, just the season high for National League pitchers. It was also his first major league victory. The night game also really happened. The date was August 23, 1957, and the Dodgers beat the Braves, 3–2. Aaron did hit a homer, and he drove in the other Milwaukee run as well. The Dodgers not only scored the winning run in the bottom of the ninth, they scored all three runs in the bottom of the ninth. But it was Gino Cimoli who drove in Furillo to send us home happy. So my memories are pretty good, but far from perfect. As for that elusive third game, well, who knows?

1

Abner Doubleday and the "Invention" of Baseball

THOMAS L. ALTHERR

Ten or fifteen years ago, most serious baseball historians subscribed to the line that Abner Doubleday did not invent baseball in Cooperstown in 1839, that such a claim was the product of spurious evidence from a quasi-demented mining engineer named Abner Graves and the jingoistic crusade of Albert Spalding to revel in baseball's "American" origins. Indeed, around that time, I composed a short encyclopedia entry, the gist of which went, in paraphrase:

> One of the most bedrock and celebrated myths in sports is that Abner Dou-
> bleday invented baseball. In 1889, allegedly following a friendly dispute with
> New York City sportswriter Henry Chadwick over a claim that baseball has its
> roots in the British game of rounders, baseball player-manager and sporting
> goods magnate Albert Spalding set up a commission that launched a nearly
> twenty-year campaign to establish indisputably that baseball was an American
> invention. After years of collecting evidence that proved no such American
> origin, Spalding and Abraham Mills, the rather reluctant commission chair,
> seized on testimony in 1905 from one Abner Graves that Graves himself had
> witnessed the Cooperstown creation and Doubleday's display of genius as
> a boy from the nearby hamlet of Fly Creek. Emboldened by Graves's asser-
> tions, the Mills Commission anointed Abner Doubleday as the creator of the
> National Pastime.

According to this long-cherished version, Doubleday, a West Point cadet, home for the summer in Cooperstown in June 1839, gathered a group of boys from local academies in Elihu Phinney's pasture, drew up the rules, and laid out the ball field for the first baseball game. For Spalding and many other

Abner Doubleday, Civil War general, but did he invent baseball? (Brady-Handy Photograph Collection, Library of Congress.)

American patriots and Anglophobes, this "Immaculate Conception" myth tidied up the nagging suggestions that baseball had derived from European games along a circuitous path. Toss in the fact that Doubleday became a bona fide Union Army Civil War hero, at Fort Sumter as well as at Gettysburg, and the ingredients calcified into an unshakable mix of myth.

Baseball historians and other scholars began discrediting this story as early as 1938, the year before the Baseball Hall of Fame opened its doors in Cooperstown. Robert Henderson, a librarian at the New York Public Library, launched the first salvo with some "Notes on Rounders," descriptions of all sorts of European ball games (and a few American ones) preceding baseball, and compiled this evidence into a 1947 book, *Ball, Bat, and Bishop*.

Other historians centered their critique on Doubleday's surmised role as inventor. The major arguments against it focused on Doubleday's absence from Cooperstown in 1839, his exemplary attendance at West Point that year, the fact that until his death in 1893 he himself never claimed to have invented the game, even in his autobiography, and the increasing number of discoveries by Henderson and others that bat-and-ball games had long antedated the hallowed date. Indeed, in 1816, Cooperstown itself had en-acted an ordinance against ball play in the streets. How remarkably pre-scient of the village fathers to prohibit a game that would not be invented until twenty-three years later!

Then there was the matter of Abner Graves, a quirky character to say the least, whose checkered past and inconsistencies hardly inspired credibility. How convenient that he held on to not only his memory but the very ball from that first game! As cynical Catholics and non-Catholics alike are wont to point out, there are enough pieces of the "true" cross on altars across the world to construct another Notre Dame cathedral. Hardly a choirboy, Graves had left a long trail of shady investments and failed mining ventures. Later, in the 1920s, he married a woman quite his junior and then killed her dur-ing a marital dispute. Saved from execution by an insanity defense, Graves spent his waning years in a mental institution.

Yet a few supporters of the Doubleday creation story persist, even today. They maintain that Graves remembered the year wrong, that Abner, the young cadet, was in and out of town in years before and after 1839. Some argue that there was another Abner Doubleday who Graves mixed up with the future famous military leader. Yet others hold out hope that more evi-dence will surface to lock in the nationalist pedigree. Several members of the extensive Doubleday clan cling loyally to the legend, even to the point of occasionally sending a hate letter to anyone who may dare impugn their beliefs. For its part, the Hall of Fame acknowledges the substantial skepti-cism about Graves's evidence but still exhibits the ball Graves alleged he kept from that supposedly historic 1839 event. And as one waggish Hall of Fame official declared, "Well, maybe baseball wasn't invented in Cooperstown, but it should have been!"

As I now revisit the same topic after years of study, I find myself retreating from categorical statements. So much new research about the early phases of baseball and ball play history has appeared in the past ten or fifteen years that I hesitate to close the case on the whole Doubleday episode. One of the first things my dissertation advisor at Ohio State said in our first historiography seminar many years ago still rings in my ears: "Historians should never say 'never.'" Although I retired from teaching a couple of years ago, I spent the better part of my career counseling students to be wary of rushes to judg-ment, that just when they thought the answer was clear, some historian or two, evil creatures to be sure, would discover new evidence, reinterpret old evidence, or apply some new diagnostic tool. That third possibility may not figure in here unless we exhume Doubleday and find some baseball gene in his body, but it is more than likely that new evidence and reinterpreted older evidence will continue to muddy this intellectual fray.

In 2005, David Block published a monumental book on the roots of baseball, *Baseball before We Knew It.* As he developed a new interpretation, Block checked out the hoary assumption that baseball had derived from rounders and found little evidence to support Chadwick's claim. Spalding may not have cared either way, but even today too many baseball historians adhere like lemmings to the rounders theory. Block was skeptical. Essentially, he asked, "If not rounders, then what?" and he pitched us back to some drawing board, some proverbial square one. In 2009, Monica Nucciarone demolished claims that Alexander Joy Cartwright, a member of the Knickerbocker Base Ball Club, was "the father of baseball." She demonstrated that Cartwright's interest in baseball was transitory at best, that the assertion he spread baseball westward to California was based on fraudulent reediting of Cartwright's diaries by his grandson, and that Cartwright, once out in Hawaii, evinced much more interest in firefighting companies and American annexation of those islands than baseball. Following Nucciarone, John Thorn published *Baseball in the Garden of Eden* (2011), in which he challenged much of what we thought we knew about early baseball. Down went the assumed importance of the Knickerbockers. Up went an array of new finds, including a 1791 town ordinance prohibiting baseball in Pittsfield, Massachusetts, and new evidence that other New York clubs predated the Knickerbockers and played games in the 1830s. My own research on pre-1845 ball games (not only baseball, but anything played with a ball or similar projectile), which awaits publication, resulted in two awards from SABR, the Society for American Baseball Research, and also helped break new ground.

Possibly the most ambitious record of research on early baseball has been the Protoball Project, the brainchild of Larry McCray, who teaches at the Massachusetts Institute of Technology. For more than ten years, McCray has logged digitally thousands of references to baseball and similar games, all the way from ancient times to 1870. Just the most cursory view of the Protoball Web site (www.protoball.org) will amaze any historian or researcher just how extensively ball games figured into humans' play and ritual repertoire long before Doubleday. Another fertile source for pre-1839 baseball history is the periodical, *Base Ball: A Journal of the Early Game.* Many essays published therein concern later years, but others, especially those edited by McCray for the Spring 2011 special issue on origins, attest to the frenetic pace of research and publication about the earlier periods.

In 2013, two books tossed the verdict up for grabs one more time. The first, *Baseball's Creation Myth: Adam Ford, Abner Graves and the Cooperstown*

Story, by Brian "Chip" Martin, substantially re-researched the Doubleday/ Graves episode. Martin performed the most exhaustive search for new information, spending much time in archives in Denver, Iowa, and South Dakota, read newspapers and manuscript collections, consulted local historians, and constantly broadened the scope of his investigations. Graves came up for respectful reconsideration as Martin gained access to Masonic Temple records that rehabilitate Graves's reputation, at least somewhat.

Moreover, Martin became intrigued with possible connections between Graves and Adam Ford, a Denver-based physician, who had grown up and trained for the medical profession in Ontario, Canada. In April 1886, for reasons still not clear, Ford wrote a letter to *Sporting Life,* a weekly devoted to baseball, and gave a thorough rendition of a baseball game he witnessed played in his hometown of Beachville, Ontario, on June 4, 1838. Although Doubleday's coronation as creator was years away, Canadian baseball enthusiasts later celebrated this game as predating Cooperstown's by more than a year. Martin maintained that because Graves and Ford traveled in many of the same circles in Denver, Graves would have most likely heard Ford's story and maybe felt prompted to tell his own about Doubleday.

But just when the story seemed more complex than ever, another 2013 book, *The Farmer's Game,* by David Vaught, stirred the pot even more. In this work, ostensibly about baseball in rural places out West, the Midwest (Iowa and Minnesota) and back East (North Carolina), Vaught tucked in a chapter on dear old Otsego County, New York, where Cooperstown is situated. While Vaught didn't prove Abner Doubleday invented the game, he made a strong case for reexamining Graves's testimony. Vaught dredged up hitherto overlooked information about Doubleday's progenitors in the Cooperstown region. He especially singled out Seth Doubleday, somewhat renowned for playing town ball, a baseball ancestor, in the area in the late eighteenth century.

Vaught also described Cooperstown as a village fraught with class tensions and generational anxieties. For example, the 1816 ban on ball play, according to Vaught, resulted less from trepidation about property damage than from fears of the old Federalist-leaning elite that they were losing power to a new generation of Jeffersonian Republicans far less propertied and concerned with order. Ball play, baseball, or some similar game, threatened not only windows but social proprieties. Vaught then brilliantly pushed the comparison ahead in time to the 1830s and 1840s and showed how these clashes persisted in the writings of James Fenimore Cooper, son of William Cooper, one of the town's Federalist founders. If Abner Doubleday did anything in 1839, it happened within the context of this visible social turmoil.

So where do we stand? What further questions beckon us? One thing we can categorically state is that whatever the young West Point cadet did or didn't do in 1839 in Cooperstown, he did *not* "invent" baseball. No one invented baseball. Unlike basketball's attempts to give sole credit to James Naismith for his 1891 version, and some weaker claims that Amos Alonzo Stagg created football, baseball grew topsy-turvy from an evolutionary tree—sorry, creationists—of a variety of predecessor, competing, isolated, or now-lost games. Further research may elevate one or more of these games to special status as the likely progenitor(s) of baseball or, just as likely, leave us awash in a dazzling array of possibilities. My own wild speculation with no more evidence than gut feelings is that baseball historians, no longer tethered to the British origins, may locate the origins of baseball, along with einkorn agriculture and certain forms of social organization, in what is now Iran, Afghanistan, and/or Kazakhstan.

But back to the Doubleday controversy. If he did draw up some rules and playing dimensions, shouldn't he receive due congratulations and Abner Graves some vindication? To the point critics level that Doubleday never claimed any credit, perhaps he knew that his game was not the only one, so why celebrate something not unique? As a cadet at West Point, he surely studied mathematics, engineering, and surveying. The raucous chaos and inefficiency of town ball may have offended his own search for precision, and he slapped a temporary application of such on the boys' game. Already demonstrating the leadership abilities that would carry him through the Civil War, Doubleday may have commanded respect and admiration from boys eager to obey his directions.

Regarding other criticisms, such as his failure to mention baseball in his autobiography, perhaps we should step back. In his autobiography and other Civil War writings, Abner discussed virtually nothing of his childhood, adolescence, or pre–Civil War experiences. Perhaps lost manuscripts about his younger days still exist, but until they surface, why require Doubleday to write on matters other than military?

Additionally, historians should pay closer attention to his post–Civil War life. Doubleday retired from military duty in San Francisco, moved to Texas in 1873 and then New York City, and listed himself as a lawyer. By 1878, however, he had moved to New Jersey and became immersed in theosophy, a strain of spiritualism, eventually becoming president of the American Theosophical Society. Would his spiritualist beliefs have precluded interest in baseball as too worldly, something separate from the true path? Or, as an adult, a Civil War hero, did he see baseball as just a boys' game, unworthy of his manly bearing and regard?

And what of baseball itself during those years? Admittedly, the organized major leagues had rebounded from the National Association days and the initial missteps of the National League. The arrival of the American Association in 1882 had invigorated rivalries. But by Doubleday's last years, major league baseball was on the brink of the doldrums era. The Players' League fiasco of 1890 had brought down the American Association and left the National League weakened. As a New Yorker, Doubleday may have found little to cheer about as Boston, Baltimore, and Brooklyn (a separate city from Manhattan then) carried off all the Temple Cup trophies during the decade. New York teams were mediocre. Maybe Doubleday, probably a staunch moralist, was embarrassed by baseball's unsavory connections to gambling, alcohol, and prostitution. Perhaps the immigrant-filled team rosters awakened in him some nativism akin to that of the Know-Nothings of the 1850s.

One of the key players in the Doubleday drama still deserves more scrutiny, namely, Albert Goodwill Spalding. First, given his nationalist/jingoist bent and his personal feud with Chadwick, why did Spalding pursue his crusade to establish baseball as an American game so passionately? Were there other motives? Did Spalding organize the argument at first as a stunt, a promotional gimmick to stimulate public interest in baseball and thus increase the bottom line of his sporting goods business? Did he then feel himself trapped by his own rhetoric? Did he dig in his heels when the first committee findings illustrated non-American origins? How much did he badger Abraham Mills into buying the Graves story? Was he one of the great American showmen, such as P. T. Barnum in an earlier generation, seizing on and manipulating spectacle for all its crowd-pleasing worth?

Second, patriotism certainly played a role in Spalding's efforts, and Anglophobia was not difficult to spot in those decades, but there may have been a deeper personal desire. The dinner at Delmonico's welcoming Spalding and the Chicago White Stockings home from their 1888–1889 world tour was definitely a bash of hoopla and braggadocio. But even Spalding understood that the tour did not spread baseball to such British Empire countries as Australia and Egypt, let alone Great Britain. Spalding's entourage undoubtedly, maybe even unwittingly, acted as cultural ambassadors of American imperialism, as Thomas Zeiler described in his book about the tour. But for Spalding, any shorter-term hopes of baseball flourishing around the globe were dashed. Did Spalding then disavow British origins evidence as part of a revenge campaign against the Britons?

Third, maybe we had better take another look as Spalding's own embrace of theosophy by 1900, even to the extent of his moving to California to join a community there. Was this a coincidence, or did Abner Doubleday's own involvement with that variety of esoteric spiritualism somehow intrigue Spalding? During this period, Spalding oversaw the consolidation of the Doubleday creation story, published his own large history of the game, *Base Ball: America's National Game,* and remained an enthusiastic champion and ferocious defender of the Mills Commission report. Yet he subscribed to a belief system that sought an underlying, connective truth in the universe. As Casey Stengel once wondered, "Who would have thunk it?"

On the subject of belief systems, have we scoured all the evidence available in Masonic archives? Thanks to Jim Brown, one of my former students and a great friend, author Brian Martin gained unprecedented access to Masonic archives in Denver. But Brown, who had a flair for the conspiratorial, confided to me when he read Martin's book that either the author had chosen to leave certain items out, or there was more to look at. Jim was a Mason, and he promised me he could either research the matter more himself or secure entrée for me. Our schedules did not triangulate with the Masonic librarian soon enough, and in July 2014, Brown died unexpectedly. As I am not a Mason, I have little hope of access. Perhaps some historian with Masonic credentials will take this cue to heart and action.

Last, here is something of a wish list. The Doubleday story may continue to befuddle historians or even get murkier, but we can approach related topics with more vigor. If, as David Block discovered, the German Johann Christoph Gutsmuths included a four-page description of *Das Englische Baseball* in his compilation of European sports and games extant in the 1790s, let's look assiduously for similar texts in whatever language. If, as Thorn reported, Pittsfield banned baseball in 1791, let's plunge into the tedious work of scavenging through town histories, bylaws, and other archival materials stored in a multitude of places in a multitude of towns. If Seth Doubleday, Abner's relative, was an avid town ball player in the 1780s and 1790s, let's ransack genealogical records not only about the Doubleday family but allied branches, and other residents of Otsego County. If Americans, taken prisoner during the War of 1812, were playing ball when British troops at Dartmoor Prison gunned them down in 1815, let's investigate every avenue of that horror. If, as later New York politician Thurlow Weed remembered, he and some other gents playing baseball a couple of afternoons a week in Rochester in 1825, let's track down who those gents were and look into their later careers and connections. If a game of "bass-ball" took place that same year, 1825, in Delhi, New York, a hamlet near Cooperstown, let's be alert to the possibility of other games in newspapers, ephemera, and manuscripts.

See you at the archives!

For Further Reading

Block, David. *Baseball before We Knew It: A Search for the Roots of the Game*. Lincoln: University of Nebraska Press, 2005.

Martin, Brian. *Baseball's Creation Myth: Adam Ford, Abner Graves and the Cooperstown Story*. Jefferson, N.C.: McFarland, 2013.

Thorn, John. *Baseball in the Garden of Eden: The Secret History of the Early Game*. New York: Simon and Schuster, 2011.

Vaught, David. *The Farmer's Game: Baseball in Rural America*. Baltimore: Johns Hopkins University Press, 2013.

2

The "Stars and Stripes" at the Olympic Games

MARK DYRESON

On the night before the Opening Ceremony at the 1992 Olympic Winter Games in Albertville, France, American cross-country skier Bill Koch attempted to sleep. Sixteen years earlier in Innsbruck, Austria, Koch became the first Nordic skier from the United States to win an Olympic medal when he finished second in the 30-kilometer race. That silver medal made Koch an iconoclastic hero in his home nation—a quirky individualist pursuing a sport embraced in the Nordic world but ignored by the American masses. After his stunning Olympic performance in 1976, Koch crafted a solid international career in Nordic racing, but he never again approached the medal stand at the Olympics. As the American media favorite at the 1980 games in Lake Placid, New York, Koch finished out of medal contention, his endurance sapped by asthma. In 1984, he again finished far behind the leaders in Sarajevo. When he failed to make the U.S. team for Calgary in 1988, his Olympic career seemed over.

In the early 1990s Koch staged a memorable comeback and earned a spot on the 1992 squad, his fourth Olympic berth. His teammates honored his perseverance as well as his breakthrough as the first American to cross-country ski at a world-class level by electing Koch to carry the American flag in the Parade of Nations. Ever the nonconformist, Koch pondered breaking with a longstanding American tradition and submitting to Olympic protocol by lowering the "Stars and Stripes" as he passed in review before the French president. At a press conference on the morning of the Opening Ceremony, Koch told the press what he was planning to do with the flag. "We're the strongest nation on earth," he said. "We want to be good world citizens. A dip demonstrates a little humility."

Koch's musings about breaking with American Olympic tradition ignited a media firestorm. U.S. Olympic officials insisted that they told Koch he had no choice in the matter and that he must not dip the flag. The American media pointed out that for more than eight decades, since the very first Olympic Parade of Nations in 1908 at the London games, American teams had followed a national custom and refused to lower the "Stars and Stripes" before foreign leaders. That night, the American television audience watched the parade unfold, wondering whether or not Koch would dip the flag. CBS, the network covering the games, perhaps fearing that a break with custom would provoke a jingoistic furor at home, cut away to commercial as Koch approached French President Francois Mitterrand in the official box. While an advertisement played on U.S. airwaves blocking the live feed, Koch decided to maintain the sacred American ritual of refusing to dip. Afterward he told the press that while he did not necessarily agree with continuing the tradition, he had deferred to the wishes of his teammates.

In 1936 another American cross-country skier, Rolf Monsen, had carried the American flag at an Olympic Opening Ceremony under very different circumstances. Monsen, a Norwegian immigrant, carried the "Stars and Stripes" proudly aloft in the parade at the Bavarian Alpine towns of Garmisch-Partenkirchen, refusing to dip it before Adolf Hitler at the start of the winter games. German spectators and the German press groused that Monsen's actions amounted to a deliberate snub of Chancellor Hitler, while many in the United States cheered Monsen's refusal to kowtow to the dictator.

In the *New York Times*, sportswriter Arthur J. Daley, who would become the most popular, if not the most accurate, historian of American flag behavior at the games, offered a different explanation for Monsen's gesture. Daley asserted that Monsen and the Americans intended no disrespect toward Hitler or Germany. Instead, the Norwegian immigrant proudly continued an American tradition of refusing to dip the "Stars and Stripes" at the Olympics, a tradition that had begun at London in 1908. Daley recalled that the U.S. flag-bearer in London, a weight-thrower from California named Ralph Rose, had marched past King Edward VII without lowering the American flag, thereby subverting IOC protocol. Daley assigned to Rose a nationalistic—but not an entirely American—motive for the controversy. The evening before the parade, a contingent of "Irish Whales," as the immigrant strongmen from New York City's Irish-American Athletic Club (IAAC) who dominated field events such as the shot put, hammer throw, and discus were known, threatened to pummel the 6′6″, 250-pound Rose if he dared to lower the U.S. flag before the English king. Daley declared that Rose's desire to escape a beating from the "Irish Whales" began the custom of refusing to dip the "Stars and Stripes" at the Olympics—a custom Monsen had continued with Hitler. Daley contended that the gesture had nothing to do with American distaste for Adolf Hitler and the Third Reich.

Daley, who in 1956 became just the third American sportswriter to win a Pulitzer Prize and who from his perch atop the sports page of the nation's leading daily newspaper shaped opinion for more than half-a-century, was fundamentally wrong about two important elements of his story. American distaste for Hitler and the Nazis had in fact a great deal to do with the U.S. refusal to dip the flag to Hitler at Garmisch-Partenkirchen and in Berlin at the summer games later that year. A strong protest movement to boycott the "Nazi Olympics" and oppose a variety of German racial, religious, and political policies came very close to keeping the American team at home. The boycott issue deeply divided American Olympic leadership, and even supporters of sending the team expressed anxieties about participating in any international endeavor with Nazi Germany. Other American correspondents in Germany reported that anti-Nazi sentiments played an important role in Monsen's refusal to dip the flag, a crucial fact Daley missed.

Ralph Rose at the 1912 Summer Olympics. (Official Olympic Report.)

Daley's second error was his claim that ever since Rose's refusal to dip the "Stars and Stripes" in London, the United States has adhered to this convention without fail. The U.S. refrained from dipping in 1908 but from that date until 1936, American flag-bearers sporadically dipped and did not dip. The U.S. flag-bearer lowered the flag to the Swedish king in 1912 at Stockholm. After an interruption in the Olympic quadrennial for the Great War, American flag-bearers refused to dip the flag to Belgian leaders in Antwerp in 1920, but then they decided to dip the flag to French officials at Paris in 1924. These two decisions were even more mysterious considering the same person served as flag-bearer in both parades. Patrick McDonald, one of the "Irish Whales" who in 1908 had been a member of the posse that allegedly threatened Rose with a beating if Rose dipped, refused to dip to the Belgians but lowered the American flag for the French.

In 1928 the American Olympic team, commanded by General Douglas MacArthur on leave from his military post to burnish his credentials for future political ambitions, refused to dip the flag to Dutch leaders in Amsterdam. MacArthur insisted on following U.S. military flag protocol, which dictated that soldiers not dip the "Stars and Stripes" to anyone, not even to the commander in chief, the president of the United States. In 1932, with MacArthur back at his army post, American flag-bearers ignored military standards and dipped the flag, first at Lake Placid to New York Governor Franklin Roosevelt and then at Los Angeles to U.S. Vice President Charles Curtis. Daley thus had no valid excuse for claiming in 1936 an unbroken lineage for American refusals to dip. In 1932 as the lead Olympic correspondent for the *New York Times,* he had watched the Parade of Nations from the press box in the Los Angeles Coliseum as Morgan Taylor, the American flag-bearer, lowered the "Stars and Stripes" to Curtis.

Since 1936 U.S. flag-bearers have unswervingly held the "Stars and Stripes" high and defied International Olympic Committee regulations at Olympic parades. An increasingly elaborate mythology, much of it spun by Arthur Daley in a series of Olympic histories, evolved to justify this American practice. The refusal to lower the "Stars and Stripes" in Nazi Germany clearly represented a dramatic act of political theater and not the mere replication of a venerated tradition. Daley and the rest of the American press, however, glossed over that story and instead linked American flag behavior to an older and more sanitized protest against despotism, an Irish American gesture of defiance toward an English king in London in 1908. "Shades of Brian Boru and George Washington" exclaimed Daley in one of his *New York Times* columns, simultaneously evoking icons of both Irish and American resistance to British imperialism. Since that original protest, Daley and his followers insisted, U.S. flag-bearers had unceasingly repeated the refusal to dip until it became a harmless tradition, a mere national habit that did not express any sentiments about the regimes that hosted the Olympics. Daley pushed that notion vociferously in 1948 when the Olympics returned to London and an American flag-bearer again marched past an English king, reassuring British allies that no affront was intended and that the refusal to dip was merely a quirky if hallowed American habit. For Daley, who was born in New York City in 1904 and grew up in the Irish Catholic community venerating the "Irish Whales" and their athletic kin, this particular fable fit his ethnic and political sensibilities.

The inescapable murkiness surrounding the origins of the tradition allowed Daley to spin his later justifications of the habit. While Daley got some major facts wrong, in all probability he rendered the sentiments of the tale accurately. Amazing as it seems to a twenty-first century audience that inhabits a world in which the media records every minute detail of each Olympic games not only in thousands of print narratives but also in high-definition digital depictions, records of earlier modern Olympics leave many details obscured in the unrecorded mists of the past. Still photographs and even a few moving pictures of the 1908 London Olympics survive, but a photographic record of the moment at which Ralph Rose refused to dip the "Stars and Stripes" to the English king has yet to be discovered. Contemporary accounts and later chronicles, differing in many key aspects, also fail to provide resolute clarity.

A few eyewitnesses to the 1908 Parade of Nations mention that the American flag-bearer dipped the "Stars and Stripes," but most accounts insist that he did not lower the banner. Different writers even provide multiple identities for the flag-bearer, not only Rose but also some of the "Irish Whales" themselves. Later chroniclers asserted that the flag-bearer or one of his comrades not only refused to dip the flag but shouted in defiance at the English monarch that "this flag dips for no earthly king." Such a dramatic oath seemingly would have captured the attention of the droves of reporters covering the Olympics, but even a brief mention of any such utterance is universally absent from stories written at the time. Sifting through multiple accounts, the best a historian can offer is that it seems relatively certain that the American flag-bearer was Ralph Rose, that in all probability he did not dip the flag to King Edward VII, and that the gesture was unaccompanied by any shout or explanation.

Reconstructing a motive from the existing historical record is even more difficult than establishing basic details. None of the athletes involved in the flag-dipping controversy in London left an explanation to justify his actions.

The Parade of Nations now so familiar to Olympic audiences was in 1908 brand new. The IOC had requested that the national teams dip their flags to the British officials in accordance with well-established diplomatic customs. Whether Rose simply forgot those instructions or whether he deliberately held the "Stars and Stripes" aloft remains uncertain. Martin Sheridan, one of the "Irish Whales" who won two gold medals and one bronze medal in London, filed stories for the *Chicago Record Herald* on the 1908 Olympics and confirmed that Rose did not dip the flag—like Rose, Sheridan failed to shed any public light on a rationale.

The British press covering the Olympics did not even bother to mention the flag-dipping incident, a stunning surprise as "Fleet Street" covered the Anglo-American animosity in the stadium and in the stands that suffused the 1908 Olympics. The American press covered the story, but opinion on the "snub" was deeply divided. Some American reporters cheered Rose's combative gesture as an appropriate response to British rancor toward the American team, citing a long train of questionable decisions by British umpires and boorish behavior by British spectators. Most of the American media, however, decried Rose's actions. Several correspondents mentioned Rose's reputation as an immature hothead who regularly engaged in indecorous hijinks. They blamed U.S. Olympic officials for trusting a well-known miscreant with flag-bearer responsibilities. Others observed that the act was not simply a defiant gesture by Rose but clearly a plan hatched by some of his teammates as well, given the hearty congratulations Rose received from his American mates after the parade. No contemporary account mentioned any hint of an Irish component to the fracas, a development that became a central explanation for the affair only in later retellings. Instead, reporters linked Rose's refusal to American nationalism, mentioning the "Spirit of '76" and other manifestations of American identity making in their break from Great Britain's imperial grasp. In the *Washington Post,* Ed Grillo decried the refusal to dip the American flag as sign of rabid and regrettable jingoism. "What if the games had been held in this country and some foreign athlete had refused to salute our President? Isn't it a good guess that a free-for-all fight would have resulted?" Grillo queried. "Every true American will deplore this exhibition of indecency and failure to observe the rules of good behavior," the reporter concluded, predicting an American flag-bearer would never again repeat Rose's performance. Whatever motivated Rose for doing what he did followed him to an early grave. When he died in 1913 from typhoid fever, his eulogists prominently mentioned his refusal to lower the "Stars and Stripes" in his obituaries.

The impossible task of expressing the sentiments of "every true American" has fallen to U.S. flag-bearers ever since Ralph Rose's original act. In 1936 the on-again, off-again custom hardened into a permanent tradition as a protest against the Nazi regime. Jesse Owens, the quadruple gold medal star of the Berlin games, proudly recalled the protest in a later documentary film about his exploits, proclaiming, inaccurately, that the United States was the only nation that refused to lower its banner to Hitler. In fact, a curious coalition of Bulgaria (a future Axis member), Iceland, and India joined the Americans in refusing to lower their national standards.

Since 1936, a few American athletes have considered breaking with tradition to convey a variety of sentiments, from international solidarity to opposition to war. Most famously, the 1956 Olympic hammer-throw champion and peace activist Harold Connolly campaigned for the flag-bearer position at the 1968 Mexico City Olympics by promising to dip as a gesture of international harmony and a sign of his solidarity with protests against racism at home and abroad. U.S. Olympic officials declined Connolly's offer. After those same officials booted John Carlos and Tommie Smith from the American team for their black-gloved medal-stand protests of racism as an unacceptable intrusion of sport into politics, supporters of the banished athletes decried the hypocrisy of allowing "official" political expressions by refusing to dip the flag while sanctioning black Olympians for exercising their free speech rights. At the 1972 summer Olympics in Munich, many thought that American flag-bearer Olga Fikotova Connolly would surely dip. A 1956 gold medalist in the discus for Czechoslovakia, she had engaged in the most famous romance in Olympic history, meeting and a year later marrying fellow Olympic champion Harold Connolly. Their Cold War fairy tale warmed hearts around the globe, and when the Olympians of her new nation elected her to carry the "Stars and Stripes" in Germany, it burnished the romantic allure of their story—though no amount of burnishing would prevent the couple from divorcing a year later. Connolly, who shared her husband's views on flag-dipping, surprised prognosticators and refused to break with tradition. She told the press afterward that she refused to lower the national standard in deference to the wishes of her American teammates and the American public.

In the decades since 1936, American athletes, officials, journalists, and fans have pondered the U.S. flag-dipping tradition and wondered if it should continue. On a stage where billions watch the Parade of Nations, flag symbolism carries powerful meanings. While many Americans, following Jesse Owens, assume that only the United States refuses to dip the flag, the practice is not unique. From the Soviet Union's entry into the Olympic movement in the 1950s through the dissolution of the Soviet state in the 1990s, flag-bearers from the U.S.S.R. refused to dip. Though Soviets articulated a different history and rationale for their actions, their imitation of American habits ironically earned the wrath of many American commentators who condemned this insertion of "politics" into the Olympics by Soviet athletes, while at the very same moment explaining American behavior as quaint custom entirely devoid of political sentiments.

Confusion over the complex history of the American refusal to dip the flag endures. What began as a seemingly sharp rebuke of King Edward VII and the United Kingdom a few years before World War I and solidified with a seemingly overt condemnation of Adolf Hitler and the Third Reich on the eve of World War II has evolved into a custom that allegedly has little to do with the host nation and represents a broader expression of American exceptionalism. Though many of the details about the original perpetrators are lost, it seems clear that athletes and not governmental policy makers nor Olympic administrators created the practice. Although U.S. Olympic officials are currently committed to continuing the tradition while International Olympic Committee leaders would like to see it disappear, the flag-bearer and the Olympians who select her or him for that honor continue to hold ultimate power over whether or not the "Stars and Stripes" dip. As to my own sentiments, I admit to sympathies with both sides. As for predictions on how long the tradition will continue, I will play the old historian's card. My efforts to try to see the past more clearly leave my eyes pointed in the wrong direction to predict the future. Of one thing, though, I am certain. The *Washington Post*'s correspondent in 1908 was absolutely correct in the aftermath of the very first Olympic parade that how the American flag is handled before the eyes of the world in Olympic parades requires an effort to calculate the sentiments of "every true American." Such arithmetic is always essentially political.

For Further Reading

Dyreson, Mark. *Crafting Patriotism for Global Domination: America at the Olympic Games*. London: Routledge, 2009.

———. *Making the American Team: Sport, Culture and the Olympic Experience*. Urbana: University of Illinois Press, 1998.

Llewellyn, Matthew P. *Rule Britannia: Sport and Nationalism, Identity, and the Modern Olympic Games*. London: Routledge, 2012.

3

The Black Sox Scandal Redux

DANIEL A. NATHAN

Many years ago, historian Carl Becker argued, "in order to understand the essential nature of anything it is well to strip it of all superficial and irrelevant accretions—in short, to reduce it to its lowest terms." This makes sense to me. We will add complexity and nuance to the Black Sox scandal later. For now, this version of the event should suffice as a refresher for those who know about the scandal and as an introduction for those who do not.

In 1919, some veteran, talented baseball players on the Chicago White Sox conspired with gamblers, taking money to play poorly and intentionally lose the World Series to the Cincinnati Reds. As a result, the underdog Reds won the best-of-nine-game series, five games to three. Almost a year later, the ballplayers' perfidy was discovered and revealed to the public. Nationwide, many people—especially baseball fans and some members of the media— were upset by the news. They felt duped and betrayed. Some were hurt and disillusioned. This event quickly became known as the Black Sox scandal. In 1920, a Cook County, Illinois, grand jury indicted eight White Sox and five small-time gamblers on a variety of conspiracy charges. The indicted men were put on trial in July 1921. Despite the fact that some of the ballplayers had testified before the grand jury that they had taken money to "fix" the Series, they were all acquitted, due in part to the complicated nature of the charges against them. Many people in Chicago cheered when the accused White Sox were legally exonerated. Nonetheless, the newly hired baseball commissioner, Kenesaw Mountain Landis, a federal judge, banned them from the major leagues. In the short run, Major League Baseball's reputation was damaged by this event, but the game survived and soon thereafter thrived.

"Fix These Faces in Your Memory." (*Sporting News.*)

All these years later, the Black Sox scandal has not faded into obscurity. Far from it. The infamous fixed World Series has been remembered and retold countless times in myriad mediums for almost a hundred years. It has retained its cultural resonance and relevance. Why? There are several reasons.

For one, contemporary events—including all manner of cheating and sports scandals, from Pete Rose to BALCO to Lance Armstrong—often resurrect or reinvigorate Black Sox narratives and memories. Here are a few examples. In 2003, when the Major League Baseball steroid abuse scandal was becoming public, sports columnist Filip Bondy argued, "This is the lowest moment in baseball since the Black Sox threw the Series. Maybe lower." A few years later, Bob Eckstein drew a clever series of cartoons for the *New York Times*. One of the images featured a basketball player shooting a free throw, a referee at his side, and was accompanied with the caption: "Gambling allegations involving a N.B.A. referee may be the biggest sports disgrace since the Black Sox scandal of 1919." In September 2013, a NASCAR team manipulated a race by having its drivers do less than their best. Among the many losers in this incident, mused motorsports writer Nate Ryan, was "NASCAR and its credibility among mainstream sports fans and media who might have been curious about how the sport would handle its own version of a Black Sox Scandal." In these instances, and many others, the Black Sox scandal provided people with a benchmark or a cultural touchstone for malfeasance in the sports world.

The Black Sox scandal has also become a thriving cottage industry. The amount of money made from Black Sox–related products—films (dramas and documentaries), television shows, plays (including an opera), books (fiction and nonfiction, for adults and children), magazine and newspaper articles, memorabilia, and sundry collectibles—is incalculably more than what the banished ballplayers received (or in some cases allegedly received) for fixing the World Series. The sentimental movie *Field of Dreams* (1989) is an extreme example. Based on W. P. Kinsella's novel *Shoeless Joe* (1982) and starring Kevin Costner, it is about an Iowa farmer who builds a baseball field because an unidentified voice tells him, "If you build it, he will come." In the process, the mystical field conjures Joe Jackson's ghost and grossed the film-makers more than $64 million at the box office. There are many other less lucrative examples of the Black Sox scandal doing a steady business. One can visit, for example, the not-for-profit, all-volunteer-run Shoeless Joe Jackson Museum in Greenville, South Carolina, the ballplayer's hometown. One can also purchase Black Sox trading cards for $2.99 online. It is the other end of the spectrum, however, that usually receives more attention. In February 2015, for instance, a baseball signed by six of the Black Sox ballplayers sold at auction for more than $81,000.

Additionally, a surprising number of people remain intrigued by what occurred during and just after the 1919 World Series. For some of these people, their thirst to know seems unquenchable. The late Gene Carney, author of *Burying the Black Sox: How Baseball's Cover-Up of the 1919 World Series Fix Almost Succeeded* (2006) and the most passionate and dogged Black Sox researcher I have met, helped found a Google discussion group on the subject, as well as a Society for American Baseball Research (SABR) committee devoted to researching and reexamining the scandal. Comprised of baseball fans, antiquarians, and scholars from across the country, these groups continue to dig for new evidence and debate its possible meaning. The SABR Black Sox Research Committee publishes a semiannual newsletter and many of its members collaborated on *Scandal on the South Side: The 1919 Chicago White Sox* (2015), edited by Jacob Pomrenke, SABR's director of editorial content.

Scandal on the South Side is an interesting example of the ongoing historical research on the Black Sox scandal. A collection of biographical portraits of all the White Sox ballplayers in 1919 and many other men with the team (including owner Charles Comiskey, front office executives, and even batboy Eddie Bennett) and several thematic essays, the book, Pomrenke explains, is intended to "clear up some of the misconceptions about the 1919 White Sox team that have been passed down through history." Some of the chapters are based on "new information" that many previous journalists and scholars lacked. It is an impressive, fact-filled, useful book. At the same time, it "isn't a rewriting of *Eight Men Out*," Pomrenke clarifies, referring to Eliot Asinof's 1963 popular history, which is still widely considered the most authoritative version of the Black Sox scandal, "but it is the complete story of everyone associated with the 1919 Chicago White Sox, told in full for the first time. We'll help bring you up to date on what we collectively know about the Black Sox Scandal and the infamous team at the center of it all. We won't take sides on whether certain players were guilty or whether they were punished fairly. We just present the best available information to you—and as you can tell by now, there's a lot of new information out there." Pomrenke and the book's contributors want "to challenge" their readers' "assumptions" and help people "gain a better understanding" of the 1919 World Series and its aftermath.

Like many of the books and articles about the Black Sox scandal published in the last ten-plus years, *Scandal on the South Side* represents the quest to recover the Black Sox past, the desire to know (with something close to certainty) what happened just before, during, and soon after the 1919 World Series. For some, like Susan Dellinger, author of *Red Legs and Black Sox: Edd Roush and the Untold Story of the 1919 World Series* (2006), this desire is rooted in the yearning for vindication. Roush was the best player on the Reds, a future Hall of Fame outfielder, and the last living participant of the 1919 World Series (he died in 1988). He was also Dellinger's grandfather. She claims, "It is time to give the Cincinnati Reds of 1919 the respect they deserve. They have suffered the humiliation of being 'synthetic champions' long enough. The best team did win the 1919 World Series." Well, the morally superior team won.

More numerous and prominent are those writers and researchers (and fans) who want Joe Jackson and his reputation redeemed. Daniel J. Voelker and Paul A. Duffy's 2009 article, "Black Sox: It ain't so, kid, it just ain't so," is an excellent example of this. Voelker and Duffy, Chicago attorneys, argue: "Direct evidence, such as 'Shoeless' Joe's performance during the 1919 Series and his repeated denials of wrongdoing, suggest nothing more than Joe's bad judgment in taking money from his teammate and roommate, [Claude] Williams, and not being more aggressive and timely in reporting his suspicion of the 'fix' to Comiskey, White Sox Secretary (General Manager) Harry Grabiner, or William 'Kid' Gleason, the White Sox manager in 1919." Unconvinced of Jackson's alleged misconduct, Voelker and Duffy assert that he "deserves recognition for his contribution to the sport, and vindication of his name." Many reasonable people agree. Some sentimental people do, too.

The same redemptive impulse has animated those who think the supposedly miserly Charles Comiskey and the banished White Sox third baseman Buck Weaver have been mistreated by history, their legacies besmirched. In *Turning the Black Sox White: The Misunderstood Legacy of Charles A. Comiskey* (2014), Tim Hornbaker declares, "Instead of attempting to separate fact from fiction, writers have embraced the standard theories of Comiskey and labeled him a scoundrel on par with the 'Black Sox' conspirators themselves. It is easy today to be affected by the standard lore surrounding Comiskey, but everything is not always as it seems. The deeper clarification of his career and the circumstances of the 1919 World Series have been ignored for far too long." The book is intended to counter "the movement to demonize Comiskey" as a cheapskate despot who contributed to the conditions that made the Black Sox scandal possible. It is unclear that any such "movement" exists, although many people who have written about the Big Fix have asserted that Comiskey was arrogant, insensitive, and exploitative when it came to his ballplayers.

In addition to the relentless work of Dr. David J. Fletcher, founder of www .clearbuck.com and the Chicago Baseball Museum, "to clear Buck Weaver's name and reinstate him to Major League Baseball," so he can become eligible for induction to the National Baseball Hall of Fame, the *Chicago Tribune* took up Weaver's cause in the summer of 2015. In a lengthy, compassionate profile of Weaver's eighty-eight-year-old niece, Patricia Anderson, journalist John Owens writes, "Almost from the time he was banned from the game, Weaver's supporters have been trying to get him back in, saying he was unfairly punished because he was not involved in the fix. Weaver appealed unsuccessfully six times to Landis and his successors, Happy Chandler and Ford Frick, before dying in 1956." Less than a month after this story was published, Commissioner Rob Manfred declined to reconsider Weaver's case, "citing information that Weaver had participated in players-only meetings in 1919 to discuss the scheme to fix the World Series." This was disappointing news for those who consider Weaver a blameless victim of circumstance, but a number of his supporters remain undaunted. "Despite Manfred's decision," notes Owens, "historians familiar with the case say that they will continue to try to uncover new evidence that could help determine Weaver's innocence." Always, the quest for "new evidence."

More than once, I have wondered: What kind of new evidence can possibly exist that could conclusively exonerate Joe Jackson or Buck Weaver? What lost but now found faded scrap of paper could convince the unconvinced of their integrity and lack of wrongdoing?

How about reliable, quantifiable player salary data? That is, in part, the premise of Bob Hoie's well-researched article, "1919 Baseball Salaries and the Mythically Underpaid Chicago White Sox" (2012). "For more than ninety years," Hoie writes, "it has been widely believed that the perfidy of the Black Sox was prompted by low player salaries paid by Chicago team owner Charles Comiskey." Hoie ascribes this idea to numerous people, including the Black Sox's defense attorneys in 1921, the cantankerous syndicated columnist Westbrook Pegler, Eliot Asinof, the "premier chronicler of the Black Sox saga," and numerous historians (who seem not to have done their due diligence by repeating this notion). After carefully scrutinizing newly available Major League "transaction cards" from 1919—which contain salary, bonus payments, and other contract information for most ballplayers—Hoie reveals that Asinof and all the others were wrong: the Chicago payroll (which was about $90,000) was not among the lowest in the American League. It was among the highest, in the same neighborhood as the Boston Red Sox ($93,475) and New York Yankees ($91,330), and greater than the Detroit Tigers, Cleveland Indians, St. Louis Browns, Washington Senators, and Philadelphia Athletics. This is good to know. It is a persuasive rebuttal to Asinof's poorly supported claim that "no players of comparable talent on other teams were paid as little" as the star players on the 1919 White Sox. And to his assertion, "Many second-rate ballplayers on second-division ball clubs made more than the White Sox. It had been that way for years." Hoie has convinced me that Asinof was incorrect about the White Sox's collective salary in relation to their contemporaries.

At the same time, this finding lacks much explanatory power. It is possible, of course, that, regardless of the team's overall payroll, the men involved in the conspiracy felt or believed they were being exploited or treated poorly, by the labor system (which effectively diminished their earning power), if not by Charles Comiskey. Regardless of their salaries, they may have, as Asinof puts it, thought of Comiskey as "a cheap, stingy tyrant" who paid some ballplayers more generously (say, second baseman Eddie Collins, who made $15,000 in 1919 and who was not part of the fix) than others (say, Joe Jackson, who made $6,000). It is possible that (like me) some of the conspiring ballplayers were not well informed about how much their peers were paid. It is also possible that they were ethically challenged men who saw an opportunity to make some quick, easy money and took it, not having thought too much about the possible consequences. No spreadsheet of neatly organized player salary data can reach the complicated jumble of thought processes, emotions, grievances, and rationalizations that motivated men like Eddie Cicotte, Happy Felsch, Chick Gandil, and the others to fix the World Series.

Maybe the most important thing to recognize and perhaps embrace when considering the Black Sox scandal is its indeterminacy. Simply put, some aspects of the Black Sox story are forever unknowable, such as who approached whom and when: Did the ballplayers hatch the idea and go looking for gamblers who would and could finance it? Or did the gamblers bring the scheme to the ballplayers? Or did both things happen practically simultaneously? As sportswriter Frederick G. Lieb declared many years ago, "The complete story of the great fix never will be known." He was and remains correct. There are few certainties when it comes to the Black Sox scandal. But there are a few. We know that the Reds were a good team and won the 1919 World Series and that some of the White Sox admitted to taking money to play poorly and intentionally lose games. Another thing "certain about the 1919 Series," observes historian Steven Gietschier, "is that the whole truth will never be known. The principals have gone to their graves, and the evidence that survives is confusing and inconclusive."

With the recent publication of *The Betrayal: The 1919 World Series and the Birth of Modern Baseball* (2016), Charles Fountain is the latest (and certainly not the last) writer to revisit the Black Sox scandal. As far as I can tell, his years of thorough research have not yielded anything novel about the Big Fix. Yet to his credit he does understand its inscrutability. "The Black Sox story," he explains, "is like a puzzle with a thousand pieces. Any five hundred pieces come together nicely and make a clear picture. That leaves a lot of pieces left on the side. Fit some of the extra pieces in and those too make a clear picture, but now some of the pieces in the first picture have come out. Try to force them all in and you're breaking off the edges, or layering the pictures on top of one another to the point where all sense of order and clarity is blurred." It is a good analogy. For almost a hundred years, many people have sought clarity when it comes to the Black Sox scandal, but many pieces of the puzzle are lost and irretrievable, if they ever existed. And so despite all the words and pages written about it, and all time and energy people have devoted to it (and will continue to do so), the Black Sox scandal is as elusive as it is resilient.

For Further Reading

Asinof, Eliot. *Eight Men Out: The Black Sox and the 1919 World Series.* New York: Henry Holt, 1963.

Dellinger, Susan. *Red Legs and Black Sox: Edd Roush and the Untold Story of the 1919 World Series.* Cincinnati: Emmis Books, 2006.

Lamb, William F. *Black Sox in the Courtroom: The Grand Jury, Criminal Trial and Civil Litigation.* Jefferson, N.C.: McFarland, 2013.

Nathan, Daniel A. *Saying It's So: A Cultural History of the Black Sox Scandal.* Urbana: University of Illinois Press, 2003.

Pomrenke, Jacob (ed.). *Scandal on the South Side: The 1919 Chicago White Sox.* Phoenix: Society for America Baseball Research, 2015.

4

The Creation of the Negro National League

LESLIE HEAPHY

On Friday, February 13, 1920, a gathering of baseball businessmen and newspapermen in Kansas City, Missouri, made history. Led by Andrew "Rube" Foster, a club owner and former pitcher, this unlikely group came together hoping to establish a permanent league for black baseball. They succeeded. The Negro National League, their creation, began play in 1920 and, with one interlude, competed through 1948. How the men involved arrived at that February day and what happened when they met is a story filled with intrigue, scandal, closed doors, and so much more. Why was Kansas City chosen as a meeting place when Chicago was Foster's home and black baseball flourished there? What did Foster say to convince most of the leading men in black baseball to come to Kansas City and work together? Who decided which newspapermen to invite? What kind of agreement did these businessmen hammer out? More generally, why did Foster succeed when Beauregard Moseley, Frank Leland, and other black baseball magnates had failed so many times before? These and other questions are what we want to answer as we follow Foster, Moseley, and others through the steps that led to the creation of what was officially named the National Association of Colored Professional Baseball.

African Americans played baseball before and during the Civil War. After the war ended, the Philadelphia Pythians, an all-black club, applied for membership in baseball's first major league, the National Association. They were turned down, but along with numerous other black clubs, they continued to play regularly. Individual black players, including George Stovey, Frank Grant, and Bud Fowler, also found opportunities on white ball clubs until the mid-1880s. Moses Fleetwood Walker and his brother, Welday, played for the Toledo Blue Stockings of the major-league American Association in 1884. They were the last African Americans to play in the majors until Jackie Robinson joined the Brooklyn Dodgers in 1947.

With the onset of Jim Crow, blacks found themselves pushed out of all aspects of white mainstream society, including baseball. As a result of this unofficial color line, separate teams developed, beginning with the Cuban Giants in New York. These ball clubs had to seek out other African American teams as regular opponents. Beginning in 1886, black baseball entrepreneurs tried to establish a league for their segregated sport, but each of these early attempts failed. That year in Pittsburgh, delegates from seven cities met to form a colored baseball league of professional baseball players. Cities represented were Baltimore, Boston, Cleveland, Louisville, Philadelphia, Pittsburgh, and Washington, with Nelson M. Williams of Washington facilitating the meeting. Delegates unanimously adopted rules to establish an African American National Agreement, and they appointed committees on a constitution and schedule, with the next meeting scheduled for March 1887 in the same city. Unfortunately, the league never really got started. There were too many uncertainties, ranging from travel and accommodations to ballparks and attendance.

A number of other attempts followed, but none succeeded. Chicago Republican politician and entrepreneur Beauregard Moseley came the closest in 1910 after Foster had called for a proper league with strong finances and fan support. Moseley proposed a seventeen-step plan that appeared in the *New York Times* on December 4, 1910. Cary B. Lewis, managing editor of the *Chicago Defender,* one of the country's leading black newspapers, lent his weight to this effort by attending one of the league's few meetings. But the effort failed, partly owing to in-fighting between Foster and Leland, owner of the Leland Giants from Chicago. They battled over the ownership and even the name of the Giants. Foster, who pitched for the Leland club, believed Leland was not being fair to his players in the amount of money he paid them, and so he tried to break away and start his own team named the Chicago American Giants. Most of the players he took from Leland's club. Foster learned a great deal in the legal battles that ensued. The disputes also affected the players and their contracts as well as scheduling, which helps explain the emphasis on such topics at the meetings in 1920.

In December 1911, Foster wrote an article for the *Indianapolis Freeman,* another black newspaper, describing the troubles of the business of black baseball as he saw them. He laid most of the blame for the game's instability on "petty jealousy" and how that resulted in guerrilla warfare tactics between teams, especially those in Chicago. In 1913, Foster again argued that unless black baseball organized, there would be no long-term success. And in 1914 when a couple of Cuban players found their way into major league baseball, Foster thought black players would follow, but this did not happen. Blacks continued to be forced to play on segregated teams.

At the close of the 1919 season, Foster wrote a five-part series called "The Pitfalls of Baseball" for the *Chicago Defender*. In addition to laying out the ills of the game again, he talked about what a new league would need to succeed, starting with a strong leader. It is clear from his comments that Foster thought himself the best and maybe the only logical candidate, as all the other owners had failed along the way. Foster's attitude would surely make the meeting in 1920 a bit heated at times. He also talked about the need to pay higher salaries, noting immodestly that his Giants had been the best at paying their players well. Foster ended the series by saying that he would soon try one more time to get owners together to organize a league. There was a threatening tone to his writing as he basically said, "It is now or never."

Students of black baseball would like to know why the 1920 meeting occurred where it did. Why convene at the YMCA in Kansas City when Foster, the organizer, was from Chicago? Did he have ulterior motives? Was he trying to curry favor with certain Kansas City people, such as J. L. Wilkinson, owner of the Kansas City Monarchs? Did all the previous in-fighting in Chicago between Foster and Leland make that city an unsuitable choice? Or was it simpler than that?

The Paseo YMCA building in Kansas City, where these men gathered, had opened its doors in 1914 and counted Felix H. Payne among its charter members. Payne was a successful black businessman in the Kansas City music industry, and he had an early connection with black baseball in 1909 as the owner of the Kansas City (Kansas) Giants. Payne's prominence in black Kansas City and beyond put him in a position to be important to Foster's dream. He had used his money and his connections to help raise the funds to build the Paseo Y, and during the meeting, he hosted Lewis, a key participant, and his wife, at his home. So maybe the reason Foster picked Kansas City was to play to the egos of those he thought needed to be involved.

The meeting might have taken place in Indianapolis. The Senate Street YMCA in that city had opened its doors in 1913 and shared one name in common with its counterpart in Kansas City. Prominent businessman and philanthropist Julius Rosenwald had helped provide funding for both YMCA building projects. The Senate Street Y was a centerpiece for the black community, even more so than the Paseo Y, but it did not seem like a good candidate to host such an important meeting because it was not the economic center of the Indianapolis black community. Madame C. J. Walker and her cosmetics industry served that role. Walker had no involvement with the 1920 meeting because she died in 1919, but Indianapolis was represented by ABCs manager/owner C. I. Taylor, who could not be left out if the league were to succeed. As early as 1915, Foster and Taylor had published a series of strong letters to the public airing their differences but acknowledging that they would need to work together to create any kind of successful league. Interestingly perhaps, the NNL's 1921 league meetings would take place in Indianapolis.

While Detroit did not serve as a potential meeting place, it had a strong black community that could not be ignored, and by 1920 a team, the Stars, that was economically successful. As a result, Foster invited Stars owner John "Tenny" Blount to the Kansas City meeting. But there was another reason. Foster and Blount had prior ties. In fact, this is where some of the intrigue comes into play, as researchers wonder just exactly what had taken place between Blount and Foster to make Foster willing to set up a team in Detroit and invite Blount to run the club when John Roesink had been the Stars owner since the early 1910s and even built his club a stadium in 1914. This is a particularly interesting question given Blount's connections to the numbers game and Foster's later decision to push Blount out of the league over a monetary dispute. Was Foster simply looking for someone who would do his bidding and vote the way he wanted?

C. I. Taylor wrote an impassioned letter to the *Pittsburgh Competitor* shortly before the 1920 meeting imploring Foster to step up and make a league happen. He even said that he thought there was no one better than Foster to do this. He suggested a midseason meeting in Chicago to accomplish this goal. There was no mention of Kansas City at all in his letter, just Chicago, leaving open the question of how the meeting wound up in Kansas City.

Now for a little more intrigue. Sometime before the Kansas City meeting, Foster reportedly held secret meetings in both Detroit and Chicago with some owners and Nat C. Strong, a booking agent from the East. Strong was the man all the teams went to in the East to book games because he controlled access to all the New York ballparks. The purpose was to iron out some disagreements and hammer out some new understandings between Strong and clubs in the Midwest so that the meeting in Kansas City could even happen. Most of the disagreements had to do with how Foster was handling players' contracts. Strong told Foster that eastern owners did not like to work with him. What exactly they agreed to in these secret meetings is not known, but Foster must have used his best persuasive powers to convince Strong not to stand in the way. Foster also decided that his league would need a new team in Kansas City and that he needed to court J. L. Wilkinson, owner of the All Nations team, to strengthen what would be a western circuit. So that's how Kansas City became the new meeting place.

When Foster first proposed his new league, it was to be called the Western Circuit Negro National League because there were plans for an eastern circuit to be added later. Organizers also suggested that only western teams should be included because they were solid and located in cities that allowed Sunday baseball. As it turned out, the planned eastern circuit did not come to pass until 1923, and it developed as a separate entity. Foster could not work out the details with Strong, and so the eastern teams followed the lead of Philadelphia's Ed Bolden and created the Eastern Colored League (ECL).

Picture yourself as a club owner anxiously awaiting the start of the 1920 baseball season, suffering through another winter with no baseball, when a telegram arrives from the great Rube Foster. You read excitedly that you are being invited to take the train to Kansas City to join a gathering to create the new Negro National League. You agree and make your travel plans and hope that a February meeting in the Midwest will not get snowed out. As February draws closer, you wonder who else has been invited and what will happen this time. Maybe you have conversations with others, but maybe not. All you can do is wait for everyone to arrive at the railroad depot in Kansas City.

February 13 arrives, and you learn that Foster had gathered a group of owners, newspapermen, and lawyers to discuss the organization of a new league. After introductions are made and everyone settles in for the day, the first order of business is deciding who will run the show. Everyone knows it will be Foster because he called the gathering. Tenny Blount of Detroit handles this first order of business by nominating Foster, who is elected chairman. This task alone may be why Foster invited Blount, who did not have the finances to own a team on his own. Foster was the power in the room because he also carried the proxy vote of August "Tinti" Molina, owner of the New York Cuban Stars. After explaining what he saw as the purpose of the meeting, Foster made it clear that the nuts and bolts of a constitution, bylaws, and even player selections should be hammered out by the newspapermen present. They included Lewis, Elwood Knox of the *Indianapolis Freeman,* and Charles Marshall from the *Indianapolis Ledger.* Marshall had written a strong article supporting a new league and extolling the virtues of both Foster and Taylor in January. Added to this group was Topeka attorney Elisha Scott. Some newspapers reported that writer Dave Wyatt from the *Indianapolis Ledger* was present and said he may have been the primary writer of the constitution, but most talked only about the work of Lewis and Knox. We may never know for sure, but Wyatt wrote a number of articles immediately after the meeting with details that only could have come from his being present. It should also be noted that no players were involved. In fact, Foster had previously indicated that many players he had talked to were not in favor of a league because they were worried about being controlled. They wanted the freedom to be able to move where the money was.

Immediately after Foster's election, the group selected Lewis as secretary. Then things got interesting as Foster pulled out a charter he already had written and incorporated in six different states. This raises another question as to why he would have invited all the newspapermen if he already had written a charter. Foster's bold move showed he meant it when he said it was now or never. Unfortunately, there are no recordings or photos to reveal anyone's reaction to this ploy, but it is easy to assume that everyone was stunned. (These incorporation papers were not actually signed and registered in Illinois until 1924, and when they were, all the signees and stockholders were from Illinois except for Wilkinson, again showing how important he was to this endeavor. One of the majority stockholders, in addition to Foster, was his half-brother, Willie Foster, the only player involved.) Those present then retired for entertainment and smoking, hosted by Payne, Clarence Houston, and a local attorney named Calloway. One can only imagine what some of those conversations must have been like.

The local hosts in Kansas City wanted to make sure their visitors had a grand time while in their town. Wilkinson provided the resources for a ten-course meal at the Deluxe Café to go with some entertainment, putting the attendees in good spirits for the remaining meetings. On the second night, the attendees left the community center for another fine dinner at the Deluxe Café, hosted this time by the Elks and Quincy Gilmore, Wilkinson's right-hand man. After all the business had been completed on Sunday, Mrs. Payne hosted a dinner for Foster and a few select guests, including Blount, Wyatt, and Knox. Was this a thank-you for their support of Foster's plans? Again, all we can do is imagine the conversations taking place at each of these events. By Sunday, the group had to have been satisfied with the results.

The first major area of discussion on that first day among the owners, not surprisingly, dealt with the selection of players. Blount and Taylor were particularly heated in talking about other owners not respecting player contracts in the past. This matter would need to be addressed in any league documents to ensure the league's survival. Once again Foster saved the day. He rose and told those assembled that he had more to lose than anybody else, but he was willing to throw everything he had on the table and let the newspapermen divvy up the assets, the players. When Foster spoke, people listened.

After some discussion, the writers and Scott were sent off to work on a document for consideration that addressed more specific issues than Foster's charter. They worked all night and came back on Saturday with a draft to be adopted. The writers read the preamble first, and the owners adopted it easily. The constitution itself took longer. According to newspaper stories, the document went through many corrections before it was finally accepted. Unfortunately, there was no James Madison present to keep meticulous notes of what was proposed, argued over, and changed. What little we know today is what was published in newspapers. That mainly consisted of who was there, who signed the final document, and what the basic text was. So many questions remain unanswered. For example, how did they decide on $500 as the proper membership fee for the league? How would schedules be set? Would there be standard contracts for the players? What kind of penalties would there be for not abiding by the bylaws and constitution? How would umpires be selected and trained, if at all? Who made each proposal? How did the voting take place?

What we do know is the league did not plan to start play until 1921. The delay centered on each team's need to find a ballpark to use as its home base. Foster believed that might take a year. It turned out, however, that the Western Circuit was able to play in 1920, and by the end of the season was being referred to as the NNL.

Another thing we know is exactly who signed that first constitution and paid the $500 fee. The list included Foster of the Chicago American Giants, Blount of the Detroit Stars, Wilkinson of the Kansas City Monarchs, Taylor of the Indianapolis ABCs, Joe Green of the Chicago Giants, and Lorenzo Cobb of the St. Louis Giants. John Matthews of the Dayton Marcos was unable to attend in person because of illness, but he sent his consent and his payment to be included with this initial group.

Deciding which players would play for which teams consumed much of the rest of the weekend. These discussions must have been fascinating as the owners argued the merits and skills of each player and decided who would play for whom. The group agreed that the writers would arbitrate all disputes over players. The players selected for the various clubs represent a veritable who's who of black baseball stars. For example, Blount's Detroit team included future Hall of Famer Pete Hill, Bruce Petway, Frank Warfield, and Mack Eggleston. Wilkinson's Monarchs were assigned John Donaldson, Rube Currie, and future Hall of Famers Jose Mendez and Wilbur "Bullet" Rogan. Bingo DeMoss, Dave Malarchar, Dick Lundy, and future Hall of Famer Cristobal Torriente helped fill Foster's American Giants roster. Walter Ball and John Beckwith were assigned to the Chicago Giants, and Taylor's ABCs got future Hall of Famer Oscar Charleston and Dizzy Dismukes. The St. Louis team included William "Plunk" Drake and Tully McAdoo. The roster for the Dayton Marcos remained blank, but no one explained why. It may have been simply that because Matthews was not present, the other owners wanted to inform him before his roster was sent to the newspapers.

Little else about the dealings of these baseball men in Kansas City became public knowledge, but we know the end result. The Negro National League began play in May 1920 and changed the fortunes of African American ballplayers forever. Who had to compromise and who got left out of the meeting became a moot point in the face of the new league's success. The organization finally created what had failed many times before. Foster and Taylor had recognized the need for the owners to put aside their differences and work together. There remained many details to work out as the signers left Kansas City and headed home, but the atmosphere in their train cars must have been one of optimism, joy, and a little apprehension as they ventured into uncharted territory.

For Further Reading

Lester, Larry. *Rube Foster in His Time.* Jefferson, N.C.: McFarland, 2012.

Lomax, Michael. *Black Baseball Entrepreneurs, 1902–31.* Syracuse, N.Y.: Syracuse University Press, 2014.

Newman, Roberta, and Joel Nathan Rosen. *Black Baseball, Black Business: Race Enterprise and the Fate of the Segregated Dollar.* Jackson: University Press of Mississippi, 2014.

5

George Gipp, Knute Rockne, and the Post-Mortem Faux Pas

RONALD A. SMITH

"Win one for the Gipper" is in the American lexicon, but not because Notre Dame star George Gipp actually uttered the phrase in 1920 as he lay dying from pneumonia. Rather, Notre Dame coach Knute Rockne made the words up eight years later when he used the memory of the great running back to rally the Fighting Irish, tied at half-time with undefeated Army, 0–0, before about 78,000 in Yankee Stadium. Journalist Frank Wallace, a Notre Dame grad, recounted Rockne's speech. "On his deathbed," Rockne said, "George Gipp told me that someday, when the time came, he wanted me to ask a Notre Dame team to beat the Army for him." Wallace continued the story told to him by an eyewitness. "It was not a trick. George Gipp asked it. When Notre Dame's football need was greatest, it called on its beloved 'Gipper' again."

The concocted expression "Win one for the Gipper" became so well known that Arthur Daley of the *New York Times* used it during World War II when former Notre Damer Jack Chevigny, a Marine, died fighting the Japanese on Iwo Jima. Lt. Chevigny, present at Rockne's halftime oration, was in a foxhole when he was killed by a Japanese shell. Using the words made famous by actor Ronald Reagan when he played Gipp in the 1940 movie, *Knute Rockne-All American,* Daley wrote that Chevigny "never had a chance to whisper 'Win one for the Gipper.'"

When Gipp died in 1920, only days after Walter Camp had named him Notre Dame's first All-American, he was probably more famous than Rockne. Biographer Jack Cavanaugh claimed that Gipp's football exploits may have "overshadowed those of such football immortals as Jim Thorpe and Red

Grange" as the best passer of his era, averaging eight yards as a running back his senior year, booming kicks over fifty yards, and once drop-kicking a sixty-two-yard field goal—all this, Cavanaugh claims, while never allowing a completed pass in his area as a defensive back. This is the stuff of what legends are made, especially after a tragic death.

The tale is mythic, perhaps, but what was not invented was that Rockne and Notre Dame administrators refused to pay Gipp's medical expenses after he died in a South Bend hospital following a game against Northwestern on a cold and miserable day. The difference between the origin of "Win one for the Gipper" and the strange case of Notre Dame's parsimony is that the details of Gipp's medical treatment are quite well documented. The controversy over the nonpayment of Gipp's medical bills is little known, but it sheds unusual light on both Rockne and Notre Dame.

Rockne began his head coaching career at Notre Dame in 1918, two years after the school recruited the mature, twenty-one-year-old Gipp, without a high school diploma, to play baseball. Gipp, however, was soon engaged to play football. In his first season as head coach, Rockne, with Gipp playing until hurt, achieved a modest 3-1-2 record. But in Gipp's final two years, his

Tribute to George Gipp by illustrator B.H.B. Lange. (University of Notre Dame Archives.)

fourth and fifth at Notre Dame, he was Rockne's unquestioned star in two undefeated seasons.

It is no wonder that Rockne pandered to Gipp, who missed classes, drank, gambled, and womanized throughout his stay at Notre Dame, for the coach would not likely have been undefeated without him. As Murray Sperber, the top historian of Notre Dame football, has stated, Rockne "was willing to overlook some player transgressions, especially those committed by his star."

Gipp was very nearly a nonstudent. In his freshman year, he passed just enough courses to be eligible for the 1917 varsity football season. For the next two years, the school allowed him to play both baseball and football even though he earned no class credits at all. He left school in the spring of 1919 but returned in the fall to continue his football career. Yet, he received no academic credits while starring on Rockne's first undefeated team. In the spring of 1920, President James A. Burns finally booted him out of school, yet he remained in South Bend, and local townsmen pressured Burns to re-admit him. The expulsion lasted only about a month. A petition signed by eighty-six South Bend businessmen was particularly important to Burns, as local contributions were vital to his fund-raising possibilities.

Burns was the first Notre Dame president to take raising an endowment seriously. He saw that winning football, made possible by a dynamic coach like Rockne and star athletes like Gipp, could generate large crowds and sig-nificant money so Burns could build dormitories, classrooms, and a greater Notre Dame.

With Gipp reinstated, Rockne could look forward to another successful season. Gipp dominated play, including starring in a key game against Army in New York. The following week, fans filled Notre Dame's small, makeshift stadium to see Gipp, the "Babe Ruth of the gridiron," help defeat Purdue. Gipp then helped prevent an upset by Indiana when Rockne taped up Gipp's injured shoulder, sent him back into the game, and escaped with a 13–10 victory. Despite his injury, described as a separated shoulder and broken collarbone, Gipp did not return directly to South Bend, but went on to Chi-cago to demonstrate dropkicking to some high school players. In Chicago he developed a cold and was treated by Dr. C. H. Johnson, an ear, nose, and throat specialist, before returning to Notre Dame.

With two games remaining on the schedule, Gipp was basically done for the season. His shoulder injury had not healed, and he was sick with ton-sillitis, but he still traveled with the team to Evanston for its game against Northwestern. Notre Dame alumni and fans from the Chicago area were a significant part of the crowd, and the alumni created "George Gipp Day" because they wanted to see the football hero participate. Rockne kept Gipp on the sidelines for almost the entire game, but he gave in with Notre Dame safely in the lead. With ten minutes left in the game, Gipp entered in his weakened condition. He completed five of six passes, connecting for two touchdowns. He played no more—in his life.

Chilled and with a fever, Gipp returned to South Bend with the team and even attended a football banquet two days later, only to be admitted to St. Joseph's Hospital the next morning. He stayed there while Rockne took his team to play a Thanksgiving Day game against Michigan State. Gipp took a turn for the worse, developing pneumonia. Soon, Dr. Johnson arrived on the scene, evidently at the behest of Gipp's mother and brother. He apparently felt that the treatment Gipp was receiving was appropriate and returned to Chicago. However, when Gipp's condition worsened, his mother and his brother, Matthew, asked if Johnson could return, and for the next eight days until Gipp's death on December 15, Johnson attended to him.

The disconsolate Gipp family rejected any help from Notre Dame with the funeral, even though they mortgaged their home to pay the expenses. When Johnson sent his first bill, the family told him to send it to Rockne and Notre Dame. Johnson did so, but received no reply. Burns quickly agreed with Rockne that Notre Dame had not summoned Johnson and therefore should not pay for Gipp's treatment.

The Chicago doctor claimed, "Mr. Rockne guaranteed that the athletic association would pay me for my services." Shortly after Gipp died, Johnson sent a statement to the Athletic Association, but got no reply. After more than two months, he contacted Burns. "Father, this is a rank injustice. I dug down in my pockets and paid all of my expenses and don't feel I have earned such treatment."

Notre Dame asked Dr. James McMeel, a local physician who also treated Gipp, to give his account of what had occurred. McMeel reported that he and Dr. T. A. Olney had counseled with Johnson and outlined a course of treatment. Johnson returned to Chicago, but one week later, Gipp's mother and brother requested that Johnson come to South Bend again. McMeel stated, "I acquiesced," and just before Johnson returned the next day remarked, "I remember very distinctly hearing that Mr. Rockne said that he wondered who was going to pay him."

Burns accepted McMeel's version. He tersely replied to Johnson that the Gipps "assumed responsibility for this." Send your bill, he told Johnson, to Matthew Gipp, "who sent for you."

Upset, Johnson soon replied to Burns, "My bill is $750 [and] this includes eight days services, expenses and treatment" including treating Gipp in Chicago before the Northwestern game. Apparently, Burns ignored the inquiry. After almost a year elapsed, Johnson proceeded with legal action. His counsel told Burns that there were several eyewitnesses who had overheard Rockne request that Johnson go to South Bend to take care of Gipp. Burns was curt in his response: "The University of Notre Dame has no responsibility for the employment of Dr. Johnson. . . ."

The stalemate may have continued had Burns decided to stand for a second three-year term as Notre Dame president in July 1922, but he did not. Johnson soon met with the new president, Matthew Walsh, and while he was hopeful that his bill would soon be paid, it was not. A month later, he asked Walsh, "What can be the matter, . . . surely I am entitled to some courtesy." The "courtesy" soon came, but in a rather backhanded manner. Walsh decided to pay Johnson something to settle the matter, but he refused to admit that the medical payment was a responsibility of Notre Dame. He wrote the doctor, "The University was under no obligation to you," but "we have decided to send you the enclosed check for three hundred and fifty dollars." Walsh then closed his letter with the admission that the settlement was being made because Burns said "it was possible that [Knute Rockne] had committed himself in some way but had no definite recollection of so doing." When Walsh asked the Notre Dame treasurer to pay the $350, he wrote, "Please charge this amount to football expenses for 1923."

Knute Rockne's greatness was not based on his integrity. Rockne may well have given permission to bring Johnson in to treat Gipp. The dispute over Johnson's claim fit into Rockne's habit of agreeing to a proposition and then abruptly changing his mind. Rockne would sometimes make arrangements for games with other colleges, and then, if a better deal came along, he would break the contract with the lesser school. More troubling was Rockne's breaking his own contracts with Notre Dame to pursue more lucrative positions at other universities.

Rockne had several offers to coach at other schools following Gipp's great career, but two stand out because of contracts evidently agreed to but then rejected—the University of Iowa and Columbia University. In early 1924, Rockne, with forty-eight wins and only four losses since becoming head coach, was open to receiving offers, and Iowa was ready to offer him a change of scenery. Rockne was having difficulty with the Notre Dame Board of Athletic Control for a variety of reasons, and he used the opening at Iowa to extract changes from Notre Dame, including raising his salary.

Whether Rockne made a verbal agreement with Iowa is not clear. Iowa's athletic director, Paul Belting, later said that Rockne agreed to a three-year contract at $8,000 per year, nearly 40 percent more than he was making at

Notre Dame. If Rockne did not agree to the Iowa contract, at least Iowa's president, Walter Jessup, believed he had done so. Still, five days after negotiating with Iowa, Rockne and President Walsh agreed to a ten-year, $10,000 per year contract, one of the highest salaries and longest contracts for any football coach. Rockne told the press, "Notre Dame is a part of my life, and my one ambition . . . Notre Dame is my school."

Columbia's attempt to entice Rockne to New York the next year was more complicated and involved greater maneuvering by the coach. With the "Four Horsemen" leading the team in 1924, Rockne had achieved his third undefeated season, topped by defeating Stanford in the Rose Bowl. Rockne was probably the leading candidate for open coaching positions. No one had a better record, as Rockne had achieved sixty-five wins, six losses, and four ties in his first eight years. The Columbia Athletic Board decided to offer Rockne what was reported to be a three-year contract worth $15,000 the first year, $17,500 in the second, and $20,000 in the third. If he had accepted, Rockne would almost surely have become the highest-paid football coach, earning more than university presidents and multiple times more than the highest-paid professors.

Rockne had good reasons to leave Notre Dame. He had for several years called for the construction of a football stadium to meet the increasing demand for tickets at home games. Little progress was being made, and Walsh was quite content to use excess football money, mostly from away games, to build academic and residential facilities on campus. Walsh and the Notre Dame Board of Athletic Control had become thorns in Rockne's side. Following the Rose Bowl victory, Notre Dame officials decided to decline all future invitations to bowl games, thus joining the Big Ten in opposition to postseason games and the increased commercialism of football. Then, too, anti-Catholic activity during the Notre Dame–Nebraska game in Lincoln convinced the Board of Athletic Control to recommend to Walsh that Notre Dame drop the series with Nebraska, a traditional moneymaker. Even though Nebraska had won three of the previous four games, Rockne opposed ending the series. However, the priests running Notre Dame felt that the school should no longer tolerate anti-Catholic insults. Rockne was offended because he created the Notre Dame schedule, but he did not leave. In fact, he added the University of Southern California to the schedule, beginning one of the great rivalries in twentieth-century college sport.

Following the 1925 season, Rockne went to New York to help choose the 1925 All-American team. While in New York, he met James Knapp, chair of the Columbia Athletic Board. After signing the extraordinary contract,

Rockne indicated that he would have to return to South Bend and get permission to break his contract there. A cynic could certainly conclude that he might use the Columbia contract to gain further concessions, financial and otherwise, from Walsh. When Knapp released confirmation of the contract before Rockne returned to Indiana, Rockne immediately repudiated the agreement. This caused major confusion and indicted both Knapp and Rockne. New Yorker James M. Byrne, a member of Notre Dame's Board of Trustees, confirmed to Walsh that "Rock was wrong in ever entering into any negotiations with Columbia while under contract with Notre Dame." Byrne, who knew Rockne well, stated that Rockne "was not morally strong enough to stand up and assert himself when he should have. I know he has embarrassed the University and himself greatly, due to his thoughtless dealing on many occasions."

When Rockne returned to South Bend, he expressed regret for the embarrassment he caused Notre Dame, and then he added, "At no time had I the intention of leaving the University of Notre Dame. . . ." He told Arch Ward, sportswriter for the *Chicago Tribune* and a Notre Dame graduate, "Don't ever pay attention to rumors about me going elsewhere to coach. Notre Dame took me in as a poor boy years ago. It gave me an opportunity for an education. It enabled me to make good in the field I have chosen for my own. I am indebted to the school as long as I live. Nothing will tear me away, no matter what the inducements. When I quit coaching at Notre Dame, I am through with football." Rockne was an enigma in action and in telling the truth.

Sometime after the Columbia fiasco, Ray Eichenlaub, who had played football with Rockne in Notre Dame's great 1913 win over Army, wrote to Walsh about Rockne's "unethical action with regard to the general interests of Notre Dame." Eichenlaub noted first the Columbia debacle and recounted the Iowa situation, stating, "Rock had absolutely signed a contract with the University of Iowa." The Notre Dame grad then noted "that Rock had accepted a date on the football schedule of The Ohio State University only later to cancel same and that he had scheduled a game with Gus Dorais at Detroit only later to cancel this game for another." If Rockne's behaviors raised ethical issues at the Catholic institution, it is little wonder that the issue of Gipp's medical expenses as he lay dying was raised again.

The school's refusal to pay for Dr. Johnson's services was little known in 1920, but it became nationally known in 1926 and embarrassed Notre Dame. Right about this time, Red Grange turned professional after a great career at the University of Illinois, a move that raised the ire of those who gloried in amateurism and rejected professional sport. Grange's coach, Robert Zuppke, defended him and made comments that could be used to condemn Notre Dame's refusal to pay Gipp's medical bills. "I blame no players for becoming professionals," Zuppke stated. "When you cross the goal line, nobody is with you, nothing but your shadow." He told athletes, "Take care of yourselves when you are running through a broken field. Nobody else will."

Grantland Rice, probably the best-known sportswriter in America in the mid-1920s, picked up on the idea that Notre Dame was making a huge profit on football and that Rockne was earning far more money than any of the school's professors, and yet the institution was unwilling to pay for medical care for one of its players. Rice wrote in early 1926 that Gipp's parents "had to mortgage their small home to pay the charges" from the medical expenses. "It was," Rice told his national audience through his popular column, "a financial burden Notre Dame should have carried." Rice, using the Red Grange pro signing, reasoned that if Notre Dame did not repay the Gipps, "there should be no other complaints about other Red Granges jumping into the pro game to clean up every dollar in sight." W. O. McGeehan, sports columnist for the *New York Herald Tribune,* agreed with Rice. Gipp "was an amateur at heart," he wrote. "He never would consider the overtures of professional promoters" like Grange. In fact, Gipp was no amateur. He played baseball for money, earned his living at Notre Dame by gambling in cards and in pool, and bet on his own team to win, but there was still strong opposition to Grange when he turned professional.

In early 1926, Notre Dame attempted to enter the Big Ten. The fact that the school did not have a stadium as large as the Big Ten's smallest did not, for some reason, become a major factor in Notre Dame's rejection. How Notre Dame dealt with Gipp's medical expenses may not have been the deal-breaker, but it was likely one of a number of issues, the largest of which was that Notre Dame was a Roman Catholic institution. The university had applied for Big Ten membership several times before, always unsuccessfully. The expressed reason for exclusion was never that it was a Catholic institution, but that the Big Ten did not want to expand or that Notre Dame's academic standards were subpar. Big Ten officials could point to numerous athletes, such as Gipp, who attended only to play football. There is truth to the latter charge, according to Jack Cavanaugh. "That Rockne had skirted the normal entrance process and academic standards to acquire some players," Cavanaugh stated, "was undeniable."

By 1926, Notre Dame had cleaned up its academic standards somewhat, was athletically worthy of Big Ten membership, and felt it had a good chance at joining the conference. Rockne toured Big Ten schools lobbying for admission, but he met resistance for a variety of reasons. When Big Ten faculty representatives voted following the season, Notre Dame was again left out of the most prestigious conference in America. As a result, the Irish remained a football independent without conference affiliation into the twenty-first century.

George Gipp and "Win one for the Gipper" have remained in the American vocabulary, but the knowledge that Notre Dame and Knute Rockne had resisted paying the medical bills accumulated during the attempt to save Gipp's life has been forgotten. That says something about the nature of myths. Few want to despoil heroic events such as Gipp becoming Notre Dame's greatest athletic hero or to question Rockne's use of Gipp's death to tell a fabricated story to fire up a team in a heroic comeback eight years later. It is likely that few will care that Rockne earned a bonus for being undefeated, a bonus greater than the total of Gipp's medical expenses. Nor will they likely be concerned that Notre Dame refused to pay for Gipp's medical treatment, though officials paid a token amount, when pressured, nearly three years later. Myths endure. The legend of George Gipp will surely last for more than a century, and Knute Rockne will likely continue to be considered America's greatest collegiate football coach.

For Further Reading

Cavanaugh, Jack. *The Gipper: George Gipp, Knute Rockne, and the Dramatic Rise of Notre Dame Football.* New York: Skyhorse Publishing, 2012.

Rockne, Knute. *The Autobiography of Knute Rockne.* Indianapolis: Bobbs-Merrill, 1930.

Sperber, Murray. *Shake Down the Thunder: The Creation of Notre Dame Football.* New York: Henry Holt, 1993.

6

Babe Didrikson at the 1932 Olympic Games

LINDSAY PARKS PIEPER

On a hot July afternoon in 1932, Mildred Ella "Babe" Didrikson single-handedly won the Amateur Athletic Union (AAU) National Track and Field Championships. Representing the company for which she worked, the Employers' Casualty Insurance Company of Dallas, the one-woman show hurdled, jumped, and threw in eight different events over the course of just a few hours. To the spectators' delight, the "Texas Whirlwind" earned six first-place finishes and outscored the second-place team, the Illinois Women's Athletic Club (IWAC), all by herself. Didrikson gained national recognition and simultaneously secured a position on the 1932 U.S. Olympic track and field squad. Her impressive exploits continued a month later in Los Angeles. In the 1932 Olympic Summer Games, she won two gold medals and settled uneasily for a controversial silver.

Didrikson was the greatest female athlete of the twentieth century. Prior to gaining celebrity in track and field, she led her company's basketball team, the Golden Cyclones, to a pair of national basketball championships in 1930 and 1931. The "Texas Thunderbolt" also won the 80-meter hurdles, baseball throw, and running broad jump in the 1931 AAU meet. Sadly, however, her tremendous AAU and Olympic achievements were marred by hostile rumors and cruel innuendos. Didrikson's brazen self-promotion irked her teammates, and her unfeminine, athletic appearance troubled the larger society. While the "Texas Tomboy's" impressive feats afforded her national recognition, the same accomplishments allowed some to cruelly label her a member of a "Third Sex."

Babe Didrikson (right) competes in the 80-meter hurdles. (Babe Didrikson Zaharias Collection, Mary and John Gray Library, Lamar University.)

Track and field was a popular and prestigious sport in the 1930s. It was also a physical activity reserved almost exclusively for men. Doctors' orders, physical educators' teachings, and widespread public beliefs limited women's access to but a few athletic events. Medical practitioners believed the vigorous nature of running, jumping, and throwing damaged women's reproductive capabilities, physical educators embraced these claims and implemented restraints, and the larger populace derided female participants in athletics as muscular, ugly, and unnatural. The sport, therefore, developed more as an avenue for boys and men to demonstrate their strength and manhood. Women who wanted to compete in track and field experienced resistance from multiple opponents.

The medical, educational, and cultural disdain for women's track and field shaped the perspectives of national and international sport organizations alike. For example, when William Buckingham Curtis founded the AAU in 1888, the organization excluded women, a practice that remained intact for more than three decades. Similarly, Pierre de Coubertin planned the first modern Olympics in Athens in 1896 without the participation of female Olympians. Although the AAU and the International Olympic Committee (IOC) eventually permitted women in track and field—the AAU in 1923 and the IOC in 1928—medical and cultural aversion to female participation continued. In this context, Didrikson emerged as both a national superstar and a social oddity.

The 1932 AAU Track and Field Championships also served as the Olympic Trials. Despite facing tremendous pressure to eschew competitive sport, two hundred elite female athletes gathered at Northwestern University's Dyche Stadium in Evanston, Illinois, each vying for a spot on the 1932 Olympic team. The runners, throwers, and jumpers competed on teams of up to twenty-five members. Didrikson, far better than anyone else working for Employers' Casualty, entered alone.

Her position as the sole representative of the Golden Cyclones fostered national interest. It also challenged the AAU's eligibility rules. Based upon archaic notions of female frailty, those rules stated that "No woman shall be allowed to compete in more than three events in one day, of which three events not more than two shall be track events." Yet, Didrikson needed to compete in multiple events to remain competitive on the scoreboard. Although the organization adhered to the belief that women were too fragile for such grueling competitions, the AAU eventually wavered. The uniqueness of "Belting Babe's" circumstances persuaded officials to overlook the rule because the potential for national attention held obvious advantages for the sport. In addition, some have also suggested that Melvorne Jackson McCombs, the manager of the Employers' Casualty athletics department and an important person in the track and field world, threatened the AAU with an ultimatum: let Didrikson participate unhindered, or he would convince other Texas teams to withdraw from the organization. The AAU therefore begrudgingly agreed to enter Didrikson into eight events, unknowingly paving the way for one of the greatest days in track and field history.

The evening before the meet, Didrikson felt ill. "I couldn't sleep," she remembered in her 1955 autobiography, *This Life I've Led*. "I kept having severe pains in my stomach." Concerned about the health of the only athlete on hand to represent the Golden Cyclones, Didrikson's chaperone called the doctor. His diagnosis? Excitement. Satisfied that her ailment was just nerves, Didrikson finally fell asleep. However, the late evening caused her to miss her alarm. By the time she found a taxicab, Didrikson had little time to prepare. She had to change into her tracksuit in the cab, and pulled up to Dyche Stadium only minutes before the opening ceremonies. Though her tardiness may have caused stress—for herself and for her coach—it also meant that the AAU did not have time to reconsider her enlistment in multiple events.

Once she arrived, Didrikson fell in line with the rest of the athletes marching around the stadium. The women paraded and waved as the Evanston American Legion drum and bugle corps played in the background. When the announcer welcomed the IWAC athletes—the home team—the crowd of five thousand erupted in cheers. Moments later, the spectators again thundered their applause when Didrikson stepped forward as the only athlete competing for the Golden Cyclones. "I spurted out there all alone, waving my arms, and you never heard such a roar," she recalled. From the opening ceremonies onward, Didrikson was the undisputed star of the meet.

The "Golden Streak from the Southwest" entered eight of the ten events contested that day, competing in all but the 50- and 220-yard dashes. Because neither race was an Olympic event, Didrikson did not want to waste her energy on the two sprints. If initially unsure of this decision, her strategy proved judicious as the temperature rose to over a hundred degrees that afternoon. Plus, with the various qualifying rounds, semifinals, and finals on the schedule, Didrikson competed in twenty-four contests in two-and-a-half hours—an average of one every six minutes. "I was flying all over the place," she remembered. "I'd run a heat in the eighty-meter hurdles, and then I'd take one of my high jumps. Then I'd go over to the broad jump and take a turn at that. Then they'd be calling for me to throw the javelin or put the eight-pound shot." It was a whirlwind day for the Golden Cyclone.

Of the eight events, Didrikson won five outright and tied for first in another. She defeated Rena McDonald, the favorite from Massachusetts, in the shot put with a throw of 39 feet, 6¼ inches, unexpectedly setting a new AAU record. In the baseball throw, she broke her own world record by heaving the ball 272 feet, 2 inches. Didrikson also beat her previous world record in the javelin with a throw of 139 feet, 3 inches, and in the broad jump, she launched herself 17 feet, 6 inches, for her fourth title.

While Didrikson earned these four first-place finishes with relative ease, she faced her stiffest competition in the 80-meter hurdles and the high jump. In the qualifying round of the hurdles, Evelyne Hall of the IWAC, the event record holder, crossed the finish line a tenth of a second faster than Didrikson. Didrikson came back to finish first in the semifinal, her time of 11.9 seconds establishing yet another world record.

All eyes, therefore, watched as Didrikson and Hall assumed their positions for the championship run, one on the track's inside lane and the other on the outside. When the gun cracked, Hall spurted to an early lead.

Didrikson quickly caught the reigning champion, and the two athletes crossed the finish line side-by-side. Although they appeared to hit the tape simultaneously, Didrikson jubilantly thrust her hands in the air while Hall waited patiently for the judges to name the victor. Unfortunately for the Illinois native, the race officials were similarly perplexed by the close finish. A look at the two competitors' contrasting postures convinced at least one judge to name Didrikson the champion. The others agreed. Unfortunately for Hall, this would not be the last time Didrikson's unabashed confidence factored into the crowning of the champion.

Yet, Didrikson's aplomb did not influence the remaining events. She went head-to-head with Philadelphia standout Jean Shiley in the high jump. Both athletes cleared 5 feet, $3^3/_{16}$ inches, set a new world record, and tied for first place. Didrikson also placed fourth in the discus and missed qualifying for the final in the 100-meters by one step. As a single-person "team," she scored thirty points, enough to win the meet by eight points over the IWAC. "Winning that 1932 national championship track meet singlehanded was the thing that first made my name big," Didrikson explained. The "Texas Tornado" left the 1932 AAU meet the undisputed star; however, when compounded with her habit of self-promotion, Didrikson's newfound publicity planted seeds of discord among her future Olympic teammates.

Sixteen women from the AAU meet made the U.S. Olympic team, and all sixteen headed to Los Angeles together. The press largely described the entourage traveling by train as the "Babe Didrikson show," increasing the dislike many already felt toward the self-proclaimed standout. For example, the Associated Press reported—in an article that appeared in numerous papers around the country—that "Miss Mildred Didrikson of Dallas, Texas . . . will lead the American women's Olympic track and field, and such assistance as she may need . . . will be provided by [fifteen] other young women." Not one to shy away from this type of coverage, Didrikson oftentimes provided the ammunition for these accounts. She told the *Los Angeles Times*, "I don't see any reason why I shouldn't win three first places. If I don't win, whoever beats me will have to set a world record." Similarly, to reporter Muriel Babcock, Didrikson boasted that "I came out to beat everybody in sight and that's just what I'm going to do. . . . I can do anything." Not surprisingly, the fifteen "other young women" resented such reports.

If these news accounts did not antagonize the athletes, Didrikson's behavior guaranteed her teammates' antipathy. She tormented them on the train, both with childish antics and unprompted descriptions of self-grandeur. Hall remembered her "running through the train, shrieking and yanking pillows out from under your head if you were sleeping." When the team stopped in Albuquerque, New Mexico, Didrikson yelled, "Did you ever hear of Babe Didrikson? If you haven't you will. You wiiillllll!!" By the time the team rolled into Los Angeles, most of the athletes despised Didrikson and desperately wanted to beat her.

The 1932 Olympics occurred in the midst of the Great Depression. Los Angeles was the only city to bid for the games, and fewer than half the athletes from the 1928 Summer Games made the trip to California. Despite the necessary austerity, the Los Angeles Olympic Organizing Committee strove for a festive atmosphere. The Opening Ceremony in the Coliseum drew 105,000 spectators, dressed in white and adorned with American flag buttons. While the lively crowd awaited the entrance of the athletes, airplanes looped overhead with advertisements. The 357 men and forty-three women from the United States entered to thundering applause and cheers. After Vice President Charles Curtis opened the games, five thousand "doves"—they were actually pigeons—were released, and the Olympic cauldron was lit. A white-robed chorus of 1,200, accompanied by a 250-person orchestra, performed the "Star-Spangled Banner."

Following the Opening Ceremony, the sixteen American female track and field athletes competed against a backdrop of unease in six events: the 100-meters, the 4 x 100-meters relay, the 80-meter hurdles, the discus, the high jump, and the javelin. Many in the IOC still questioned whether women should compete in track and field at all. Owing to the continued assertion of female frailty and the assumption that athletics masculinized women, the IOC had voted to limit each female athlete's participation to three events. Popular lore suggests this rule prohibited Didrikson from winning more Olympic medals. She also propagated this legend. "They let me in only three events. . . . I'd break 'em all if they'd let me," Didrikson informed journalist Braven Dyer in 1932. However, she actually qualified for only three events: the javelin, the 80-meter hurdles, and the high jump. In the AAU meet, Didrikson had not reached the finals of the 100-meters, removing her chances in the team relay, and finished fourth in the discus.

Despite not qualifying for more events, Didrikson sought to circumvent the Olympic rule and compete in more than three contests. She attempted to earn a spot in the discus by subverting teammate Ruth Osburn. Prior to the AAU meet, Osburn had been in a car accident that broke her ribs and strained her shoulder. Her coach, therefore, had to limit the number of times she threw in practice. Seemingly trying to cause reinjury, Didrikson challenged Osburn to an informal contest. "I can beat any discus thrower there is," she informed her. The comment predictably sparked Osburn's anger. She later recalled that Didrikson "knew she was going to make me mad." Fortunately for the discus thrower, her coach overheard the exchange and forbade her from touching the equipment until the games commenced. With Didrikson's plan foiled, she remained slated for only three events.

When the games started, track and field drew large crowds. More than 50,000 spectators observed the first day of competition, during which the "Amazing Amazon" participated in the javelin. Her first launch was both disastrous and impressive. As Didrikson started the throwing motion, her hand slipped slightly, forcing her to hop on one foot several times to regain her grasp. The unplanned movement caused a jolt of pain in her right shoulder. Additionally, faltering reduced the arc of her throw. Rather than lofting the javelin, she threw it like a line-drive into the grass. Despite her momentary slip and horizontal-propelled toss, Didrikson's effort bested the existing Olympic record by more than ten feet. But she had also torn the cartilage in her right shoulder. Her next two attempts were adversely affected by the injury, but Didrikson's first toss won her a gold medal, nine inches ahead of the second-place finisher.

The next two events proved equally challenging for Didrikson. Similar to the 80-meter hurdles at the AAU championships, she and Hall both won preliminary races. In her first heat, Didrikson started slow but sped to a new world record of 11.8 seconds. Hall then won her heat in 12.0 seconds. Just as in Evanston, the promise of a closely contested final drew the attention of the crowd. And, just as in Evanston, the two hurdlers appeared to both cross the finish line in 11.7 seconds, another world record. After thirty minutes of debate, the judges declared Didrikson the winner and named both runners world record holders.

According to Hall, Didrikson's self-assurance again had given her the victory. Speaking with the *Los Angeles Times* in 1988, Hall said that she hit the finish line first, evidenced by the blood across her neck from the finish line yarn. Yet, mirroring her antics in the AAU meet, Didrikson immediately declared herself the winner and shouted "Well, I won again." Hall remembered that her friends standing close to the finish flashed the No. 1 sign, believing she had won. "They thought I had won. I thought I had won," Hall said. But shaken by Didrikson's unconcealed confidence, Hall shook her head and held up two fingers. "Later, I learned that at that very moment a couple of judges were looking at me. It's possible they made their judgment from this gesture," she explained. Hall believed Didrikson's self-assuredness had again robbed her of a gold medal.

Hall's claim years after the fact may seem like sour grapes, but by the time the hurdles concluded and the high jump commenced, most of the U.S. team hoped to see Didrikson lose. "We were actually praying for Jean Shiley to win [the high jump]," remembered Hall. "We put a lot of pressure on Jean to beat this obnoxious girl." In one of the day's most highly anticipated events, Didrikson and Shiley outlasted all the other jumpers. The two easily cleared 5 feet, 5 inches, and set a world record. When officials raised the bar to 5 feet, 5³/₄ inches, Shiley knocked the bar off. Didrikson followed by launching herself above the designated height. "It was the most astonishing jump any woman ever dreamed about. But luck was against her," wrote sportswriter Grantland Rice. "As the Babe fluttered to earth, her left foot struck the standard a glancing blow, just six inches from the ground—and the cross bar toppled into the dust with her." She had missed.

When officials lowered the bar to 5 feet, 5¹/₄ inches, both athletes easily hopped over it. However, the presiding judge argued that Didrikson had violated the rules and awarded Shiley the gold medal. Olympic stipulations at the time mandated that competitors' feet cross the bar before their shoulders. Didrikson jumped in a western style—a predecessor to the Fosbury Flop—which meant she turned away from the bar before her launch. Although this method placed her head and feet occasionally in tandem, Didrikson never received any warnings regarding her technique. "I have jumped that way all the time," she told Rice following her disqualification. "I have kept the same style through an AAU championship. I know I never changed today." Rumors suggest that competitors, frustrated with Didrikson's boastful and arrogant behavior, reported her illegal style to Olympic officials. Many reveled in her silver medal.

Despite her surprising disqualification in the high jump, Didrikson was the most highly acclaimed athlete of the 1932 Los Angeles Games. She was "America's Girl Star of the Olympics," noted the *New York Times*. As her teammates resumed life largely unnoticed, Didrikson received a hero's welcome when she returned home to Texas. In Dallas, she participated in a ticker-tape parade and rode through the business section of the city in a limousine as the Dallas Police Department band played "Hail to the Chief." When she arrived in her hometown, Beaumont, the mayor gave her a key to the city and called her the town's "conquering daughter." Yet, outside Texas, the public admiration of the "Dallas Star" was short-lived.

Society's concerns about the appropriateness of women in sport generally, and track and field specifically, haunted Didrikson. The celebration of her achievements devolved into questions about her biology. Many publicly wondered if athletics had masculinized the "Texas Tomboy" or if she was actually a member of a third sex. The most notable example of this prejudice was an article in *Vanity Fair* in which sportswriter Paul Gallico labeled her a "muscle moll," a masculinized heterosexual deviant, and cruelly suggested she was neither male nor female but something in between. Didrikson herself recognized society's angst about her accolades. In a 1936 article in *American Magazine,* she explained that people "seem to think I'm a strange, unnatural being summed up in the words Muscle Moll, and the idea seems to be that Muscle Molls are not people."

To combat this hostility and suspicion, Didrikson shied away from her athleticism and showcased her femininity. When asked about her sporting talents, she often steered the conversation toward her skills in cooking and sewing. Furthermore, in 1935, she handed in her track spikes for golf clubs, turning to a more socially acceptable sport for women. Yet, still a true all-around athlete, Didrikson dominated the Ladies Professional Golf Association, of which she was a founding member. She then married George Zaharias, completing her transformation into the perfect homemaker.

For Further Reading

Cahn, Susan K. *Coming on Strong: Gender and Sexuality in Women's Sports.* 2nd ed. Urbana: University of Illinois Press, 2015.

Cayleff, Susan. *Babe: The Life and Legend of Babe Didrickson Zaharias.* Urbana: University of Illinois Press, 1995.

Pieroth, Doris. *Their Day in the Sun: Women of the 1932 Olympics.* Seattle: University of Washington Press, 1996.

Van Natta, Don. *Wonder Girl: The Magnificent Sporting Life of Babe Didrikson Zaharias.* New York: Little, Brown, 2011.

Williamson, Nancy P., and William O. Johnson. *"Whatta-gal": The Babe Didrikson Story.* Boston: Little, Brown, 1977.

Zaharias, Babe Didrikson. *This Life I've Led: My Autobiography.* Taylorville, Ill: Oak Tree Publications, 1955.

7

Babe Ruth's "Called Shot" in the 1932 World Series

LARRY R. GERLACH

George Herman Ruth is not only the greatest player in baseball history, but also the most iconic sports figure in American culture. People not the least interested in baseball know his name, are familiar with his monumental feats on the diamond, and have a sure sense of his place in sports history. Yet questions about the Babe abound, including the nature of his childhood, his placement in a reformatory-orphanage, his identification with the Baby Ruth candy bar, the cause of the 1925 "bellyache heard round the world," and, most of all, the legendary home run he hit in the 1932 World Series. In the annals of baseball, where controversies abound, no event has been more widely debated then and now than Babe Ruth's "called shot."

"A spiritual moment of the most gorgeous display of humor, athletic art, and championship class," wrote sportswriter Westbrook Pegler in the *Chicago Tribune* on October 2, 1932. The previous evening Joe Williams in the *New York World-Telegram* enthused that Ruth "went so [far] as to call his shot." The references, readers knew, were to Ruth's home run in the fifth inning in Game Three of the World Series between the New York Yankees and the Chicago Cubs. What so impressed the reporters was not that Ruth's homer broke a 4–4 tie leading to a 7–5 Yankees victory, but rather the circumstances that would make it the most dissected and disputed home run in baseball history.

New York was heavily favored to defeat Chicago in a World Series that would see a record thirteen future Hall of Fame players take the field. It was also the first in which both teams wore numerals on their jerseys, the Cubs being the last major league club to adopt this innovation. The Yankees, with a

107-47 record, had won seventeen more regular-season games than the Cubs. Chicago had edged the Pittsburgh Pirates by four games, while New York had easily bested the Philadelphia Athletics, three-time defending American League champs, by thirteen games despite A's pitcher Lefty Grove leading the league in wins and ERA, and MVP slugger Jimmy Foxx tallying the most homers and RBIs. Confident though they were, the New Yorkers imparted a nasty edge to the Fall Classic that erupted even before the first pitch of the first game. Bench jockeying, later called "trash talking," was commonplace, but as the two teams prepared to square off, it became unusually heated and nasty.

It was personal. The Yankees were relentless in berating the Cubs as tight-wads for voting only half a World Series share to shortstop Mark Koenig. He had been their teammate for six seasons, and, after joining the Cubs in August, had helped Chicago's pennant surge by fielding brilliantly and hitting .353 in 33 games. (The Cubs were singularly stingy in refusing even a partial share to Rogers Hornsby, who, while unpopular, had managed the team for four months until being fired on August 2.) From Game One on, the New Yorkers chided the Chicagoans unmercifully, led by Ruth's "noisy tirades." The Cubs responded by calling the Babe, now thirty-seven and near the end of his career, "grandpop," and mocking him for failing twice to become the team's manager. Chicago's pitcher in Game One, Guy Bush, the Mississippi Mudcat, as he was known, led the verbal assault, calling Ruth "a nigger," an epithet prompted by his facial features.

The Yankees came from behind to win the first two games in New York handily, 12–6 and 5–2. The convincing victories, not surprising as the team had posted a remarkable 62-15 record at Yankee Stadium, served to increase the taunting on and off the field when the Series moved to Chicago. Upon arriving at their hotel, Ruth and his wife, Claire, were confronted by "two lines of hysterical, angry women." Babe commented that they used "words that even I had never heard before" and that the verbal tirade was surpassed by "their spitting."

Rival players had vilified each other in New York, but for Game Three at Wrigley Field on October 1 a capacity crowd hoping for a Cubs resurgence created a cascade of anti-Ruthian slurs, taunts, invectives, and obscenities. Temporary bleachers had been constructed on Waveland and Sheffield Avenues to accommodate the record crowd of 49,986. Celebrities abounded. In addition to baseball commissioner Kenesaw Mountain Landis, three men recently elevated to public prominence were present: Anton Cermak, first-year Chicago mayor; Franklin D. Roosevelt, recently chosen the Democratic presidential nominee, who threw out the ceremonial first pitch; and Francis Joseph Spellman, newly appointed auxiliary bishop of the Catholic Archdiocese of Boston, soon to become Archbishop of New York. Among the youthful fans who would one day gain distinction was twelve-year-old John Paul Stevens, later to serve thirty-five years as a United States Supreme Court justice. Joining the array of nationally renowned sportswriters in the press box was a future Pulitzer Prize winner covering his first World Series, twenty-seven-year-old Red Smith of the *St. Louis Star-Times*.

Pregame attention focused not on the starting pitchers, George Pipgras, 16-9 with a 4.19 ERA for the Yankees, and Charlie Root, 15-10 and 3.58 for the Cubs, neither of whom would pitch well. Instead, fans focused on the Yankees batsmen, Ruth and Lou Gehrig in particular. Ruth was no longer the most dangerous slugger in the game, but he had a fine season, hitting .341 with 41 homers and 137 RBIs in 133 games, just shy of Gehrig's marks of .349, 34 and 156. The Babe relished batting in Wrigley's cozy confines with short fences down the lines, commenting, "I'd play for half my salary if I could bat in this dump all the time! I could bunt homers into that right field bleacher." During batting practice, initial jeers turned to cheers when the Yankees duo blasted pitch after pitch over the walls, Ruth nine, Gehrig seven. Ruth had only one hit, a single, in each of the first two games, but after this batting exhibition Gehrig remarked, "The Babe is on fire. He ought to hit one today. Maybe a couple."

He was right. Ruth hit a three-run homer off Root in the first inning, then barely missed another in the second, launching a deep fly just short of the right-field fence. He came to bat for the third time in the fifth inning with one out and the score tied. He sought redemption after being boisterously ridiculed by fans in the left-field bleachers for falling down while misplaying a low, line drive in the bottom of the fourth, a fielding gaffe that allowed Billy Jurges to reach second and eventually score to tie the game. Even before he approached the plate, the Bambino began hurling derogatory remarks toward the Chicago dugout. Responding in kind from the top steps of the dugout, Cubs bench jockeys, led by Guy Bush, razzed him unmercifully. Ruth gleefully joined in the "bitter repartee."

Upon reaching the batter's box, the Babe audaciously taunted pitcher Root, a fierce competitor. He took the first pitch for a called strike and then extended his right arm, a finger raised, perhaps pointing toward Root or the outfield. Next came two balls. A second called strike prompted "more hissing and hollering and no small amount of personal abuse" from the Cubs. Fans in the stands hurled fruit and, according to Cubs public address announcer

Pat Pieper, verbiage "you can't print in a family newspaper." Ruth reportedly laughed at the abuse, vowing, "I'm going to hit one out of the yard," and again raised his arm and extended two fingers. He then walloped the next pitch past the scoreboard and flagpole in center field into the temporary bleachers, a prodigious shot estimated at from 440 to 490 feet. The *Chicago Tribune* reported the next day that with the crack of the bat, Ruth "resumed his oratory: he bellowed every foot of the way around the bases, accompanying derisive roarings with wild and eloquent gesticulations," perhaps even thumbing his nose at the now silent Cubs. Returning to the Yankees dugout, the Babe chortled, "Did Mr. Ruth chase those guys back into the dugout? Mr. Ruth sure did." The next batter, Lou Gehrig, then hit his second homer of the day. Root was done. So were the Cubs.

Tribune reporter Edward Burns thought Ruth's home run "probably will go down as one of the classics of baseball razzing" for so dramatically and decisively showing up, even humbling, Charlie Root and the Cubs. It was vintage Ruth, another chapter of fabled aura surrounding the larger-than-life sports legend. Adding to the mystical quality of his feat, Ruth before the game had made one of his customary hospital visits to see kids; he had heard about Leo Koeppen, sixteen, who had been blinded by a bombing incident, and presented the lad with an autographed ball. That the Yankees went on the win the game and the next day completed the series sweep with a 13–6 victory was soon eclipsed by the controversy over Ruth's fifth-inning blast.

It is indisputable that Babe Ruth hit one of the most dramatic, majestic home runs in World Series history. Ruth clearly made a pointed gesture with one or two fingers raised not to the Cubs dugout, but in the general direction of the mound and center field. But to what purpose? Was he contemptuously dismissing the two-strike count, or audaciously indicating that he would hit Root's next pitch over the center-field fence, or simply vowing to get a hit that fortuitously turned into a home run?

Most of those in attendance saw his gesture—it was obvious—without discerning its significance. They interpreted things variously because they saw his gestures from different angles and perspectives and did not know what Ruth intended. Nonetheless opinions, strongly held, differed. Before Ruth's drive reached the bleachers, David J. Walsh of the International News Service shouted in the press box, "Hey, he hit it exactly where he had pointed." Pegler agreed, "Nor will you ever see an artist call his shot before hitting one of the longest drives ever made in the grounds." But Burns thought Ruth had simply "held up two fingers indicating two strikes in umpire fashion," a common view, although his fellow scribes were fairly evenly divided as to whether or not the Babe had called the home run. Positions hardened over time. Pat Pieper, seated directly behind home plate, said, "You bet your life Babe Ruth called it. I was in a perfect position to see and hear everything. Don't let anyone tell you that Ruth didn't call that shot." Radio announcer Bob Elson declared, "I definitely know he pointed to center field. There was no doubt about it. He did call his shot."

Players on the field also saw things differently. After the game, Gehrig, in the on-deck circle during the controversial at-bat, was adamant. He said, "There was never any question that Ruth called the shot." Some Yankees agreed with rookie shortstop Frankie Crosetti, who thought Ruth was signaling he had one more strike, but most of his teammates sided with pitcher Charlie Devens, "It was quite extraordinary to see him point, then hit the very next pitch out of the ballpark." Deniers there were. All but one of the Cubs, including Koenig, rejected the notion that Ruth called the homer, agreeing that he was pointing toward Root to indicate the count. The dissenter was Guy Bush, who had so caustically vilified Ruth. "I believe Ruth meant to call the home run," he said. "I believe that he pointed, and I'll always believe that he pointed." (On May 25, 1935, Ruth hit the final two home runs of his career off Bush in Pittsburgh. As the Babe rounded the bases, the "Mississippi Mudcat" doffed his cap in respect.)

Most relevant are the three persons close enough to hear what Ruth said and see how he gestured. All three agreed that Ruth challenged Root, vowing to hit his next pitch. Catcher Gabby Hartnett recalled that the Babe raised one finger and shouted, "It only takes one to hit it." Umpire Roy Van Graflan remembered him saying, "Let him put this one over, and I'll knock it over the wall out there." While Gehrig said Ruth pointed at Root and shouted, "I'm going to knock the next one down your goddamn throat," Root dismissed the idea, disingenuously saying if Ruth had "pointed as they say, he would have been knocked on his fanny." Instead of wasting a pitch and going to a 3-2 count, foolish for such a dangerous hitter, Root was determined to strike out his tormentor by throwing the most difficult pitch to hit, a slow curve low and outside that, according to Root, "wasn't a foot off the ground and was three or four inches off the outside of the plate, certainly not a good pitch to hit." Babe won the one-upmanship battle by bashing the ball into the far reaches of the center-field bleachers.

The basic facts are clear—a gesture followed by a home run—the decision uncertain. While on the Supreme Court, Justice Stevens, who as a lad from his seat behind the Cubs dugout looked directly at the left-handed-hitting Babe, ruled that Ruth called the shot. "He definitely pointed toward center field. There's no doubt about that. That's my ruling," he said. But the jury is still out. Indeed, the ongoing debate is moot. There is no definitive visual or audio evidence. There is no recording of the radio play-by-play account or commentary from Ted Husing or Graham McNamee, who broadcast the game nationwide for CBS and NBC, respectively. Newsreels do not capture the moment. The grainy images on the lone extant home movie taken by Matt Miller Kandle Sr. from the left field stands are tantalizingly inconclusive.

In truth, Babe Ruth alone knew the answer. No one asked Ruth after the game what his gesture meant, and his subsequent recollections were contradictory and inconclusive. Ever the showman, he characteristically played it to the hilt with braggadocio, relishing the notoriety. He changed his story first and then the details over the years. Upon returning to New York after the Series, he repeatedly told interviewers that he intended to hit a home run without mentioning pointing to center field. The next year he told a Chicago broadcaster, "I wasn't pointing anywhere. I never knew anybody who could tell you ahead of time where he was going to hit a baseball." But then told columnist Walter Lippmann that he intentionally indicated center field as the destination for the home run. From then on, he consistently affirmed signaling the home run with ever-greater embellishment and bravado. Perhaps his most accurate account was serendipitous. "I didn't exactly point to any one spot, like the flagpole," he admitted. "Anyway, I didn't mean to. I just sorta waved at the whole fence, but that was foolish enough. All I wanted to do was give that thing a ride . . . outta the park . . . anywhere."

Since 1932 there has been much pro-and-con speculation by historians and journalists who were not present at the game and thus do not know what happened. Given the disparity of views of players then and in later reminiscences and the absence of verifiable reportorial or visual evidence, accounts of Ruth's "called shot" are based on hearsay, speculation, and personal opinion. For all the attention given the Babe's immortal blow, there is no consensus as to what actually happened, and there never will be.

Two days before his death in 1970, Charlie Root, the winningest pitcher in Cubs history, told his daughter, "I gave my life to baseball, and I'll only be remembered for something that never happened." But something dramatic and remarkable had happened. Hartnett stared seemingly in awe at Ruth as he crossed home plate and Gehrig, after shaking the Babe's hand, looked at him admiringly as he trotted toward the dugout. The Babe had done something extraordinary. But did he point to signal his intent to hit a home run?

The debate over whether Ruth actually pointed to center field as the destination of his home run misses the point: The Babe called his shot, even if he didn't. Perhaps he didn't point to center field. Perhaps he did not knowingly think he would hit a home run. But he did make an obvious gesture toward Root, a sign of contempt and brazen confidence to hit the ball. Challenging the pitcher was an act of bravado that put additional pressure on Ruth. He was on the spot either to put up or shut up. And he did, hitting it up and out. He had called attention to himself, put himself on the line in front of a hostile crowd in the World Series, and, true to form, made good on his boast. He delivered a dramatic blow properly referred to not as a "called homer" or "called home run" but as the "called shot" since it was a fatal shot to the heart of Charlie Root and the Cubs. And it added another chapter to the book of Babe Ruth heroics. Grantland Rice said it best: "No one else in sport could have developed such a plot and then finished the story with such a flaming finale."

George Herman Ruth changed the offensive nature of the game with his prodigious slugging, winding up with season (60) and career (714) home run records that stood more than thirty years, yet the solo shot in 1932, the last World Series home run in his storied career, remains the feat most remembered. Ruth challenged Root and delivered. It was a terrific performance, another larger-than-life feat in the Babe's storied career. Perhaps the most remarkable aspect of Ruth's home run is why that singular event achieved legendary status and eight decades later remains an impassioned topic of debate. The salient question is not what happened, but why do we care?

The contemporary controversy was the understandable product of the time, place, and circumstance, but how to explain the continuing fascination and dispute? The circumstances of the home run—gestures, comments—added to the aura of incomparable exploits on and off the field by the game's greatest player. It provided a thrilling, conversational antidote to the economic and social malaise of the Great Depression. The ambiguity of Ruth's gestures and retorts, noted but unverified by newspaper accounts and audio-visual sources, fueled the making of fable. Moreover, the decentralized journalism network allowed controversy to take shape and then the legend to grow with embellishments over time, something impossible with modern, technological sports reporting and the impact of mass communication. Then, too, the Babe's mythical exploits on and off the field still invite scrutiny intended to embellish or diminish his seemingly unfathomable feats.

Perhaps, too, we embrace the "called shot" as a welcome mutant achievement in the world of sport, one of those rare human endeavors still haunted by uncertainty. Baseball, especially with its geometric and arithmetic precision, creates clear, precise, unambiguous outcomes. The "called shot" clashes with the observable certainties of the game. It is a reminder that there lurks in human achievement an element of the mysterious, the unknown, the unfathomable. Hence the legend and the controversy.

And maybe that's for the best. Myth is often more serviceable than truth. Baseball historian John Thorn wrote, "It doesn't matter whether Ruth called his shot. What matters is that we're still talking about it." As usual, the Babe had the last word, reportedly telling Crosetti after the game, "You know I didn't point, and I know I didn't point, but if those bastards want to think I pointed to center field, let 'em."

For Further Reading

Creamer, Robert W. *Babe: the Legend Comes to Life*. New York: Simon and Schuster, 1974.

Montville, Leigh. *The Big Bam: The Life and Times of Babe Ruth*. New York: Doubleday, 2006.

Sherman, Ed. *Babe Ruth's Called Shot: The Myth and Mystery of Baseball's Greatest Home Run*. Guilford, Conn.: Lyons Press, 2014.

Smelser, Marshall. *The Life That Ruth Built: A Biography*. New York: Quadrangle, 1975.

8

March Madness or Madness in March?

CHAD CARLSON

The Division I Collegiate Men's Basketball Championship—the tournament known as "March Madness"—is one of the premier events on the American sporting landscape. Each year millions fill out their brackets, and television generates billions of dollars for the NCAA and its members. Amid all this success, it is hard to believe that the first tournament in 1939 lost money and did not show much promise. As tournament officials scratched their heads with doubts and concerns, looking back, we can only wonder, "What were they thinking?"

Postseason basketball was not a new idea. Private promoters had organized such events in the past. In fact, the previous season, 1937–1938, had concluded with two postseason tournaments for the first time ever. Emil Liston, coach at Baker University in Baldwin City, Kansas, ran one, the second edition of an eight-team tournament in Kansas City that he called the National Intercollegiate Basketball Championship tournament. Two years later, Liston formed the National Association of Intercollegiate Basketball (NAIB)—later the National Association of Intercollegiate Athletics (NAIA)—to assume sponsorship of this event.

The other postseason event in 1938 was the inaugural National Invitation Tournament hosted by the Metropolitan Basketball Writers Association (MBWA) in New York City's famed Madison Square Garden. The writers envisioned this event as a way to build upon the massive spectator interest surrounding college basketball in the Garden. In 1941, the MBWA turned over this tournament to the new Metropolitan Intercollegiate Basketball

Committee, comprised of representatives from eleven New York City universities, and the public increasingly referred to the tournament as the NIT.

Set against this background, the National Association of Basketball Coaches (NABC), the voice of college coaches across the country, convened in Chicago in early April 1938 for its twelfth annual meeting. Legendary Kansas coach Phog Allen helped create this group in 1927, and he remained a prominent member. A late blast of winter weather in the Windy City caused NABC members to shudder and brace. Unseasonably warm temperatures throughout March suddenly plummeted below freezing. The Hotel Morrison on South Clark Street downtown provided a shield against the bitter cold, enabling the convention delegates, 109 in all, to meet and cook up a new plan. A small group of prominent NABC members eyed the two existing tournaments with both envy and disdain. They saw success and wanted a piece of the action, but they thumbed their noses at the methods Liston and the MBWA used to run their galas.

Ohio State coach Harold Olsen requested the podium on the second day to propose that the NABC should hold its own event in 1939—a third "national" postseason tournament—that would be sponsored by the NCAA. He presented four arguments. First, there was a demand, he said, and the coaches' association should be the sponsor. Second, an NABC tournament would bring revenue to the coaches' association without cutting in an outside sponsor, an accusation the NABC hurled at both Liston's tournament and the NIT. Third, a coaches' tournament would help boost college representation at the next Olympic Trials basketball tournament. And fourth, an NABC tournament would be a fitting end to the season if held in conjunction with the annual coaches' convention.

Olsen's argument found great, if not unanimous, favor with convention delegates. Basketball historians, though, know very little about where he got his idea. To be sure, Olsen had allies with whom he must have caucused beforehand. Allen, he must have known, would favor any event that would increase the chance of collegiate representation on the American Olympic team. The Kansas coach had worked tirelessly in the early 1930s to get basketball added to the Olympic docket and expected to be rewarded for his efforts in 1936 with an honorary coaching position. That did not happen, and, as AAU teams swept through the Olympic Trials tournament—defeating college teams—and AAU players won roster spots, Allen burned with fury.

John Bunn, former Kansas Jayhawk cager, assistant coach under Allen, and just retired from coaching at Stanford, may also have shared his views

Harold Olsen, 1933. (Ohio State University Archives.)

with Olsen. Bunn and his Stanford Indians had come to national prominence over the past few years thanks to superstar guard Hank Luisetti. In December 1936, Bunn brought his team to Madison Square Garden to face Long Island University (LIU) in one of college basketball's early intersectional games. LIU came in riding a forty-three-game winning streak that ended abruptly. Luisetti, the junior sharpshooter, awed New York fans with his fearless and innovative offensive tactics—jump shooting and dribbling with speed both left and right. Luisetti became one of the first nationally recognized college basketball stars.

The following season, Bunn took his team across the country again, and Luisetti cemented his legacy. Most of the basketball establishment—including New York City's powerful media—believed that Stanford was the best team in the country, but this claim was little more than speculation. Stanford, like many other teams, followed a strict policy against postseason basketball play. Bunn must have been aching for an opportunity to showcase Luisetti and his team in a postseason event to validate their prowess. Stanford would have allowed Bunn's boys to participate in an NCAA-sanctioned postseason event. The NCAA president, Stanford law professor W. B. Owens, would have condoned the Indians' participation in any association event. Although it was not in his nature to be aggressive, Bunn may have lobbied Olsen that an NCAA-sponsored tournament was long overdue.

Thus, Olsen clearly had powerful allies, and he spoke to a membership that had college basketball's best interests in mind as a first priority. Although the NABC delegates would have been split if forced to support only one of three tournaments, the membership wanted to promote college basketball. Olsen's tournament would do this, and, if backed by the NCAA, Olsen's idea would grab the support of even more NABC members.

After the April convention, Olsen drafted a proposal and sent it to the NCAA. President Owens and the executive committee quietly and earnestly reviewed the document before officially approving it in early October 1938. What took them so long? The NABC had already discussed the only impediment to this proposed event—the fact that two national tournaments already existed.

Owens did not indicate any hesitation on the NCAA's part when he approved the event, but his delay through the summer months handicapped Olsen. The Ohio State coach must have been elated when he received the good news, but that joy likely preceded strong anxiety. He had only five months to prepare a national basketball championship tournament worthy of the reputation of both the NABC and the NCAA!

Olsen formed an executive committee that included, not surprisingly, both Allen and Bunn. Olsen consulted these two reputable colleagues in every decision he made in the early going, down to the smallest details. Unfortunately, this proved too slow. So when Allen told Olsen in early November that he did not need to be included in every decision, Olsen's confidence rose, and he picked up the pace.

The tournament he created included eight teams. For administrative purposes, Olsen followed the NCAA's eight geographic districts, and the tournament featured one team from each. The four districts west of the Mississippi River would each provide one team to square off in a Western Regional tournament, the four eastern districts did the same, and then the two regional champions would meet in an East–West Final. That much was easy.

Securing tournament locations was not so simple. Showing his competitiveness, Olsen eyed New York City and Kansas City as sites for the Eastern and Western Regionals. These cities, of course, hosted the NIT and NAIB tournaments, respectively. They were basketball-mad, and Olsen wanted to enter these markets and push the existing tournaments out. But neither event would relinquish its dates in the cities' prized arenas, and Olsen was forced to pursue Plan B.

In hindsight, it is clear that the refusals from the NAIB and the NIT to move doomed the inaugural NCAA basketball tournament. Bunn convinced Olsen to hold the Western Regional in San Francisco, where a municipal exposition would cover the tournament's expenses. Olsen chose Philadelphia as the site for the Eastern Regional, and he selected Chicago to host the East–West Final. The spacious Chicago Stadium was booked the night Olsen wanted for the final game, so he used Northwestern University's Patten Gymnasium instead. None of these cities panned out.

Allen did not agree with the decision to hold the final in Chicago, and he queried Olsen about why he had not been consulted, despite his earlier half-step removal from the decision-making process. When Olsen chose not to respond, the relationship between these two men began to deteriorate much to the detriment of the tournament's future.

When the first NCAA tournament began in mid-March, Oregon breezed through the Western Regional in front of roughly six thousand fans over two nights. This small turnout was not totally unexpected, nor did it worry Olsen and his committee, for the regional could not lose money.

Olsen had higher expectations for the Eastern Regional. Philadelphia's blossoming college basketball establishment had grown, featuring a handful of prominent college teams that packed their home gyms, including Penn's 10,000-seat Palestra, Olsen's chosen site. Contests featuring two local teams in Philadelphia's Convention Hall had drawn as many as 12,000 fans. Temple won the NIT in 1938 and Villanova would play in this first Eastern Regional, so Olsen must have felt comfortable with Plan B.

And yet, even though Villanova reached the Eastern Finals, losing to Olsen's Ohio State squad, the arena remained virtually vacant. Only 2,200 fans came to the opening round, and a meager 1,400 attended the final. As Olsen sat on the bench coaching his team, he must have wondered what had happened. Where were the fans? Why didn't they show up? Why didn't they support Villanova, at the very least? Was the tournament too late in March? Did fans see it simply as a pale competitor to the NIT?

After winning the Eastern Regional championship—a title that, without many fans, seemed to have little luster—Olsen and his Buckeyes traveled to Chicago for the national championship. Many of the 132 NABC attendees greeted him and watched as part of a crowd generously estimated at 5,500 as the Oregon Webfoots took down Ohio State, 46–33, to win the inaugural championship. Oregon's return home via train became a virtual victory parade once they reached the eastern border of the Beaver State. Locals petitioned the railroad to stop the train at every little burg on the route so fans could hail the champions. And once the Webfoots reached Eugene, they disembarked to encounter a crowd thousands strong lauding their feats.

Ohio State, on the other hand, returned to an empty campus. It was spring break. The Buckeyes received no parades, no celebrations, and only little season-ending publicity. Indeed, the pep rally after they won the Big Ten conference title became the highlight of their season's recognition. The lack of celebration gave Olsen more time to mull over the most appalling part of the inaugural tournament. It had lost more than $2,500. If the NCAA had not agreed to cover the debt, the new tournament would have been dead in the water.

As a basketball historian, I wish I could have been there with Olsen, Allen, and Bunn in the immediate aftermath of the tournament. Huddled in a hotel, I would have loved to hear their unfiltered thoughts. Bunn, the youngest of the group, probably would have been the least vocal. The former Stanford coach, who went on to coach at Springfield College and then at what is now the University of Northern Colorado while also serving as chairman of the Naismith Memorial Basketball Hall of Fame, was known as a good, modest, and honest man. His fellow coaches liked him because he was sincere and reasonable and would not stoop to "win at all costs."

Bunn had a deep relationship with Allen that would have resulted in deference to his mentor. When Bunn took over Stanford's program in 1933, he stayed in contact with his former coach despite one notable recruiting battle in which Allen literally pulled a Kansas high school star out of Bunn's arms. It is a tale that reveals Allen's personality. He was forceful, aggressive, and impulsive. While his reputation for manipulation and bias grew over time, he was always an activist and a leader. Further, he rarely found himself at fault—at least in his own mind. In the tournament's post-mortems, he probably would have been the most vocal.

Olsen put enough into this tournament and possessed enough administrative experience and acumen to fight back if pushed by Allen. When this occurred in correspondence, Olsen always responded diplomatically or simply moved forward if he thought Allen was being unreasonable. Olsen's peers and players liked him. His troops believed that his physical stature—he was as wide as he was tall, they said—belied his kindness. But he was no pushover. He required his players to reciprocate his kindness with their own etiquette and strict behavior.

While I cannot picture Allen entering a room at the Hotel Morrison with a smug grin on his face ready to confront Olsen—Allen was not a smug person—I can see him initiating conversation forcefully. "I told you so!"

may have come from his lips. "Why didn't you choose Kansas City as a host site?" And "Who was in charge of publicity for the regionals?"

"Every basketball tournament that I have ever hosted in Kansas City has been a success and has made a lot of money," Allen may have mentioned, for he was never shy about reviewing his accomplishments. In 1905, at the age of nineteen, Allen hosted the self-proclaimed "World's Championship of Basket Ball" featuring the local Kansas City Athletic Club team he starred on and the Buffalo Germans team that won the 1904 Olympic basketball exhibition. And in 1936, Allen hosted a district playoff series for entrance into the Olympic Trials. Both of these events made money hand over fist.

"I don't understand how the tournament in New York can make so much money and we can't even make a penny," Allen may have lamented pointedly. For as abrasive as Allen could be, he was also very sharp and knowledgeable. He had a great memory for details and events that furthered his causes— whatever they were—and embellished when he felt necessary. Allen surely would have known the size of the crowds at Madison Square Garden and surely would have fabricated the unspecified amount of money that the NIT made. In fact, the six-team NIT in 1939 averaged more than 15,000 spectators for each of its three nights of play. Each evening of action outdrew the entire NCAA-NABC tournament in total!

But it was not the attendance specifically that bothered Allen. Over the following years, he publicly disagreed with the way the NCAA remunerated teams because they could make a lot more at the NIT. Thus, even though attendance mattered, Allen focused on the money.

Olsen may not have had answers to Allen's questions, but he would not have cowered in a corner. He knew that Kansas City would have been a strong host site, but he had not been able to work out acceptable dates for NCAA games there. On this point, Bunn clearly agreed with him. Olsen also had tried hard to get his tournament into Madison Square Garden—the Holy Grail. His failure to obtain dates in the basketball mecca forced him to draw some battle lines. He felt that he had been locked out, kept out, and even blackballed by the New York City basketball establishment. And he felt similarly about Kansas City, though not to the same extent.

He must have thought, "Why wouldn't the NAIB and NIT cease their operations or move over for the NCAA-NABC event?" And he would have voiced this complaint to Allen and Bunn. For his ensuing public remarks showed his more aggressive and defensive side. He lamented to the NABC that other so-called national tournaments had created barriers that he could not overcome, resulting in poor attendance and the financial deficit.

Allen may have ended the three-way conversation with an eye toward the future and an ultimatum. "You better give me this tournament to host in Kansas City next year or else . . ." Indeed, Allen publicly voiced that exact idea as Olsen and colleagues discussed the future of the tournament. Many NABC members felt that the unsuccessful event should end—an early version of "one and done"—because it lost money. At the back end of the Great Depression and with the grim realities of international conflict rapidly escalating, these coaches shared in the American collective mindset: Losing money is bad, being indebted to anyone else is worse, and the best way to dig out of a hole is to stay conservative.

Allen, for all his bluster, put his neck on the line to continue the tournament. After pleading to host both the Western Regional and the East-West Final in Kansas City, he guaranteed that he would not only pay back the 1939 debt to the NCAA, but that he would also make money for the NABC. Loads of hard work paid off, aided by the fortuitous forces of Lady Luck. Allen's Jayhawks, who qualified for the 1940 Western Regional, had to travel less than fifty miles to compete, and they won the event. In the Eastern Regional, the Indiana Hoosiers qualified, had to travel only a bit farther to the Indianapolis host site, and they won, too. Thus, home crowds came out in droves to cheer on their teams all the way to the end. And after the Hoosiers took down Allen's squad in the East-West Final, the balance statement showed a net profit of more than $9,200. Allen had done as he said he would. He saved the tournament.

But he may have burned some bridges in the process. After the tournament, he was asked to step down from his position as selection committee chair in the NCAA's District 5—the role that allowed him to be the Kansas City site host. The official reason for this administrative action—likely implemented by Olsen—was that Allen had overseen District 5 basketball for thirteen years and it was time for a change. Olsen may have requested this change to be fair. He may have felt some embarrassment at finishing as runner-up of his own tournament in 1939 and assumed Allen felt the same as host in 1940. He may have wanted to avoid such situations in the future. By naming Missouri coach George Edwards as the new District 5 chair, he selected a much less successful coach.

Or Olsen may have been fed up with Allen's complaining. Immediately after the 1940 tournament, Olsen, Allen, and the NCAA could not agree on how to disperse the profits. Allen wanted the bulk to go to the competing teams, thus putting the tournament on financial par with the NIT. However, with Olsen's approval, the NCAA disbursed some monies to the teams but kept much more for itself. This decision heightened tensions between the two coaches. Allen thought Olsen sold out to the NCAA and was not arguing forcefully enough for the participating teams. Olsen, on the other hand, understood his place and knew he had to go along with the NCAA's wishes. After all, it had covered his debts in 1939.

Regardless of the true reason for Allen's dismissal from the committee, the NCAA tournament continued to grow. The 1941 event made more than $9,000 again. Kansas City continued to host the Western Regional Finals until 1951, and it hosted the East-West Final until 1943, when Olsen finally found his Holy Grail. Getting dates in Madison Square Garden took him four years, but the wait paid off. Attendance and profits skyrocketed, and the NCAA tournament used the Garden for its Eastern Regional and East-West Final until 1949 when the championship game moved to Seattle for a year.

The decision to move to New York City, more than anything else, put the young tournament on track to become the mega-event it is today. But in its early years, before becoming stable and sustainable in Kansas City and then New York, it was very tenuous. As a basketball historian, I wish I had been there.

For Further Reading

Carlson, Chad. *Making March Madness: The Early Years of the NCAA, NIT, and College Basketball Tournaments.* Fayetteville: University of Arkansas Press, 2017.

Frei, Terry. *March 1939: Before the Madness: The Story of the First NCAA Basketball Tournament Champions.* New York: Taylor Trade Publishing, 2014.

Kerkhoff, Blair. *Phog Allen: The Father of Basketball Coaching.* Indianapolis: Masters Press, 1996.

9

Kenny Washington, Woody Strode, and the Reintegration of the National Football League

DAVID K. WIGGINS

In 1947, Jackie Robinson made history when he integrated modern major league baseball. It was an extraordinarily important event received enthusiastically by the African American community and covered widely by black and white newspapers and other publications throughout the United States. Noted NPR broadcaster Scott Simon wrote recently that, "The story of Jackie Robinson's arrival in the major leagues is a heroic American legend. It is a story that endures all the nicks and nits of revisionism because, when the last page is turned, it plays on in our minds and lives: a bold man, dark skinned and adorned in Dodger blue, who displays the daring and audacity to stand unflinchingly against taunts, strike back at beanballs, and steal home with fifty thousand people watching. . . ." Historian Jules Tygiel called Robinson's breaking the so-called color line a "tale of courage, heroics, and triumph. Epic in its proportions, the Robinson legend has persevered—and will continue to do so—because the myth, which rarely deviated from reality, fits our national perceptions of fair play and social progress." Anthropologist John Kelly claimed that Robinson's tenure with the Brooklyn Dodgers "was the proving ground for most U.S. citizens for the prospect of black and white races integrating into one nation."

Standing in sharp contrast to the Robinson saga was the reintegration of the National Football League a year earlier. In 1946, African Americans Kenny Washington and Woody Strode signed contracts with the Los Angeles Rams. Close friends, Los Angeles natives, and local legends, Washington and Strode were Robinson's teammates on the great UCLA football team of 1939. Often referred to as the "Gold Dust Trio," the three players were all gifted athletes.

Robinson, who distinguished himself in four sports, excelled as a running back and in the defensive backfield. Strode, described by famous *Los Angeles Times* sportswriter Jim Murray as "strong enough to strangle a horse and fast enough to catch one," was a 6'4", 200-pound end who demolished opponents across the line of scrimmage. Washington was a great all-around athlete, a talented baseball player whom Rod Dedeaux, the highly successful coach at Southern Cal, contended was even better on the diamond than Robinson. Washington was one of UCLA's all-time gridiron stars, an outstanding runner and passer from a single-wing offense. He was a second team All-American in 1939, played for the College All-Stars in 1940 against the world champion Green Bay Packers, was chosen by the Helms Athletic Foundation along with USC's Morley Drury as "Los Angeles' greatest all-time collegiate football players," and was selected in 1956 to the College Football Hall of Fame.

Tellingly, the signing of Washington and Strode did not translate into a "heroic American legend" and has never been considered "epic in its proportions." On the contrary, when juxtaposed with Robinson's integration of major league baseball, Washington and Strode's reintegration of the NFL has nearly faded from view. The few individuals who have written about the event have correctly noted that the limited popularity of professional football was largely responsible for this neglect. In my view, however, the story has limited appeal because it lacks a white benefactor who pointed the way toward racial progress by interceding on behalf of two black athletes denied equality of opportunity. As noted by historian Richard C. Crepeau, the Rams' signing of Washington and Strode was "a matter of necessity rather than choice." Only after the Rams realized they would not be able to use the Los Angeles Coliseum, a publicly funded facility, with an all-white roster, and that the new All-America Football Conference (AAFC) would not bar black players did they ink Washington and Strode to contracts. The Rams hoped that signing two local athletes would boost attendance, which it did, but that was probably more a result of the Rams being the new team in town rather than from Washington and Strode's presence. The role of the two men in the reintegration of professional football would soon be forgotten, while Robinson would go on to a Hall of Fame career.

The early involvement of African Americans in the NFL is well documented. In 1920, Robert "Rube" Marshall of the University of Minnesota and Frederick "Fritz" Pollard of Brown University were the first African Americans to play in the NFL, then called the American Professional Football Association. A bit more than a decade later, the University of Oregon's Joe Lillard and Duquesne University's Ray Kemp would be the last, until

1946 Los Angeles Rams, including Kenny Washington (13) and Woody Strode (34). (Associated Press.)

1946. Neither player's contract was renewed for the 1934 season, Kemp after playing for the Pittsburgh Pirates and Lillard for the Chicago Cardinals. For the next twelve years, the league was lily-white.

Owners drew the color line at their annual meeting in 1933. Why they decided to bar black players is open to speculation, but many blamed George Preston Marshall, the southern-born owner of the Washington Redskins, who adamantly opposed race mixing. When once asked why there were no African Americans on the Redskins, he proclaimed, "We'll start signing Negroes when the Harlem Globetrotters start signing whites." Others claimed that some well-meaning owners feared that African American players would suffer serious injuries at the hands of southern-born players. Others contended that letting African Americans play would create logistical problems because special arrangements would have to be made for separate housing, travel, and dining accommodations when teams were on the road. Others argued that there were not enough quality African American players in the college ranks that could seriously be considered candidates for the NFL. Still others claimed that the NFL simply did not have the financial resources to scout African American players and simultaneously blamed the color line on Joe Lillard, whose volatile personality dissuaded owners from signing other black players.

African Americans did not immediately protest the new color line. As historian Thomas G. Smith noted, "Even after the color barrier was established in professional football, blacks were slow to attack it because they were reluctant to admit it existed." Although Smith is correct, there were additional reasons for the relatively slow and intermittent show of protest against the ban. The primary factor was the limited popularity of pro football at the time. African Americans were just as interested in the sport as anyone else, but football did not resonate and hold the same symbolic importance as baseball. Perhaps no sportswriter was more aggressive and committed to erasing baseball's color line than Wendell Smith of the *Pittsburgh Courier*. Together with other black sportswriters and a few enlightened white journalists, Smith hammered away at baseball's owners for their exclusionary policies. In 1938, he launched a vigorous campaign that included chiding African Americans for their continued support of major league baseball, proposing the creation of an NAACP effort on behalf of African American players, and conducting interviews with National League president Ford Frick, numerous managers, and players to determine their position on the color line; calling on President Roosevelt to implement a Fair Employment Practices Policy in baseball; admonishing Washington Senators owner Clark Griffith for his racist views; helping to arrange a meeting with Commissioner Kenesaw Mountain Landis; and organizing tryouts for black players. During World War II, Smith ingeniously drew on the status of baseball as America's national pastime and the great leveler in society by pointing out the hypocrisy of excluding African Americans from Organized Baseball while many were in the military fighting against a country that believed in racial superiority.

Smith's sustained effort was not duplicated by others in the black press during the twelve-year period when the NFL barred African American players. Black sportswriters occasionally wrote about African American success in predominantly white college football, but they did so primarily out of a sense of racial pride and to make it clear that blacks and whites could compete against one another without incident. There were two well-known attacks on racial discrimination in the NFL. One came from white radio broadcaster Sam Balter after no African American players were selected in the 1939 NFL draft. Calling out the league for not drafting Kenny Washington, Balter complained, "What you [leaders of the NFL] did Saturday was a source of bitter disillusionment to me—not on Mr. Washington's behalf, but on behalf of the millions of American sport fans who believe in fair play and equal opportunity." Black journalist William Brower also attacked the NFL in a 1940 essay called "Has Professional Football Closed the Door?" "When you simmer everything down," Brower wrote, "there is only one direction in which to look when you go to attach the blame—categorically in the faces of the national professional football magnates. There is no record of any authenticated commitment by them on the issue of the color line in the professional's game."

The games black athletes played against whites for charitable causes during World War II were important. Although they showcased the talents of African American footballers to a large audience, these games were, in some ways, high-reward, high-risk contests. Performing well against good white professionals could help prove that African American players were worthy of participating at the highest levels of the sport. Defeat, though, could prove otherwise. A highly publicized game between the Chicago Bears and a team of "Negro College All-Stars" attested to the high-risk nature of these contests. The game was not close. The Bears thrashed their opponents, 51–0, and punished the team of African American players, who lacked the depth and extended practice time to put up a fight.

On March 21, 1946, the NFL finally reintegrated when the Rams signed Washington to a contract. A short time later, the team signed Strode, who, according to some, was brought in only to room with Washington on the road. These signings, while receiving some media attention, generated little enthusiasm, even when compared to Robinson's season with the minor league Montreal Royals in 1946. Wendell Smith, for instance, wrote that he believed 1946 was the greatest year yet for African American athletes, even "greater than in 1936 when Jesse Owens led a caravan of 'Black Ambassadors' to Berlin and handed Hitler his first major setback. At the top of the list, of course," wrote Smith, "is Jackie Robinson, who is athlete of the year and the 1946 International League batting Champion."

Signing Washington and Strode was not the result of any prearranged player tryouts or investigations by white owners to determine whether African American footballers had the "correct" personal attributes to succeed at football's highest level. Instead, they sprung from a confluence of factors that forced the hand of NFL owners—who were practical, financially driven, and media conscious. The catalyst that ultimately led to the signings was the NFL's war with the All-America Football Conference. In 1944, Arch Ward, the well-known sports editor of the *Chicago Tribune,* organized this new league with franchises in New York, Brooklyn, Buffalo, Miami, Cleveland,

Chicago, San Francisco, and Los Angeles. The AAFC became an immediate threat to the NFL. In the upstart league's first draft, AAFC teams took several stars and by 1946, they had signed ninety-five players who had spent time in the NFL, including Frankie Sinkwich, the NFL's Most Valuable Player in 1944. The AAFC, along with the first United States Football League (USFL), which never materialized, also proclaimed that race would not be a barrier to signing players.

This announcement by the AAFC caught the attention of the NFL, which was having trouble controlling costs, despite the upsurge in the popularity of professional football. Notwithstanding these circumstances, NFL owners continued to discriminate until one of their own was forced to sign African American players. In 1946, Cleveland Rams owner Dan Reeves moved his financially strapped but championship football team to Los Angeles after a protracted fight with his fellow NFL owners, who probably agreed to the move only because the AAFC also had a team (the Los Angeles Dons) in the city. The Rams had not yet relocated when they and the Dons began to receive pressure to sign African Americans. Leading the charge for reintegration was the outspoken *Los Angeles Tribune* sportswriter Halley Harding, an outstanding all-around athlete who had played for the Kansas City Monarchs and the Harlem Globetrotters. With the assistance of two members of the Los Angeles County Board of Supervisors and a pair of African American sportswriters, Herman Hill of the *Pittsburgh Courier* and Edward Robinson of the *California Eagle,* Harding argued at a January 15, 1946, meeting of the Los Angeles Coliseum Commission that no team that discriminated against African American players should be allowed to use the publicly supported Coliseum.

Harding made an impassioned speech. No transcript survives, but the *Pittsburgh Courier* summarized the meeting. Harding recounted the exploits of African American athletes who had once played in the NFL. He blamed Marshall for the league's color barrier, questioned why a player as talented as Kenny Washington had never been offered a contract, and concluded by describing the sacrifices made by black soldiers during World War II. The speech undoubtedly touched many. Woody Strode's son, Kalai, recently posted on YouTube an actor's rendition of what Harding supposedly said over a montage of pictures of professional football's early black pioneers.

The Coliseum Commission meeting was followed a week later by a "get together" at the Last Word Club in Los Angeles. This gathering included Chile Walsh, general manager of the Rams; Bill Schroeder, general manager of the minor league Hollywood Bears in the football version of the Pacific

Coast League; and several members of the black press. Walsh expressed an interest in signing Washington, Strode, and a third player, Chuck Anderson. But he said he would not ink the famous "Negro" trio to professional grid pacts if they were under contract to any other club. Schroeder, who owned the rights to Washington, countered that he would not block the signing of any player by the NFL, but expected to be compensated for anyone taken from his club. Schroeder got compensation, and the Rams signed Washington on March 21 and Strode several weeks later. Other NFL owners did not receive the news well, and Rams backfield coach Bob Snyder supposedly admitted that the team would not have signed Washington if it had remained in Cleveland.

The decision to sign Washington and Strode, born of pragmatism because the Rams found themselves in an untenable situation regarding the use of the Coliseum, made sense from a competitive standpoint only if the two local players could return to their glory days. But as great as they were as collegians, the passage of time and, in the case of Washington, injuries, prevented them from enjoying long and productive careers with the Rams. Strode played sparingly during his one year with the team and then played two years with the Calgary Stampeders of the Canadian Football League, helping the team capture the 1948 Grey Cup Championship. He retired from the Stampeders in 1949.

Washington's career with the Rams lasted three years. Over that period, he gained 859 yards and in 1947 led the league with 7.4 yards per carry. He was not, however, the player he had been at UCLA or later with the Hollywood Bears and San Francisco Clippers professional football teams. He was nearly twenty-eight by the time he joined the Rams and suffered a serious knee injury that required surgery before he had stepped on the field for the NFL club. In his final game with the Rams against the Pittsburgh Steelers on December 12, 1948, a day declared "Kenny Washington Day" by Los Angeles Mayor Fletcher Bowen, the player they referred to as "Kingfish" was showered with gifts at halftime and given a thunderous ovation by those in attendance.

If Washington had been born a generation later, he certainly would have been paid handsomely for his prodigious talents. While Strode remained in the public eye because of his long acting career, Washington lived in relative anonymity following his football days. He is probably, in spite of being one of the greatest college football players of his era, the least well known of the "Gold Dust Trio." Washington and Strode, however, will always be linked because they were the first African Americans to reintegrate the NFL. Just a few months after the Rams signed Washington and Strode, the Cleveland

Browns of the AAFC signed Marion Motley and Bill Willis. Unlike the sign-ings of Washington and Strode, which were completed under duress and in a seemingly perfunctory fashion, the Motley and Willis signings were ulti-mately the choice, albeit with advice and perhaps even pressure from others within the Browns organization, of legendary coach Paul Brown. The elevated level of importance attached to these signings had a great deal to do with the success of Motley and Willis, who played in the NFL for nine and eight years, respectively, and were selected to the Professional Football Hall of Fame. But it also was a story in which the central figure was a white man who made the signing of the two players possible. Like some of the more famous stories of integration in sport, whether it was Alice Marble's efforts to see that Althea Gibson was permitted to play in the U.S. Tennis Championship or Don Haskins's decision to start five black players for Texas Western in the 1966 NCAA basketball title game or Branch Rickey's signing of Jackie Robinson, Brown was the white man who delivered Motley and Willis from oblivion. It is why he is often referred to as the "Branch Rickey of football." No such moniker could be attached to anyone associated with the Washington and Strode episode.

If Willis and Motley overshadowed Washington and Strode, Robinson's entry into Organized Baseball overwhelmed all other stories of integration in sport and remains one of the most significant events in the history of race relations in the United States. This fact was both a matter of pride and source of some frustration to Washington and Strode, because the three of them had been celebrated teammates at UCLA. "Next to me, Jackie was the best competitor I ever saw," Washington once noted. "But when he became a baseball star it kind of shook me. I out-hit him by at least two hundred points at UCLA." Robinson, for his part, once told *Gridiron* magazine, "I'm sure he [Washington] had a deep hurt over the fact he never had become a national figure in professional sports." Irrespective, no circumstances during their time together at UCLA would have prefigured such divergent experi-ences in professional sport and in their post–playing careers and how they would ultimately be remembered.

Though Robinson has been the subject of movies and countless number of books and articles, and immortalized by Major League Baseball with the retirement of his jersey number, 42, Washington and Strode have received scant attention from journalists and academicians. Their names resonate only with football aficionados or the staunchest of UCLA fans or scholars with a particular interest in race and sport. Strode wrote his own memoir, but no one has published a serious book specifically devoted to either of these two men. In the end, the story of two local black players with no white benefactors who reintegrated a sport that did not resonate with the public paled in comparison to the Robinson story. It was merely one of a countless number of unanticipated and largely unplanned events that helped chip away at the racial discrimination in one of America's most significant cultural institutions. While not, as some scholars might claim, a critical event, the signing of Washington and Strode deserves to be remembered because it led to the reintegration of the sport that is now, ironically enough, considered by many to be America's national pastime.

For Further Reading

Crepeau, Richard C. *NFL Football: A History of America's New National Pastime.* Urbana: University of Illinois Press, 2014.

Smith, Thomas G. *Showdown: JFK and the Integration of the Washington Redskins.* Boston: Beacon Press, 2011.

Strode, Woody, and Sam Young. *Goal Dust: The Warm and Candid Memoirs of a Pioneer Black Athlete and Actor.* New York: Madison Books, 1990.

10

Althea Gibson, America's First African American Grand Slam Champion

MAUREEN SMITH

Jackie Robinson was not alone. For a good chunk of the twentieth century, African American athletes in many sports found themselves marginalized, confined to the sidelines, confronted by systematic restrictions preventing their participation in mainstream sporting organizations limited to whites. Gradually these bans fell, creating a long list of "famous firsts," epochal moments in the history of American racial relations and American sports, and equally famous athletes. Althea Gibson's name is on this list, recognized as the first African American, male or female, to win a Grand Slam tennis title. More often than not, Gibson is hailed as the first African American, man or woman, to win the sport's most prestigious title, the singles championship at Wimbledon, in 1957. Less clearly remembered, except by the sport's dedicated fans, is Gibson's earlier Grand Slam win at the French Championships in 1956. Yet, it was her triumph at the All England Club and not at Stade Roland-Garros that earned her a fabled ticker-tape parade in New York City.

As Robinson's career with the Brooklyn Dodgers was coming to an end in 1956, Althea Gibson's career was taking off. She had been competing for more than ten years, but because the United States Lawn Tennis Association (USLTA) had denied her entry into its events, the tournaments she had dominated were sponsored by the all-black American Tennis Association (ATA). Gibson found great success in ATA events, and eventually, after much pressure from the ATA and a scathing letter from tennis legend Alice Marble, the USLTA relented and extended Gibson an invitation to compete in the United States National Championships at Forest Hills, New York, in 1950. This was a token invitation at best, and Gibson did not advance very far, losing a three-set match in the second round to Louise Brough, the reigning Wimbledon champion. Sportswriter Lester Rodney, who had ardently campaigned against baseball's color line, also covered Gibson's debut in the world of white tennis. "No Negro player, man or woman, has ever set foot on one of these courts," he wrote in the *Daily Worker*. "In many ways, it is even a tougher personal Jim Crow–busting assignment than was Jackie Robinson's when he first stepped out of the Brooklyn Dodgers dugout." Yet, after her first appearance at Forest Hills, Gibson's tennis career did not take off as expected, and she recorded mostly mediocre results through much of the first half of the 1950s.

Beginning in December 1955, Gibson traveled to Asia, Africa, and Europe, playing in tournaments as part of a State Department–sponsored goodwill tour. Far away from home, she put together a winning streak that saw her capture title after title. Occasionally, American newspapers gave her some coverage, providing their readers with short updates on her overseas victories. By the time Gibson entered the French Championships in the summer of 1956, she seemed unbeatable although, as the *Los Angeles Times* noted, "Many of the titles were won in tournaments where tennis nobodies and second raters filled out the field."

Clyde Reid, writing in the *New York Amsterdam News,* called the French Championships Gibson's "last continental competition" before Wimbledon, and she made the most of it. She was the lone American woman to reach the tournament quarterfinals, and in her semifinal match, the first she played on center court at Roland-Garros, she faced her doubles partner and close friend, Angela Buxton of Great Britain. During the match, Gibson's shoulder strap broke, a result of her "energetic swing." Reid suggested that the cheers and boos of the French fans affected Gibson's play, too, and that her reaction to the crowd, especially their booing when her strap broke, was an exhibition of "fine sportsmanship." In the end, Gibson earned her way into the finals, beating Buxton, 2–6, 6–0, 6–4.

In the finals, Gibson faced defending champion Angela Mortimer, also of Great Britain. In their previous four meetings, Mortimer had defeated Gibson each time, but this match was different. The front-page story in the *New York Times* provided the details: "Althea Gibson, the United States' only big winner on the European tennis circuit this spring, smashed a year-old jinx and won the women's singles title in the French tournament today with a 6–0, 12–10 victory over Angela Mortimer of Great Britain." The *Times* noted that the 1-hour, 45-minute match "overshadowed" the men's final between Australia's Lew Hoad and Sven Davidson of Sweden because Hoad needed only one hour and twenty minutes to beat Davidson in three sets. Gibson was so "happy" to have finally beaten Mortimer, the *Times* said, that she "leaped over the net to put her arms around her erstwhile jinx." Gibson's victory in Paris was her seventh consecutive title and the thirteenth since the start of her overseas trip the previous December. Gibson and Buxton then teamed up to meet Americans Darlene Hard and Dorothy Head Knode in the doubles final, winning in three sets, 6–8, 8–6, 6–1.

Mainstream newspaper accounts of Gibson's historic win hardly mentioned her race. In the days following the French tournament, there was no acknowledgment of Gibson's victory as a "famous first," a racial barrier broken, a milestone to be celebrated. Still, Gibson herself reflected on the historic nature of her win two years later in her autobiography. "I had become the first Negro ever to win the championship of France," she wrote in *I Always Wanted to be Somebody,* "in fact, the first Negro ever to win any of the world's major singles tennis championships." She remembered, too, the low-key nature of her celebration, recalling that Angela Buxton's father took the pair out to dinner and that she was back in her hotel room by ten o'clock that evening.

For the most part, the American sporting press was much more interested in Wimbledon, the upcoming tournament viewed as the pinnacle in the world of tennis, the championship above all others, the coveted prize and ultimate symbol of success. Gibson's win in France served to heighten expectations that she could become the Wimbledon champion.

Stories in the black press did identify Gibson's race, making it a point of pride and celebration, and they, too, looked ahead to her prospects at the All England Club. In the *Pittsburgh Courier,* Bill Nunn Jr. thought "the lithesome net queen" was poised to become the "first Negro woman to ever win the coveted" title at Wimbledon and at Forest Hills. A month later, Nunn viewed Gibson as a "definite threat" to become "the first of her race to ever win the tournament that has existed since 1877."

After Gibson's victory in Paris, and in anticipation of an encore win at Wimbledon, the *New York Amsterdam News* editorialized that the tennis star be applauded in "the true New York tradition . . . a ticker tape parade up Broadway!" upon her return. Gibson, the paper noted, "armed with only her brown skin and tennis racket," had brought "honor and glory" to the country, winning fourteen tournaments. She deserved to be celebrated. The editorial did not argue that her French victory merited a parade. Rather, the paper argued that "Negro Americans who conduct themselves in exemplary fashion while on foreign soil today are an effective propaganda weapon for this nation in the cold war with the Communist world."

Gibson started her quest at Wimbledon with a straight-set win over Edda Budding of Germany. On her way to the quarterfinals, she then beat Pat Hird, Anne Shilock, and Pat Wheeler, all British, before losing to the eventual champion, Shirley Fry, in three sets, 6–4, 3–6, 4–6. Despite her failure to win the singles title, Gibson did not leave empty-handed. She and Buxton repeated what they had done in Paris, winning the doubles. In her autobiography, Gibson explained her poor showing at Wimbledon as a result of being "a little overtennised," but "mostly . . . overeager." When she returned to New York, the *Amsterdam News* tabled its idea for a ticker-tape parade, basing its change of heart on logistics and poor timing. Clyde Reid went on to explain Gibson's poor showing in the singles as a result of her "weakening service" and "troubled" backhand. Her American friends, Reid noted, blamed it on "stage fright." A New York parade, if there were to be one, would have to wait.

Althea Gibson's 1956 Wimbledon doubles trophy.

Gibson's approach to Wimbledon the following year took a much different tack. While she played a few warm-up tournaments, she skipped the French Championships, forgoing defense of her title to focus on the elusive larger prize. In her first-round match against Hungary's Suzi Kormoczy, Gibson "advanced shakily," winning, 6–4, 6–4. She then beat Australia's Margaret Hellyer, 6–4, 6–2, before facing Gem Hoahing of Great Britain, in her "easiest match so far," winning 6–1, 6–1. In the quarterfinals, Gibson faced eighteen-year-old South African Sandra Reynolds, whom she "whipped," 6–3, 6–4. Her opponent in the semifinals was Great Britain's Christine Truman, "the 16-year-old child prodigy who blossomed into the big time." Gibson "rudely spanked" her, 6–1, 6–1, earning a coveted spot in the final against fellow American Darlene Hard. Gibson had defeated Hard in all three of their previous matches, and this final proved to be more of the same. Gibson won, 6–3, 6–2, to claim the Wimbledon singles title. Of her Wimbledon win, the new champion exclaimed in the *Pittsburgh Courier,* "Winning this title is the greatest thrill since I started playing tennis."

If Americans slightly ignored Gibson's "historic" victory a year earlier in Paris in anticipation of a Wimbledon victory that did not happen, the nation's press celebrated her Wimbledon crown in 1957 as if she were American tennis royalty. Her photo with Queen Elizabeth appeared on the front page of the *New York Times,* with full coverage of her match in the sports section, as well as a story about her welcome-home celebrations.

At the center of many newspaper stories was the social significance of Gibson's race. The caption on page one of the *Times* told readers Gibson "became the first Negro to win a Wimbledon singles title." Another story claimed Gibson "fulfilled her destiny at Wimbledon," becoming "the first member of her race to rule the world of tennis." The *Los Angeles Sentinel* thought the victory "crowned a life-long ambition" by becoming the first "Negro" to win the tournament. The *Los Angeles Times* identified Gibson as "a Negro from Harlem's teeming sidewalks" and later noted that never before had a "Negro champion" held the singles title in the eighty-year-long history of Wimbledon. A *New York Times* profile compared her to Jackie Robinson, "the first of her race to break a big league barrier," and like Robinson, "she went all the way to the pinnacle." A *Pittsburgh Courier* editorial cartoon captured the significance of the moment by depicting Gibson jumping over the net into "champ territory," where she is greeted by Sugar Ray Robinson, Joe Louis, Jim Brown, and Jackie Robinson, who "welcome Althea." The title of the cartoon proclaimed that there was "Always Room For a Lady." L. I. "Brock" Brockenbury, writing for the *Los Angeles Sentinel,* viewed Gibson's win as a "most significant achievement for the race." He clarified his position, explaining that Gibson's victory was evidence that "any one with similar determination can go to the top in any field." Seen as "another milestone in the long hard fight for equality," Brockenbury hailed Gibson as an inspiration for all.

At least one reporter, instead of focusing on Gibson's status as a racial barrier breaker, called attention to the racism she faced on the tennis court of the All England Club. Writing for the *Pittsburgh Courier,* Rudolph Dunbar claimed the tennis player "fought British color prejudice" for two weeks. By the time Gibson reached the finals, Dunbar was amazed she was able to forget the "slanders, slurs, insults and injuries" to claim victory in front of "thousands who did not want a colored girl to win." Dunbar suggested that even "white Americans resented the treatment accorded" their fellow American, victimized by "cat-calls and ugly names."

A year after the *Amsterdam News* called for a ticker-tape parade, New Yorkers welcomed Gibson home with another historic first. Returning to her neighborhood in Harlem, she told her neighbors, "My victory was your victory," acknowledging the racial symbolism of her win, despite her later resistance to being considered a representative of her race. Gibson was feted at City Hall by Mayor Robert Wagner, who told her "It's a long, long way from 143rd Street to Wimbledon, but you did it in a dignified way." She received a congratulatory telegram from the governor of New York and was the first African American woman honored with a parade up New York's vaunted Broadway. In an editorial, the *New York Times* celebrated Gibson's inclusion among royalty, presidents, generals, and other athletes who had received such an honor. She "attracted especial attention because she was the first member of the Negro race" to win Wimbledon, but the editorial claimed that "race was not precisely the reason why she had the ride up Broadway." The editorial suggested that the United States honored individuals of "any" race "who have achieved greatly in spite of difficulties" and concluded that Gibson's significance extended beyond her symbolic sporting victory, indicating that "the social atmosphere of our country is changing." Gibson stood as someone who "exemplified this change and did what she could do to bring it about," suggesting that "our country is changing." Her parade was "evidence that we are becoming a land of diminished discrimination and or greater opportunity." The *Los Angeles Sentinel* thought it "probable" that the parade "made quite a few American hearts quicken at the thought that another stride toward democracy" was taken with Gibson's win. To Gibson herself, said the *Los Angeles Times,* the historic parade was "amazing, wonderful, the greatest moment of my life."

With her Wimbledon triumph, Gibson had won "the big one," said the *Pittsburgh Courier,* but the sporting press quickly turned its attention to the upcoming U.S. Nationals title that had so far eluded her. Sportswriters predicted that the title would finally be hers, and they were right. Gibson continued her winning streak by claiming her first U.S. Nationals singles title, along with the mixed doubles title. After these victories, Ted Poston of the *New York Post* tried to put Gibson's success in context. He wrote that "long before Jackie Robinson, shortly after Joe Louis and a decade before the rise of Ralph Bunche, the Negroes of America had decided to scale another impregnable bastion. They were determined to tackle the U.S. Lawn Tennis Association and to remove unwritten barriers to their participation in that American sport." He added, "For their weapon, they chose a gangly, inarticulate Harlem tomboy, a street urchin named Althea Gibson." Poston felt Gibson's victories were a predictor of things to come, telling his readers, "this lissome Negro lass suggests the heights to which the descendants of those former slaves have raised their sights." In Gibson, Poston saw the collective efforts of her community, "impoverished but hopeful," and pooling resources to help advance the "most gifted." Gibson was averse to assuming the role of a racial hero. As she wrote in her autobiography, "I try not to flaunt my success as a Negro success. It's all right for others to make a fuss over my role as a trail blazer, and, of course, I realize its importance to others as well as to myself, but I can't do it." Not surprisingly, the black press and its readers were ready and more than willing to celebrate her wins as their own.

When the pioneering Gibson died in 2003, few stories mentioned her groundbreaking win in the 1956 French Championships, the victory that made her the first African American, male or female, to win a Grand Slam title, but obituary after obituary identified her as the first African American to win the prestigious Wimbledon title and the U.S. title in 1957, triumphs that she repeated the following year. Gibson insisted she was not a racial pioneer, but those who reviewed her career knew her to be just that.

In the decades that followed, few African Americans were able to make their way into USLTA tournaments, so Gibson's influence on broader participation by African Americans proved limited. African American Arthur Ashe stood out. He won his first Grand Slam title, the very first U.S. Open, in 1968, and he won Wimbledon in 1975. More recently, Venus and Serena Williams became the first African American women since Gibson to win Grand Slam titles, Serena winning the U.S. Open in 1999 and Venus repeating Gibson's Wimbledon–U.S. Open pair in 2000 and 2001. Still, fifty years after the fact, Gibson's Grand Slam victories, most notably her 1957 Wimbledon title, identify her as the "first." Celebrating her in this way is largely about the present time, of putting the present time period in context, of recognizing the past victories of those who came before and played in more challenging social conditions. It is equally indicative of the current interest in history. As a result, we celebrate Althea Gibson for being the first African American to win a Grand Slam title, sometimes remembered for her 1956 win at the "French Open," though most often for Wimbledon in 1957. Gibson, most certainly, was a champion of the courts.

For Further Reading

Festle, Mary Jo. *Playing Nice: Politics and Apologies in Women's Sports*. New York: Columbia University Press, 1996.

Gibson, Althea. *I Always Wanted to be Somebody*. New York: Harper, 1958.

Gray, Frances Clayton, and Yanick Rice Lamb. *Born to Win: The Authorized Biography of Althea Gibson*. Hoboken, N.J.: John Wiley & Sons, 2004.

Thomas, Damion L. *Globetrotting: African American Athletes and Cold War Politics*. Urbana: University of Illinois Press, 2012.

11

Blaming Walter O'Malley
for Moving the Dodgers West

ROBERT TRUMPBOUR

Who was responsible, or, to put it more bluntly, who was to blame for the Brooklyn Dodgers' leaving for Los Angeles after the 1957 season? For most fans familiar with the outline of the story, the villain is clear: Dodgers owner Walter O'Malley. Peter Golenbock dedicated his book, *Bums: An Oral History of the Brooklyn Dodgers,* to "each and every one of those Brooklyn Dodger fans who lost so much, so soon, for so little reason." Golenbock presented testimony from O'Malley himself that Brooklyn fans could use to support their accusation that their team's mercurial owner was duplicitous: "The Dodgers fans have a paramount interest in the Brooklyn club. They are more important than the stockholders, the officials, and the players, or anybody else." Golenbock was not alone in his distaste. Pete Hamill and Jack Newfield, two legendary New York journalists, agreed. Only half joking, they put O'Malley near the top of a list of the worst human beings of the twentieth century, ranking him behind only Hitler and Stalin.

Many others lined up evidence blaming the team's owner for the Dodgers' departure. But the reality was much more complex. New York politics, advances in transportation technology, economic imperatives, and a changing dynamic between owners of professional sports teams and their host cities formed an array of factors that ultimately led to the Dodgers' exodus from their hallowed birthplace.

For more than fifty years, O'Malley has been an easy scapegoat. In the minds of many, he was a calculating and cold-blooded businessman who valued the almighty dollar above all else. To cite just one example of his parsimony, he refused to allow a personal friend to travel with the team to Japan because of concerns about that individual's health. O'Malley told Harold Parrott, the team's tour organizer, that the cost of shipping a body back from Japan would be $4,800, an expense O'Malley did not want to bear. Irving Rudd, the Dodgers' promotions director, confidently asserted that O'Malley's negotiating skills were so focused on the bottom line that "if he was up against [Communist Party head and Soviet Premier] Khrushchev . . . the Soviet Union would be a Dodgers farm club today."

Despite evidence that O'Malley ruthlessly sought profit, blaming him and him alone for moving his team is an oversimplification of a highly dynamic landscape. Although O'Malley was an extremely effective negotiator, he met his match in Robert Moses, New York City's power broker and master builder, a man with his own set of priorities. Moreover, their conflict flared at a time when public officials elsewhere, including Los Angeles, were jockeying to court the owners of professional sports teams.

After World War II, many civic leaders looked to sports as a way to validate the claim that their cities had achieved major-league status. In 1953, the Boston Braves moved into a brand new, publicly financed ballpark in Milwaukee. A year later, the St. Louis Browns relocated to Baltimore and became the Orioles, and in 1955, the Athletics left Philadelphia for Kansas City. With the emergence of relatively safe and inexpensive commercial air travel, Minneapolis, Houston, and other midwestern and southern cities pushed to obtain major league teams. As California's population expanded and Los Angeles boomed to become America's fourth-largest municipality, West Coast cities, too, looked to join the hunt.

Team owners possessed more negotiating clout with city officials than ever before, except in New York. Power in New York's internal political structure was consolidated in Robert Moses, head of the Triborough Bridge and Tunnel Authority, the New York City Housing Authority, and several other key political institutions. Moses also acted as the city's liaison with the state government in Albany and the federal government in Washington, positions that further entrenched his power and brought Gotham millions in government dollars. Mayor Robert Wagner typically deferred to Moses with the hope that numerous Moses-led construction projects would cement the mayor's legacy.

For O'Malley, the root of the Dodgers' problem was replacing Ebbets Field, an inner-city ballpark that was showing its age. It had a small seating capacity and little adjacent parking, and O'Malley regarded it not as a jewel, but as an obstacle to his team's long-term profitability. O'Malley's first look into obtaining a new ballpark came in 1946, barely a year into his tenure as a major shareholder. He contacted civil engineer Emil Praeger to explore expanding or replacing the thirty-three-year-old structure. Praeger seemed well suited as a consultant. He had worked with Moses on several projects and had a stellar reputation, but nothing came of this initial encounter.

By March 1948, Norman Bel Geddes, an industrial engineer well known for designing the much-heralded Futurama exhibit at the 1939 New York World's Fair, unveiled plans for a futuristic baseball facility estimated to cost more than $6 million. O'Malley downplayed the possibility of new construction, telling a reporter, "We appreciate that the Brooklyn fans are entitled to more seats and in a modern stadium, but it just does not seem possible in the near future."

Nevertheless, O'Malley kept working on ballpark plans. A mere two days later Praeger, back in the picture, presented a report that laid out various options for a new facility, recommending placing it near mass transit facilities. By the 1950s, parking was becoming increasingly important, particularly as the postwar housing boom unfolded on suburban Long Island. Moses pushed forward plans to build additional highways, but as middle-class families moved from cramped Brooklyn apartments to communities where automobile culture flourished, O'Malley could see his fan base eroding without convenient parking. Even the rosiest calculations counted a mere nine hundred parking spaces near the park Charles Ebbets had built.

If the Dodgers were to remain in Brooklyn, O'Malley had to work with Moses, but negotiations between the two, despite a cordial veneer, were often icy and unproductive. O'Malley consistently reiterated his willingness to build a ballpark he would pay for on land he was willing to buy. All he needed, he asserted, was Moses's help to acquire such land, using New York's Slum Clearance Committee and the power of eminent domain. Moses, on the other hand, favored a publicly owned facility. O'Malley wanted to keep his team in Brooklyn while Moses preferred a plan that had the team moving to a large swath of undeveloped land in Flushing Meadows, a section of Queens. Meanwhile, as this battle between titans unfolded, Los Angeles city officials began to court the Dodgers owner tirelessly, eventually offering him a lucrative land swap that paved the way for relocation.

O'Malley's overbearing and self-serving temperament agitated Moses, but the Gotham power broker also suggested that O'Malley's inability to understand the legal and political landscape created an intractable situation. In a 1954 interview given to Frank Schroth, owner and publisher of the *Brooklyn Eagle,* Moses candidly declared that O'Malley "bores everyone to death with his endless monologue, says the same things, but shows no grasp of the constitution[al], legal, and practical aspects of the problem and keeps threatening in a rather snide way to go to Los Angeles or Long Island City." Moses further argued, "We offered him a carefully thought out suggestion which he promptly repudiated without even grasping what it was about."

Moses's broader vision for New York's future further stymied O'Malley's ability to negotiate a deal that might keep the Dodgers in Brooklyn. Moses's overarching goal was his desire to reshape metropolitan New York, including surrounding suburbs, with major highways, urban housing, and publicly controlled recreational infrastructure. O'Malley's intrusion on these plans, as the owner of a private business, was an ongoing irritant, to put it mildly.

Moses had earned a stellar reputation for clearing slums without graft or cost overruns and for getting new public projects completed on time. His political empire grew considerably in the 1930s when, under Mayor Fiorello LaGuardia, he acquired miles of beachfront property along Long Island's south shore and created superb, public recreational facilities. Moses cleverly positioned himself to take advantage of the New Deal's generous financial resources aimed at overcoming the Great Depression. He was one of the few leaders anywhere ready to move projects to fruition as the spigot of government funding opened, and he did so with competence, efficiency, and willingness to steer clear of the corruption so common in New York City.

Although not an ally of President Franklin Roosevelt, Moses's success allowed him to expand his power base further while gaining enthusiastic support from media insiders. As he racked up victories, he structured a political empire in ways that minimized insider political meddling. Moses formed public authorities that were outside the jurisdiction of legislators and even guided bills through the New York legislature when necessary. In 1946, Mayor William O'Dwyer appointed him to the nebulous position of construction coordinator, a vague title that gave him wide latitude over a multitude of city projects. As head of various government entities, Moses built parks, pools, housing, highways, bridges, and tunnels, successfully completing complex projects that might have bogged down under the leadership of a more traditional, patronage-dependent politician.

Moses shared O'Malley's concern for accommodating people driving cars. As head of the Triborough Bridge and Tunnel Authority, he amassed tolls from bridges and tunnels to fund much of his vast empire. However, he was also committed to inner-city housing and a broad range of public works projects that required him to juggle numerous political agendas as he made plans to reshape postwar Gotham. Dependent on federal and state monies to fund some projects, Moses needed to placate high-level politicians and satisfy broad public needs to maintain his considerable power. He chafed at any proposal that might put his integrity in question. To Moses, catering to a single, private enterprise like the Dodgers, with the enormous public attention it attracted, was a potential trap that could invite ongoing criticism. Moses consistently maintained a cautious posture, clearly stating that any publicly backed construction project could not favor or in any way subsidize the goals of a for-profit enterprise like the Dodgers. In one of his clearest communications, Moses warned O'Malley that Moses could not use the Slum Clearance Committee, even though he controlled it, "to encourage speculation in baseball enterprises."

That is not to say Moses never strayed from principle. In 1934, he had used land in Central Park to develop a highly profitable restaurant, and decades later he took over more park land to provide additional parking for the same restaurant. He made deals with other private enterprises, redeveloped Manhattan's West Side into Lincoln Center for the Performing Arts, and organized the massive World's Fair featuring numerous exhibits that openly promoted major American companies. However, when it came to O'Malley, Moses remained inflexible, reiterating that he was unable to bend policy to support a profit-seeking entity.

Although Moses was not all-powerful, no one individual had more control over New York's land use policies. According to Title I of the Housing Act of 1949, he had broad powers that urban expert Charles Abrams asserted were so sweeping that "Macy's could condemn Gimbels [a department store rival] if Robert Moses gave the word." Nevertheless, Moses was highly tactical in how he exerted his power. He sought to transform and reshape the nation's largest metropolitan area, not to placate a single individual.

Beyond that, Moses, with an Ivy League pedigree, favored amateur sports over professional ones and, as a former swimmer at Yale, he devoted considerable resources to building public pools and idyllic parks that raised his stature immensely with city officials and benefited citizens. More significantly, he disliked O'Malley's smooth-talking sales pitches and his attempts to align himself with powerful Brooklyn insiders. They were off-putting to Moses's pragmatic sensibilities that favored government efficiency over Tammany Hall patronage.

Moses even disliked the spots O'Malley preferred for meetings, including the Coal Hole in the Hotel Brooklyn, where initial deliberations unfolded. Moses distrusted places where the borough's political operatives and business leaders interacted, places where O'Malley seemed at home. Part of Moses's animosity might be traced back to his recollections of O'Malley's father,

Edwin, whose early career as New York's deputy commissioner of public markets linked him to Tammany Hall insiders. The senior O'Malley's political trajectory suggested he was connected to the old-style favor trading and graft Moses abhorred. Moses also did not seem comfortable with O'Malley's attempts to push grandiose proposals into a public spotlight. Moses preferred to operate quietly on the front end of projects when political infighting might unfold, with publicity more welcome on the back end, as the fruits of a given project became apparent.

Despite the antagonism between the two, O'Malley was committed to making things work out in New York, and he labored extremely hard to get his plans for a new ballpark off the ground. With fanfare and publicity in March 1952, he trotted out Bel Geddes again to announce plans for a cutting-edge stadium that would include a retractable roof, heated and cushioned seats, and such innovations as hot dog vending machines. Bel Geddes even suggested a parking deck for seven thousand cars and a synthetic, grass-like surface, predating the development of Astroturf by more than a decade. Bel Geddes suggested that construction might not unfold until "far into the future," but by June, O'Malley was pushing Schroth and the *Eagle* to support this new plan. He explained that an indoor facility with 52,000 seats "would be nearer to Wall Street and Rockefeller Centre [*sic*] than the Polo Grounds, Yankee Stadium, or Ebbets Field," and bragged that such a facility, with a moveable roof, "would provide convention facilities unequalled elsewhere."

A privately funded major-league ballpark had not been built anywhere in the nation since Yankee Stadium in 1923, making O'Malley's quest for such a facility in a city as densely populated, expensive, and complex as New York somewhat quixotic, particularly given Moses's unwillingness to assist in acquiring suitable land. Still, O'Malley held out hope that he would be able to broker a deal that would make things work out in Brooklyn.

In 1953, O'Malley proposed a Fort Greene site Moses had set aside for housing, arguing that housing could be built in many locations, but that there were few realistic options for a ballpark in heavily populated Brooklyn. By October Moses insisted that, before he could contemplate land acquisition, O'Malley's plan would require special legislation to classify ballpark construction as a public purpose. Moses countered that O'Malley was free to buy land on the open market, of course, but finding a parcel large enough for a new ballpark in Brooklyn was a problematic venture.

In 1954 O'Malley worked with Praeger again, seeking out properties that might work. He tried to arrange a meeting with George Spargo, a high-level employee of Moses, but was pushed instead to meet with Frank Cashmore,

Brooklyn's borough president. O'Malley suggested a location in Long Island City, a densely populated area with mass transit access to Brooklyn, but Long Island City was in Queens. Cashmore would never support such a location, so O'Malley next proposed a Brooklyn site near a mass transit hub at Atlantic and Flatbush Avenues. The location was a Long Island Railroad terminal with subway access, too. O'Malley thought there might also be room for parking facilities and enough land to make the ballpark part of a much larger, multipurpose development plan. Predictably, Moses dragged his feet, indicating that the ballpark was too embedded in the plan to pass the legal scrutiny required for land acquisition. He suggested that if the land was distressed, as O'Malley had argued, that he should buy it outright instead of expecting the government to employ eminent domain.

In 1955, O'Malley tried to play hardball, announcing that his team would play seven 1956 home games at Roosevelt Stadium in Jersey City, New Jersey. The Dodgers had won the 1955 World Series, and O'Malley hoped to use the enthusiasm of a world championship to break the logjam. Simultaneously, though, he continued his dialogue with Los Angeles city officials. His decision to play a few home games in Jersey City raised the ire of fans and sportswriters alike, but O'Malley hoped to demonstrate how dire the situation in Brooklyn had become. The New Jersey ballpark, he was quick to note, had a much smaller seating capacity than Ebbets Field, but five times more parking.

In 1956, O'Malley continued to work toward a resolution, but by 1957, he stepped up his discussions with officials in California, even pushing New York Giants owner Horace Stoneham to begin talking to leaders in San Francisco. A postseason trip to Japan may have pushed O'Malley further toward relocation. While on the trip, he saw a ballpark that took a mere eighteen months to plan and build. O'Malley had been working to achieve such an outcome since 1946, but he had nothing but political bruises to show for it. Still, when visiting Los Angeles later that year, he wore a "Keep the Dodgers in Brooklyn" button.

As New York's leaders continued to react with indifference, Los Angeles officials worked tirelessly to cultivate a positive relationship with O'Malley. As it became clear that a move to California was possible and maybe even likely, Moses, perhaps at the urging of Mayor Wagner, stepped up his push to build a new ballpark in Queens. Although the location offered limited subway service, and the nearby highway infrastructure was not yet fully developed, O'Malley weighed the option, but later rejected it in favor of a land swap deal in Los Angeles that proved incredibly lucrative in the long run.

Los Angeles Coliseum, 1959 World Series, Dodgers against Chicago White Sox. (*Sporting News* Archives.)

The certainty that O'Malley would have Moses administering his rental agreement in a publicly funded facility was one factor among many that worked against the Dodgers remaining in the East. The changing composition of Brooklyn's population, with a middle-class exodus and a deteriorating urban core, also pushed him to look more carefully at alternatives. Although O'Malley did not have a plan in place for a privately financed ballpark in Los Angeles and did not know that he would have to win some considerable legal battles to acquire the Chavez Ravine land he was promised, on October 7, 1957, he decided to move the Dodgers. Nearly sixty years later, the relocation remains the most significant and most contentious in American sports history.

New Yorkers, especially Brooklynites, made O'Malley the scapegoat for the Dodgers' departure, condemning what they saw as his cold-blooded negotiation tactics and strong-armed personality. The timing of the move enhanced the backlash. On January 28, 1955, after a 114-year run, the *Brooklyn Eagle* published its last issue, leaving the borough without a home-based newspaper. Although Schroth was hardly a rubber stamp for O'Malley, the newspaper, had it survived, might have offered more nuanced coverage than the Manhattan dailies. In addition, Wagner was up for reelection and was in no position to admit that his passivity throughout the long ordeal might have contributed to a franchise's move, particularly in light of the Giants' decision to move westward, too.

O'Malley was painted as the villain, while Stoneham escaped criticism as a follower whose actions a manipulative O'Malley choreographed. In fact, Stoneham had his own reasons for moving and had investigated Minneapolis before settling on San Francisco. Promises to build a magnificent, taxpayer-funded municipal ballpark in California and the certainty of a ready-made West Coast rivalry with the Dodgers were much more attractive to Stoneham than the political infighting sure to accompany a campaign to replace the aging Polo Grounds. The Giants owner stayed out of the media spotlight, so his reputation suffered less.

It could have been easy, too, for New Yorkers to paint Moses as a villain, but that did not occur. After all, if he had treated O'Malley less like an ill-informed pariah, the outcome might have been different, but by the time Moses began his push for a Queens-based solution, O'Malley no longer trusted him and was not likely to sign a long-term contract Moses would control.

Historian Peter Ellsworth argued that if Robert Moses "wanted to tear down a building to make room for an office building, he did it. No one stopped him—not presidents, governors, or mayors," but when it came to O'Malley, Moses was unwilling to expend his political capital. The motives were personal, political, or economic, or maybe a blend of all three. Moses often claimed that "once you get that first stake driven . . . no one can stop you." That first stake was never driven in Brooklyn, leaving a long legacy of baseball history to unfold in Los Angeles.

For Further Reading

Caro, Robert. *The Power Broker: Robert Moses and the Fall of New York.* New York: Vintage Books, 1974.

McCue, Andy. *Mover and Shaker: Walter O'Malley, the Dodgers, and Baseball's Westward Expansion.* Lincoln: University of Nebraska Press, 2014.

McNeil, William F. *The Dodgers Encyclopedia.* 2nd ed. Champaign, Ill.: Sports Publishing, 2003.

Prince, Carl. *The Brooklyn Dodgers: The Bums, the Borough, and the Best of Baseball, 1947–1957.* New York: Oxford University Press, 1997.

Sullivan, Neil J. *The Dodgers Move West.* New York: Oxford University Press, 1987.

Trumpbour, Robert. *The New Cathedrals: Politics and Media in the History of Stadium Construction.* Syracuse, N.Y.: Syracuse University Press, 2007.

12

The Greatest Game Ever?

RICHARD C. CREPEAU

On December 28, 1958, the Baltimore Colts played the New York Giants in the championship game of the National Football League. Just over sixty-four thousand fans were in Yankee Stadium to watch the game, and an estimated forty-five million others watched on black-and-white television sets across the nation. What they witnessed was the first "sudden death" game in NFL history, a game often called "the greatest game ever." But was it?

It was a game in which the Colts, the league's Western Conference champions, built a 14–3 lead at halftime by turning two fumbles by Frank Gifford into touchdowns. After an early field goal staked the Eastern Conference champs to a 3–0 lead, the New York halfback coughed up the ball on New York's twenty-yard line. Five plays later, Baltimore fullback Alan Ameche ran into the end zone from the one-yard line. After the second fumble, Colts quarterback Johnny Unitas connected with end Raymond Berry, alone in the end zone.

In the third quarter, a remarkable sequence of plays produced a reversal of fortune. After the Colts reached the Giants' one-yard line, the New York defense held, pushing Baltimore back to the five. From there the Giants went on a ninety-five-yard drive to close the gap to 14–10. Four minutes later, Gifford redeemed himself, catching a pass for a touchdown and a 17–14 lead for the home team.

With two minutes remaining in the game, the Colts took possession on their own fourteen-yard line. As the clock wound down, Unitas completed three passes to Berry for sixty-two yards. With no timeouts remaining and the ball on the Giants' thirteen, the Colts field goal unit raced onto the field,

Baltimore Colts quarterback Johnny Unitas. (Malcolm W. Emmons, *Sporting News* Archives.)

and Steve Myhra kicked the ball through the uprights, then positioned on the goal line, tying the game, 17–17. Many of the players, not aware of a rule put in place in 1947, did not know what to do next. They thought the game was over, but what the rules called for was a sudden-death period, the first overtime in NFL history.

The Giants won the coin toss, chose to receive, and quickly went three and out. Unitas and crew took over on their own twenty-yard line and began a drive that lasted thirteen plays and included two third-down conversions. The drive ended 8:15 into the extra period with an Alan Ameche touchdown as he went in from the two untouched. The championship drive was a dazzling display of passing, running, and innovative play calling, better even than the drive that led to the field goal at the end of regulation time.

After the fact, NFL Commissioner Bert Bell called this day the greatest in the history of professional football. *New York Times* reporter Louis Effrat said the game was the greatest he had ever seen. Writing for *Sports Illustrated,* Tex Maule spared no superlatives. His piece bore the headline, "The Best Football Game Ever Played." Down through the years, the 1958 title game has taken on a legendary aura in both popular and serious literature of the NFL, cul-

Alan Ameche bursts through to score winning touchdown in overtime. (Associated Press.)

minating with Mark Bowden's *The Best Game Ever,* published for the league's fiftieth anniversary. Three other books on the game were published at the same time, and multiple accounts of what happened on that dark and cold New York afternoon can be found in countless numbers of "greatest games" books and newspaper commemorations. An Internet search yields multiple references to it under that heading.

In his landmark history of the NFL, *America's Game,* Michael MacCambridge wrote that this game triggered a "seismic shift in the American sports landscape." Lamar Hunt, a very rich man but not yet an NFL owner, was so impressed by the game that he became inspired to move forward with the formation of the American Football League. The Pro Football Hall of Fame's Web site confirms these judgments. It identifies the 1958 championship game as "The Greatest Game Ever Played." But was it?

This sort of claim is made for particular games in most every sport. In each case the validity of the claim depends, in part, on the meaning of the phrase, "the greatest game." Was it a great game because it was highly competitive and played with great intensity and went down to the final minute or seconds with the outcome undetermined? Does the phrase mean that it was a game that had some transformative effect on the perception, popularity, or status of football? Did it redefine the nature of the sport or precipitate rules changes? Did it set off a chain of events that altered the place of football in the world of sport? Did it involve some of the greatest players and coaches in the history of the game? Does it mean that the level of play was at or near perfection throughout the contest? The phrase "greatest game" could, of course, mean any or all of these.

What about quality of play as a measure of the greatness of the game? Highly competitive games between two excellent teams often are games of mistakes forced by excellent defenses, sophisticated preparation, and pressure on the players. Pregame discussions of big games often include the view that the team that makes the fewest mistakes will win. Frank Gifford, reacting to all the books and articles celebrating the fiftieth anniversary of the 1958 championship, said, "When you think about it, it was a lousy game." Commenting on the play of both teams, Gifford said they made history that day by playing "the worst first quarter in the annals of championship football, before or since."

Many of those who think the 1958 championship game was the greatest game in NFL history stress that competitiveness is more important than quality of play. Ernie Accorsi, later general manager of both the Colts and Giants, put it this way: "You don't evaluate a football game because it's not stylistic." Rather it is the emotion, passion, and ebb and flow of play and "great players playing for the ultimate stakes."

For any number of people, it was the impact of the game that made it "the greatest." MacCambridge's reference to "a seismic shift" is bolstered by his assertion that the game marked the beginning of the rapid ascension of the NFL to the status of "national pastime." In the official program for Super Bowl XLIII, played in 2009, MacCambridge wrote of the 1958 championship: "Today it is rightly viewed as the tipping point in the game's development, the instant that pro football's barnstorming, low-rent past was transformed into its gleaming, high-tech future."

MacCambridge quoted an array of people in and around football who understood that this game had been a very special one. Chris Schenkel, who had called the game for NBC, went to the Giants' locker room afterward and told several players to remember this game because it would go down as "the greatest game ever played." Vice President Richard Nixon wrote to Gifford extolling the greatness of the game. Bert Bell recognized it as such, as did Lamar Hunt and the Giants' founding owner, Tim Mara. Tex Maule's often quoted piece in *Sports Illustrated* was followed up two weeks later by his "Here's Why It Was the Best Football Game Ever" to take advantage of the continuing buzz about the game. It also led to the magazine's decision to expand its coverage of pro football.

Even though the 1958 championship game may not have been the best-played game, it did produce an exciting second half and a heart-stopping finish that spilled over into overtime. It was sports drama of the highest order. It had an impact on many individuals who were important to the future of the NFL, and it was an important step in the burgeoning popularity of the NFL.

All that being said, it is also clear that the game did not take place in a social and historical vacuum. There was considerable context here, many decisions, developments, and personalities, both within and outside the league, that converged to make the NFL the new national pastime over the next decade. Seen more broadly, the 1958 title game is not the beginning of something, but rather the middle of something.

Where then to begin?

The National Football league did not materialize out of thin air in 1958. It was an entity nearly forty years old and, more significantly, one that had been growing steadily over the previous two decades. Average attendance at NFL games had moved upward through the '30s, '40s, and '50s. Average per-game attendance broke the thirty-thousand-mark in 1953 and increased to more than forty thousand in 1958. It never again dipped below that mark. By the mid-1960s, average attendance at regular season games would top fifty thousand.

What these numbers indicate is that a professional football fan base had been increasing for some time before 1958 and continued to grow from that point on. It is not possible to discern any major impact on that fan base from the 1958 championship game.

Another factor aiding the growth of the NFL well before 1958 was media attention. By the late 1930s, major newspapers in NFL cities were giving full coverage to their teams, though that was not the case in the remainder of the country. In both 1934 and 1937, the Associated Press voted the "growth of professional football" as the major trend in sports for that year. Motion picture newsreels were also beginning to pay more attention to the professional game. Both the College All-Star Game and the NFL championship game were covered by the newsreels shown in movie theaters, even though it would be the late 1940s before that attention was given to regular-season games on a weekly basis.

What about radio? By the 1930s, most NFL teams had their games on the airwaves. In 1934, the Detroit Lions, newly moved from Portsmouth, Ohio, established their own radio network for a Thanksgiving Day game, a practice that later translated nicely to television. However, because network radio did not carry the NFL championship game until 1940 and weekly network radio broadcasts did not come until after World War II, it is tough to say that radio was a major factor in the NFL's growth.

By the 1940s and 1950s, there was also an increase in the number of stories on the pros in both the *Saturday Evening Post* and *Collier's,* the nation's two leading weekly magazines. This growth of magazine coverage accelerated in the 1950s with additional features in *Life, Time,* and *Look,* often including a number of player profiles. In 1954, *Time* magazine was fully on-board with pro football. In a profile of Detroit's gritty quarterback, Bobby Layne, *Time* claimed that those who wanted "to see football at its best turned out to see the pros. . . . [C]ollege boys play a game, while Sunday's pros practice a high and violent art." Apropos of the Cold War, *Time* used atomic metaphors to describe the Sunday game.

Perhaps the most important development in print media was the birth of *Sports Illustrated* in 1954. In 1956, *SI* hired Maule to cover professional football, a key addition according to Michael MacCambridge because Maule understood the game better than anyone else writing about it, and had great contacts throughout the league. *SI,* in fact, treated pro football more seriously than the rest of the national press.

It was television and the NFL's comfort with the new medium that proved the key postwar development and, in the view of many, the key to NFL growth. In 1946, there were approximately twelve thousand television sets in the United States. By 1950, that number had reached more than four million, creating a potential audience of thirty million, or 20 percent of the population. In 1947, the Chicago Bears contracted with WBKB to televise all six of their home games for a fee of $4,500. The league and team owners harbored concerns that people would stay home and watch the games, but a doubling of gate receipts in that season seemed to indicate the reverse.

The first network agreement with the NFL came in 1951, with the Dumont network. By 1953, many teams had created their own regional networks. At that point, Commissioner Bell stepped in and convinced team owners to agree that no home games would be televised and no games would be broadcast into territory where another NFL game was being played. The rule was challenged in court, but Alan Grim, a federal district court judge in Philadelphia, accepted what became known as "the blackout rule." Bell was also dictating content and descriptive language to the networks, prohibiting, for example, showing injuries or fights and forbidding use of such words as "tripped up." There is no tripping in football, claimed the commissioner.

By 1956, all teams had network arrangements with CBS, and NBC had purchased the rights to the NFL championship game. Simultaneously, advertising agencies were beginning to discover television as a vehicle for sales, accentuated by the demographics of the pro football television audience. Television, in turn, found in football a solution to the content problem for what had been known as the Sunday afternoon ghetto. The NFL, in effect, offered one long reality series—although that term would not be used for decades—full of unscripted drama and excitement. The 1958 championship game highlighted these hard facts for the networks and the advertising world.

From that point on, the National Football League, using a combination of league rules and superior negotiating skills, took hold of television and exploited it. At some point it became clear that the needs equation between the two entities had been reversed. Initially, the NFL needed television, but by the early 1960s Pete Rozelle, Bert Bell's successor as commissioner, demonstrated repeatedly that television needed the NFL. Furthermore, he exploited that need mercilessly over the years, though the relationship remained symbiotic.

Football was an ideal television game. It fit nicely on the screen, while giving the viewer a better seat to see the action than could be had in the stadium. It gave an illusion of intimacy between fans and players and offered a close-up of violence and mayhem. In an age of anxiety over manliness, it offered testosterone-driven reassurance. It was a game well suited to the new suburban world described by sociologist David Riesman as being dominated by the other-directed personality.

Two years prior to "the greatest game," Jim Murray, writing in *Sports Illustrated*, assessed the state of the NFL. He predicted that 1956 would be a "banner year," with attendance topping three million for the first time. Murray, too, compared the pro game to the college game, saying the pros were like the *Ballets Russes*, while the college game was like attending a high school recital. In Murray's view, the pro game stood superior in every way. The pros were bigger and stronger, and they played a more sophisticated game.

In 1958, Bell analyzed the success of the game he controlled. Print and electronic media gave the NFL fifty million dollars' worth of free publicity, the NFL was giving the public the entertainment it wanted, and the sharp competition in the NFL added an element of suspense. Bell claimed that there were no weak sisters in his league, and he then uttered a sentence that has long been remembered. "On any given Sunday," he argued, "any team in our league can beat any other team."

Three other elements would add to the popularity and public image of the NFL, one before the 1958 championship and two following it. The first was the Cleveland Browns drafting Jim Brown in 1957. When he entered the league, Brown took the level of offensive play to new heights. In his rookie year, he led Cleveland to a 9-2-1 record and an Eastern Conference title. He led the league in rushing with 942 yards on 202 carries. The next season, Brown gained 1,527 yards, an average of 5.9 yards/carry, and scored seventeen touchdowns. As Brown moved from college stardom to professional dominance, football fans across the country took notice, and the NFL benefited. He was a singular talent, but there were others nearly as good.

The second spur to the popularity of professional football was the founding of the American Football League by Lamar Hunt and his group of fellow owners. The new league boasted a more wide-open style of play that influenced the entire professional game. The appearance of the AFL led to the expansion of the NFL and created new excitement in new markets. The competition created by the new league for players produced what were considered eye-popping salaries and signing bonuses over the following six years, and this in turn generated a flood of media interest. The AFL in its search for talent signed many more African American players than the NFL, and this in turn meant considerably better play throughout professional football as the '60s moved forward. All of this added to the interest in the professional game across the nation.

The third driving force in the growth and dominance of the NFL and professional football was the elevation of Pete Rozelle to the position of commissioner. Rozelle's first act in his new job was to move league headquarters from Philadelphia to New York. The NFL's offices in midtown Manhattan were strategically located between the headquarters of the television networks and the major advertising companies. Here, according to MacCambridge, Rozelle cultivated well-connected, powerful, and brilliant men: Herb Siegel, chairman of the board of Chris Craft, who was regarded as an "astute media man"; Jack Landry, the senior vice president at Philip Morris, the company that owned Miller Beer, soon to become a major sponsor of NFL football; David Mahoney, chairman of the board of Norton Simon, a Park Avenue public relations firm; and Bob Tisch, president of Loews Corporation. This power quartet kept Rozelle informed on media developments and advised him on television network negotiations.

Rozelle moved quickly to harness television and to cultivate and exploit CBS executives. He understood the power of professional football in the executive suites, where "jock sniffing" was an activity affirming masculinity and elevating status. In the end, the favor cost Rozelle little more than free tickets to big games and invitations to the commissioner's suite at the NFL championship and later at the Super Bowl.

Rozelle and some of his chief allies were also well connected to the power centers in Washington. At times this proved most convenient for the league and rewarding for the politicians. Connections to the Kennedy family and the willingness to dangle new franchises as bait were persuasive elements as the league grew in power and popularity.

What then might we conclude about the 1958 championship game, the epic contest between the Colts and Giants? Certainly it was an exciting game, and it happened at an important time in the history of the National Football League. But this could be said of other games as well. The "Ice Bowl" in Green Bay between the Packers and the Dallas Cowboys might be one. Some might make the case for earlier NFL championship games, such as the Giants' win over the undefeated Bears in 1934, a victory facilitated by the Giants' switching to sneakers shoes at the half for better traction on a frozen field. Others might point to the 1940 championship game, the first broadcast on radio, when the Bears used the T-formation to demolish Washington, 73–0.

Thus, even if the 1958 championship was an important game with significant consequences, it was only one game coming in the middle of a plethora of developments, both in American society and in football, that changed the landscape of professional sport. Those who led the National Football League understood what was happening in their society and knew how to exploit these changes to their advantage much better than the leaders of rival sports and entertainment entities.

Bert Bell, Pete Rozelle, and Lamar Hunt were all men of vision who saw the significance of television, grabbed it by the throat, and made it their own. They also understood that the country was making a shift economically to increased leisure and booming consumerism, which would produce the landscape for significant growth in mass entertainment. They knew, too, that sport was part of this new entertainment complex. The three of them also believed that professional football was about to take the country by storm, and they were ready to act on the belief.

Seen against the backdrop of these forces and personalities, the 1958 NFL championship game, as exciting as it was, seems to pale in comparison.

For Further Reading

Bowden, Mark. *The Best Game Ever: Giants vs. Colts, 1958, and the Birth of the Modern NFL*. New York: Atlantic Monthly Press, 2008.

Crepeau, Richard C. *NFL Football: A History of America's New National Pastime*. Urbana: University of Illinois Press, 2014.

MacCambridge, Michael. *America's Game: The Epic Story of How Pro Football Captured a Nation*. New York: Random House, 2004.

Powers, Ron. *Supertube: The Rise of Television Sports*. New York: Coward-McCann, 1984.

13

The Marichal–Roseboro Brawl and Its Coverage "Underneath America"

SAMUEL O. REGALADO

When August 22, 2015, rolled around, the Los Angeles Dodgers and the San Francisco Giants, as had been their tradition in so many baseball seasons prior, found themselves locked into yet another pennant race. Only one game set them apart in the standings as the Dodgers prepared to engage the Astros in Houston while the Giants took on the Pirates in Pittsburgh. In games against one another that season, taunts and beanball wars that had routinely enlivened past confrontations were reduced to barbs from fans in one city tweeting those in the other. And columnists from both the *Los Angeles Times* and *San Francisco Chronicle* chided each other moderately during the season. Gone was the bitter acrimony that had been a trademark of the rivalry for so long.

Still, when that August date came around, both newspapers acknowledged its significance as it represented the fiftieth anniversary of one of the most infamous brawls in baseball history and one of the sport's most violent episodes. With reckless abandon, Giants ace right-hander Juan Marichal had clubbed Dodgers catcher John Roseboro over the head with a baseball bat.

Bill Plaschke of the *Times* wrote the most extensive retrospective. Far from a condemnation of the Giants pitcher, who had since been inducted into the Hall of Fame, Plaschke instead focused on the passing years and how both players had let bygones be bygones. "At that moment, the power of forgiveness was stronger than that of an angrily swung baseball bat. One of the ugliest chapters in this sometimes senseless Dodgers–Giants rivalry had finally ended, and for once, the human spirit had won," he concluded. The *Chronicle* also commented on the day's historical significance. But perhaps as a means to get past it all, the sports department commissioned none of its current writers to reminisce about the affair. Instead, with little fanfare, the paper pulled from the archives a story that had appeared a decade earlier to mark the brawl's fortieth anniversary. Gwen Knapps's article, while providing details about the game itself, had, like Plaschke's column, given considerable weight to Marichal and Roseboro's relationship in the years since their fight.

Neither Plaschke nor Knapps included any mention of the social dynamics beyond the ballpark that had played an indirect role in what took place in San Francisco that hot Sunday in 1965. Had they done so, they might have reviewed the sentiments of two of the nation's then-leading ethnic newspapers, the *Los Angeles Sentinel,* a black newspaper, and its Spanish-language counterpart, *La Opinión,* both of whose accounts of the brawl had been quite emotional.

In 1965, the Dodgers and the Giants spent most of the season separated in the standings by only a few games, and they shared first place several times. Unlike 2015, the tension between the two teams was routinely punctuated by vocal spats and trash talking. Thus, it was no great surprise that such exchanges had already been in play during the two previous games. No one knew it at the time, but the table was most certainly being set for the now infamous August 22 game. Augmenting the scenario at Candlestick Park was the tension found 350 miles to the south and in the Caribbean during that same summer.

The Dodgers–Giants brawl occurred in the wake of the riots in Watts, an area just south of Los Angeles' city center. Though the riots had subsided by the time the baseball rivals engaged in their series, the embers remained hot, and this affected Roseboro, whose home was adjacent to where the riots had occurred. Marichal had similar concerns. The Dominican Republic that summer had exploded into a civil war, one that led to a United States military intervention and, like Watts, unrest continued to be a factor as the two teams prepared to meet. As with other Dominican players in the majors, Marichal worried about the welfare of his kin and country. Not only were people in Watts and the D.R. on edge. So, too, were Roseboro and Marichal.

Their confrontation was vicious, nothing short of grim. With Marichal at bat, catcher Roseboro, in retaliation over knockdown pitches the Giants' ace had thrown at Dodgers' hitters earlier in the game, intentionally clipped the Dominican's ear with his return throw to pitcher Sandy Koufax. Thinking that Roseboro might then attack him, Marichal swung his bat and hit the catcher in the head. News photographers and live television captured Willie Mays escorting Roseboro off the field, blood pouring down the side of his head, to the visitors' dugout and the clubhouse. By the end of the day, the melee had made the national news. Over the next several days, columnists around the country weighed in. "Picking up a baseball bat goes quite beyond the laws of civilized warfare," declared Murray Kempton. Jimmy Cannon penned, "The likes of Marichal acts like a guy trying to murder one of the opposition." In the following weeks, boos rained down upon the Giants' ace whenever the team was on the road. So demonized was Marichal that rookie manager Herman Franks altered his pitching rotation so that his turn would not come up when they reached Dodger Stadium. Charles Einstein wrote, "It was bad enough that the Giants were coming to town; you could not jam 56,000 people within the confines of four acres and expect them to tolerate Marichal, too." For his part, National League president Warren Giles fined the Dominican $1,750 and suspended him for a mere eight days. This, of course, added to the outrage. Referring to Marichal's role in the brawl as "vicious," the *Sporting News* stated, "An attacker capable of using a bat on another man does not figure to be impressed by a penalty which costs him only one pitching turn."

In an era that predated cable television and the Internet, the national audience had no choice but to understand the Marichal–Roseboro fight through the lens of the white, mainstream press. But their voices were not alone. The *Los Angeles Sentinel* and *La Opinión* also expressed their thoughts. Both

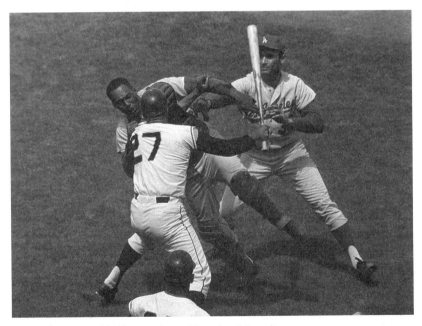

Juan Marichal attacks John Roseboro. (Associated Press.)

papers, like most media aimed at minority readers, reported the news with understandable emphasis on stories that related to their black and Latino readers. But unlike mainstream dailies, ethnic papers such as these were founded to help advance the standing of the communities and people who, in the words of a nineteenth-century Slavic immigrant, lived "underneath America." And it was this sense of mission that fueled the spirit of the two men who started each newspaper and the way they covered the news.

Leon H. Washington Jr., a black lawyer and transplant from Kansas City, founded the *Los Angeles Sentinel* in 1933 as a voice for African Americans. Throughout each year, the paper not only dispensed news but also adopted an activist role in the interest of social justice. Washington himself landed in jail for protesting white entrepreneurs who operated businesses in black communities and hired no black employees. And by sheer coincidence, the weekly's offices were located only a few miles from one of the most epic racial outbreaks in the nation's history, the Watts riots, which erupted in August 1965 and prompted the paper's columnists to advance the call for social justice on a number of fronts.

La Opinión operated a few blocks away from the *Sentinel*. Ignacio Lozano Jr., a migrant from Mexico who had launched *La Prensa* in San Antonio, Texas, in 1914, moved part of his operations to Los Angeles and established *La Opinión* in 1926. Lozano's design was to bring news from Mexico to his fellow migrants. But as their numbers grew in southern California, the conservative ethnic daily transitioned into a local newspaper with emphasis on Los Angeles–related items. By August 1965, *La Opinión* boasted a higher circulation than any of its Spanish-language competitors in the United States.

Both newspapers covered sports. And this was not unimportant. By 1965, black and Latin players on both the Giants and the Dodgers were making significant contributions to their teams' success. For their part, both clubs provided Spanish-language radio broadcasts of their games, the Giants on a part-time basis and the Dodgers with full-time broadcasters Jaime Jarrín and René Cárdenas.

But these arrangements did not necessarily mean that racial and ethnic harmony existed within each club. The Dodgers started off on the wrong foot with their Mexican American base in the spring of 1959 when owner Walter O'Malley struck a deal with Mayor Norris Poulson and the Los Angeles city council to remove Mexican residents and demolish homes in the Elysian Park district, the proposed construction zone for what became Dodger Stadium. One woman "was carried kicking and screaming from the premises," wrote Neil J. Sullivan. Los Angeles television viewers witnessed scenes in which "children cried and pets, chickens, and goats added to the chaos." The entire episode became a *cause célèbre* for the city council's only Latino member, Edward Roybal, who compared the actions to the Spanish Inquisition and Hitler's Germany.

The Giants were not exempt from similar controversy. In 1964, manager Alvin Dark told a reporter for *Newsday* that he believed his black and Latino players were "not able to perform up to the white ball player when it comes to mental 'alertness.' " Adding that his ethnic players lacked the level of "pride" and willingness to "subordinate themselves to the best interest of the team," Dark's remarks were explosive and revealed to many the tenuous racial dynamics inside the Giants' clubhouse.

When the two rivals played each other in August 1965, racial and cultural tensions were still part of the environment surrounding the close pennant race. The two principals, Marichal and Roseboro, were themselves fierce competitors and no wallflowers. Of the two, Marichal was the star. Going into that series, the high-kicking Giants ace was 19-9 and had already beaten the Dodgers three times at home. His pitching capabilities were hardly in question, and neither was his personality. Since 1958, when he first appeared in professional baseball in the United States, the "Dominican Dandy" was affable. Like most pitchers, he pouted from time to time when removed from a game, but he was likeable, and that resonated with the Spanish-language press. In Marichal's heyday, however, Spanish-language papers were few and far between in the Bay Area, and they tended to focus on politics, not sports. Hence, the lion's share of Spanish-language baseball coverage in California fell to *La Opinión* in Los Angeles, where Rudolfo "Rudy" Garcia was sports editor.

Garcia, who joined *La Opinión* in 1942, cut his teeth as a reporter on Mexican boxing, held at the nearby Olympic Auditorium. He turned to baseball in the late 1940s and in 1955 landed an extensive interview with Cleveland Indians second baseman Bobby Avila, a Mexican national who had captured the American League batting title in 1954. From that point on, the reporter wrote weekly updates on all Latino players in the major leagues. Believing that Latin players were not getting their proper due from the mainstream press, Garcia, in the spirit of the Lozano mission and legacy, emphasized the best traits of those he covered, particularly the most prominent stars. And Juan Marichal of the rival Giants was one of them.

John Roseboro made his debut with the Brooklyn Dodgers in 1957. As a result of the auto accident that ended Roy Campanella's career, Roseboro came with the club to Los Angeles as the new starting backstop. In the next few seasons, he established his big-league gravitas. By 1965, the burly catcher was, with six All Star appearances, a Gold Glove, and two World Series to his credit, one of the steadiest and toughest players in the game.

Generally amiable and quiet, Roseboro was stern and aggressive on the field. Christened "Gabby" by his teammates for his propensity to speak few words, Roseboro was one of the best in a long line of Dodgers catchers, according to pitcher Don Drysdale. Roseboro was also known for standing his ground, even off the field. During the Watts riots, near his home, Roseboro reportedly sat on his porch armed with a rifle.

The *Sentinel*'s sports coverage featured black major league stars, particularly those on the hometown Dodgers. The team, whose history included Jackie Robinson's fabled entry into the big leagues in 1947, was popular among blacks in southern California, and the team's current black players gave the *Sentinel* much to write about. Along with Roseboro, Maury Wills, Tommy and Willie Davis, and Lou Johnson were instrumental in the team's success. Wills, in fact, was the team captain, and the paper routinely referred to the shortstop as "Captain Maury Wills."

The *Sentinel*'s sports section was a generous five pages long, and its three featured writers, sports editor Brad Pye Jr., L. I. "Brock" Brockenbury, and Clayton Moore, penned their stories in charismatic fashion. Moreover, they often couched their columns in a manner that brought attention to the racial dynamics of the era. Pye, for instance, continually targeted colleges in the Southeastern Conference that, in 1965, denied blacks the chance to play football. Brockenbury was equally assertive. Only a few years earlier, the two writers had routinely targeted Washington Redskins owner George Preston Marshall for his stubborn refusal to sign black players. They even blasted the hometown Rams for having scheduled preseason charity games against the Redskins. "They bring these Washington Redskins here every year to insult their Negro customers in the first game of the season," wrote Pye. Brockenbury called Marshall "plain no-good on the Negro question."

Pye and Brockenbury, of course, were not out of step with the rest of their paper. Much like the attention they drew to college football's shortcomings on race, *Sentinel* editors took on the Los Angeles Police Department. "The image of the Los Angeles Police Department [in the black community] is getting worse instead of better," claimed the paper several months before the Watts riots broke out. Police abuse, they argued, was "adding fuel to the already smoldering fire of resentment." The *Sentinel*'s haunting observations rang true when on August 11, riots exploded in Watts. The troubles lasted through August 17, and thirty-four people died. Pictures of officers arresting black residents appeared in the *Sentinel* with the caption "Brute Force," and most of the coverage targeted Police Chief William Parker as the chief culprit.

In an effort to quell the tension, the paper's sportswriters weighed in and encouraged their black readers to adopt sports, especially baseball, as a model for tranquility. Brockenbury used his column, "Tying the Score," to write about Jackie Robinson's ability to play with whites and to argue that baseball had since made "great progress in recent years" in the area of race. Pointing to ballplayers as a group who "work together for one common goal," the *Sentinel* writer implored his readers to replicate the behavior of such athletes. Ironically, Brockenbury's sanctimonious piece appeared on the eve of the Dodgers' three-game series in San Francisco and its infamous conclusion.

Any thought that baseball was above the fray of racial acrimony collapsed only days after Brockenbury's contention that the sport was a role model for harmony. The gruesome scenes transmitted on television broadcasts into the homes of Los Angeles viewers, and eventually into newscasts across the nation, triggered anger toward Marichal everywhere outside San Francisco. Longtime Giants' beat writer Nick Peters later recalled that no one in San Francisco "really criticized him." He added, however, that "maybe we could have been more objective, but he was our guy." As awkward a position as Bay Area journalists found themselves in, the *Sentinel* and *La Opinión* sports staff, too, faced a complicated task in commenting on the brawl.

The *Sentinel* was then a weekly, so its coverage of the game appeared after National League president Warren Giles had fined and suspended Marichal. Remarkably, unlike the mainstream press, the *Sentinel* reported the pitcher's actions with measured comments. The paper said little about what Roseboro had done that led to the fight, but more descriptively couched him as the victim and saved its most animated remarks for Giles. Sports editor Pye led the charge, referring to the penalty as "Mickey Mouse." Brockenbury, perhaps slightly embarrassed for painting baseball as an example of racial harmony, was now less philosophical and called the decision a "mockery." Willie Mays, who drew little notice from the mainstream columnists, got considerably more attention in the *Sentinel* for having acted to prevent a riot on the field of play.

Down the street at the offices of *La Opinión*, there, of course, was considerable mention of Marichal. However, the paper depicted him not as an aggressor, but as a victim himself. Apparently uncertain about how to report the brawl, Garcia found himself in a spot. Having emphasized for so long the better traits of Latin players, and being a beat reporter for the Dodgers, he needed to be careful about the angle he took. Going after Marichal might alienate the Latin players from whom he had secured so many interviews. As well, he also risked losing subscribers, including Dodgers fans, who were drawn to the paper by its propensity for defending Latinos.

Context also came into play. In 1965, *La Opinión*'s subscribers ranged well beyond Los Angeles. Many, in fact, lived in the Bay Area. Not every Hispanic person read the paper, of course, but considering nearly a quarter of all Latinos in the United States lived in California, it is safe to say that the paper's influence on the Spanish-language enclave was significant, a point lost to mainstream journalists and the larger society.

With these factors in mind, Garcia took to his typewriter. In his column, "Esquina Nuetral," he opted not to vilify the Giants' pitcher. Over the course of three consecutive issues, he offered varied perspectives. In the first, he paid tribute to Willie Mays, whom he referred to as "El Pacificidor." The next week, he sought support for Marichal. Noting that his actions were indefensible on their face, he argued that baseball brawls were not uncommon. "Marichal is not perfect," he declared and went on to point out that Drysdale, Wills, and Ron Fairly were also complicit. In his third column, Garcia attributed the brawl to the pressures of the pennant race and held baseball itself responsible for its lack of proper oversight as the teams began the series at Candlestick Park. By September, while many papers continued to echo displeasure with Marichal, *La Opinión* opted, instead, to focus its attention on the final weeks of the pennant race.

As with most ethnic newspapers, the *Los Angeles Sentinel* and *La Opinión* were nonexistent to most Americans in 1965. Mainstream columnists never considered the viewpoints of either paper, and the Marichal–Roseboro fight did not raise their visibility outside their own realms. But, given the mission of each paper, the baseball brawl in San Francisco revealed a perspective that largely differed from the mainstream press. The fight also challenged each paper's sportswriters to balance objective reporting with their publications' larger mission to illuminate and advance the identity of their readership and community. Most important, these papers provided an important lens into the dynamics of sports journalism in a world "underneath America."

For Further Reading

Regalado, Samuel O. *Viva Baseball! Latin Major Leaguers and Their Special Hunger.* 3rd ed. Urbana: University of Illinois Press, 2008.

Rosengren, John. *The Fight of Their Lives: How Juan Marichal and John Roseboro Turned Baseball's Ugliest Brawl into a Story of Forgiveness and Redemption.* New York: Lyons Press, 2014.

14

What Really Happened When Curt Flood Sued Baseball

STEVEN GIETSCHIER

On October 7, 1969, the St. Louis Cardinals and the Philadelphia Phillies completed a seven-player trade. The Cards, prohibitive favorites for that season's National League East pennant that they did not win, sent four players to the Phillies: starting center fielder Curt Flood, starting catcher Tim McCarver, seasoned relief pitcher Joe Hoerner, and young outfielder Byron Browne. In exchange, Philadelphia sent a trio of players to St. Louis: starting first baseman Dick Allen (then generally called Richie), infielder Cookie Rojas, and starting pitcher Jerry Johnson.

Baseball trades happen frequently—at least they did in the 1960s—but this one was special for the players involved. Flood and McCarver had been important parts of a team that had won three NL pennants and two World Series in the previous six seasons, and they were the Cards' co-captains. Flood was one of the best defensive outfielders in the league, once playing 226 consecutive games without making an error, but he was an offensive force as well. Over the course of seven seasons, he batted .302, tying for the league lead in hits (211) in 1964, and had been named to three all-star teams. Allen's credentials were just as gaudy. In his first five full seasons (1964–1968) he batted .302, slugged .552, averaged 29 home runs and 91 runs batted in, and was also a three-time all-star.

Born in Houston, Flood grew up in East Oakland, California, and then West Oakland, where his family moved to distance itself from the hostility of local whites toward African Americans in the years after World War II. George Powles, Flood's amateur baseball coach and a coaching legend at McClymonds High School, preached racial tolerance, but Flood ran headlong into baseball's institutional racism when he signed a contract with the Cincinnati Reds organization and played the 1956 season with High Point–Thomasville in the Class B Carolina League. There, he endured all the indignities Jackie Robinson had faced a decade before: accommodations separate from his white teammates, meals taken alone, exclusion from gas station men's rooms, and uninhibited racial taunts from white fans, one of whom, Flood recalled, was a "loud cracker who installed himself and his four little boys in a front-row box and started yelling 'black bastard' at me." His manager and teammates offered little support. Most, Flood said, "were offended by my presence."

After Flood's second minor league season, in Savannah, the Reds traded him to the Cardinals. He began 1958 in Omaha but was soon promoted to the majors and batted .261 in 121 games. The Cardinals fired manager Fred Hutchinson after the season and hired Solly Hemus, a man some called a racist. He sat Flood on the bench and often avoided his presence. Hemus lasted until July 1961, and when third base coach Johnny Keane replaced him, the racial atmosphere in the St. Louis clubhouse began to improve.

Actually, as author David Halberstam explained in *October 1964,* it was August Busch, owner of the team since 1953, who began this transformation a few years earlier. Stunned to find no black players on the roster and fully aware that black Americans drank Budweiser, his company's flagship brand, Busch ordered the Cardinals to integrate despite the team's loyal fan base in the South. The club did so. In 1961, when Flood spoke out about segregation during spring training, the Cardinals broke the color line at an annual breakfast hosted by local businessmen in St. Petersburg, and shortly thereafter, Busch had a wealthy pal buy a motel so that the team could stay together in Florida and thumb its collective nose at the state's segregated housing laws.

Teams usually made a trade to obtain a particular player or two, but the Flood-for-Allen deal looked to most like a trade engineered to dispose of particular players. Despite his ability, Flood had worn out his welcome. Moreover, his personal life was in perpetual and somewhat embarrassing turmoil, including two divorces from the same woman, and his outside business interests seemed to some to distract him from the business of playing baseball. That his batting average slid from .301 in 1968 to .285 did not help.

Players are sometimes remembered for one play, good or bad, and Cardinals fans have never forgotten that Flood made a crucial misplay in the seventh game of the 1968 World Series. With the game scoreless in the seventh inning and two Detroit Tigers runners on base, Jim Northrup hit a line drive that Flood misjudged. Trying to correct his course, he slipped. Both runs scored, Northrup wound up on third, and the Tigers prevailed, 4–1. Despite the Series loss, Flood publicly asked for a raise from $72,500 to $90,000, but the club countered with an offer of only $77,500. Flood eventually got his money, but during spring training in 1969, Cardinals management expressed embarrassment when Flood's brother, a convicted felon who lived with him, tried to rob a St. Louis jewelry store and led police on a televised car chase through downtown before being apprehended.

Before Opening Day, owner Busch summoned all his players and front office personnel to a special meeting. He dressed everybody down, chastised them for being greedy, urged them to concentrate on the job at hand—winning the 1969 pennant—and scolded them for poor relationships with fans and the press. Flood, not alone among his teammates, took the criticism personally. He later wrote in *The Way It Is* that "we lost the championship of the National League on March 22, before the season started. . . . I feared . . . that I would be gone from the team in a week." He lasted the season, but after the Cardinals finished a disappointing fourth in a six-team division, "cleaning house," as it is sometimes called, was no surprise. As assistant general manager Jim Toomey said, "If he was that good, do you think we'd have gotten rid of him?"

The Cardinals had hardly become postracial, but Flood had no reason to want to leave St. Louis. He lived in an upscale neighborhood, enjoyed a vivid social life—that may have upset club officials—and helped develop a couple of successful businesses that bore his name. Thus, when Toomey called him to inform him about the trade, he was patently unhappy. On the one hand, he was upset that general manager Bing Devine had delegated Toomey to break the news. On the other, he was dismayed that he had been traded to Philadelphia, well known throughout the league as inhospitable to African American athletes.

Upon hearing about the trade, Flood told his friend, Marian Jorgensen, "I have only two choices. I can go to Philadelphia or I can quit baseball altogether. I will not go to Philadelphia." Retirement seemed to be his choice, but both Jorgensen and a St. Louis attorney he consulted told him that, if staying in St. Louis was so important, he should sue Organized Baseball, contesting the trade and the reserve clause as violations of antitrust law.

When major league clubs introduced the reserve clause in 1879, binding a player who signed a contract to his team for the following year, some players at first saw being reserved as an honor. "Reserve me," they seemed to say. "Don't you want me to continue to play for you?" Quickly, though, more astute players realized that the reserve clause not only restricted their movement but depressed their salaries. Players unhappy with a club's proffered contract had no alternative but to grin and sign. They moved from one club to another only when traded or sold.

If baseball was a business engaged in interstate commerce, then, once the Sherman Antitrust Act became law in 1890, the reserve clause would have been an antitrust violation. But no legal test came until after World War I when the former owner of the Baltimore club in the disbanded Federal League brought an antitrust lawsuit against Organized Baseball. When owners in the National and American Leagues crafted a settlement that put the upstart Federal League out of business, they excluded the Baltimore owner, and he sued for damages. The case, *Federal Baseball Club of Baltimore v. National League,* was heard by federal district court judge Kenesaw Mountain Landis well before he was approached to become baseball's first commissioner, and it went all the way to the Supreme Court. In 1922, Associate Justice Oliver Wendell Holmes, writing for a unanimous court, declared that baseball "exhibitions" (what we call "games") were neither trade nor commerce. Even though teams traveled from one state to another to play, Holmes called games "purely state affairs." Baseball was not subject to antitrust regulation, he wrote, and the reserve clause, therefore, was legal.

Make a list of the ten most wrong-headed decisions in Supreme Court history, and *Federal Baseball* is surely a contender for high honors. The Court's reasoning was tested twice in the intervening years before the Flood trade. Baseball settled with one plaintiff, Danny Gardella, after World War II, and the Court upheld its original decision in *Toolson v. New York Yankees* (1953), suggesting that because Congress had not seen fit to correct the 1922 decision, it should stand.

This was no consolation to Curt Flood. He called Marvin Miller, executive director of the Major League Baseball Players Association, and told him he wanted to sue baseball. Miller took pains to explain how arduous such a legal challenge would be, and he explained that getting the Supreme Court to reverse itself was a proposition with long odds. Miller was a labor economist, not a lawyer. He soon realized how determined Flood was and that the Players Association would have to back him for the long haul through the court system. A lawsuit would be time-consuming and expensive. Flood was already thirty-one, and Miller told him that, if he sued, he might never play again. Moreover, when Miller suggested that the Players Association might bear the considerable legal costs, Flood gave his word that he would honor that commitment. He would not be bought off by an offer to settle, and he would pay back the association if he won. Most emphatically, Flood promised he would see the case through.

Miller believed the reserve clause and baseball's exclusion from antitrust regulation were both legally indefensible. He also thought the best way to ameliorate the reserve clause was through collective bargaining and not a legal action. Nevertheless, when Flood attended the Players Association's executive committee meeting in San Juan, he received unanimous support to fund the lawsuit. Miller later wrote in *A Whole Different Ballgame* that before the San Juan gathering, he and his general counsel, Dick Moss, talked with player representatives about challenging the reserve clause. Few understood, Miller said, exactly how the reserve clause affected their lives and what changes would occur if it were abolished or even modified.

At this point, Flood signed and sent to Commissioner Bowie Kuhn one of the most famous letters in baseball history. He wrote, "After twelve years in the Major Leagues, I do not feel that I am a piece of property to be bought and sold irrespective of my wishes." The letter was made public, as was Flood's impending lawsuit. Flood's salary, $90,000, made him one of the top ten or fifteen highest-paid players, but he told sports commentator Howard Cosell on ABC's *Wide World of Sports* that "a well-paid slave is, nevertheless, a slave."

Such explosive language, of course, did not win him or his cause any friends, either among baseball's fans or most of its considerable press corps. Chalk it up to misunderstanding perhaps, but except for a few columnists with a national audience, sportswriters were, in Flood's view, "distressingly cynical and ill-informed." Many present and former players also believed baseball needed the reserve clause and that the sport could not survive without it. Among those who spoke out in opposition to Flood were Henry Aaron, Joe DiMaggio, Bob Feller, Gil Hodges, Frank Howard, Harmon Killebrew, Ralph Kiner, Robin Roberts, and Ted Williams. One former player, Joe Garagiola, even testified against Flood when the case went to court.

If Miller made one major misstep, it was his decision to hire his former colleague with the United Steelworkers of America, Arthur Goldberg, to represent Flood. Goldberg had a sterling reputation as a superb labor attorney. Moreover, he left the union to become Secretary of Labor under President John Kennedy, who later appointed him to the Supreme Court, where he wrote several decisions on antitrust law. Lyndon Johnson strong-armed Goldberg into leaving the Court to become United States Ambassador to the United Nations, and after that, he joined a prestigious New York law firm.

Goldberg was a baseball fan, too, and he agreed enthusiastically to take the case, admiring Flood's courage. But despite the sterling team Goldberg assembled, the legal representation he himself provided was substandard throughout. Early on, he assured Miller he would not be tempted by a sug-

Arthur Goldberg, 1971. (Bert Verhoeff/Anefo.)

gestion from New York Democrats that he run for governor against the incumbent, Nelson Rockefeller. However, before the case even went to trial, Goldberg was spending most of his time on the campaign trail, doing exactly what he said he would not. When the trial began, Goldberg called Flood as his first witness, conducting the examination himself. Neither was prepared. The day before, Goldberg had spent time campaigning, and even on the morning the trial began, he ate breakfast with the president of the steelworkers' union and not his client. Goldberg did not rehearse Flood in the questions he would ask or the answers the ballplayer should give. The result was two-and-a-half hours of muddled testimony that did Flood's case no good.

According to Brad Snyder, author of *A Well-Paid Slave,* there really didn't have to be a trial. The judge who handled the case could have and perhaps should have dismissed Flood's suit because federal district court judges do not have the authority to overturn Supreme Court decisions. But even though he was bound by *Federal Baseball* and *Toolson,* Judge Irving Ben Cooper wanted a trial. He was a flamboyant arbiter with an inferiority complex. As a fan, he yearned to see an array of baseball personalities parade through his courtroom, and he wanted the chance to say things like, "The Court announces a seventh-inning stretch." After Jackie Robinson testified for Flood on the second day, Cooper invited the retired Dodgers star into his chambers so he could ask for an autograph for his grandson.

No active players testified for Flood, and none attended the trial. In retrospect, Miller admitted that he erred in not arranging that players visiting New York to play either the Yankees or the Mets spend an hour or two supporting their colleague. Goldberg called former players Hank Greenberg and Jim Brosnan to testify, and then an array of sport officials including NFL commissioner Pete Rozelle, NBA commissioner Walter Kennedy, and NHL president Clarence Campbell. The lead attorney for the defense team, Mark Hughes from Commissioner Kuhn's law firm, did a superlative job. His first witness was Kuhn himself, followed by Garagiola, American League president Joe Cronin, and several other baseball executives, including Ewing Kauffman, owner of the Kansas City Royals. The trial ended after three weeks, without much drama, and in August, Cooper ruled in favor of the owners. He had no choice. District court judges do not overturn Supreme Court precedent.

Flood's lawyers anticipated an appeal because they were fairly sure of losing in district court. They were confident, too, that they would lose in the United States Court of Appeals for the Second District, and that's what happened. That court's majority opinion acknowledged the deficiency of *Federal Baseball* but admitted it had no authority to clean up the Supreme Court's mess. Judge Leonard P. Moore wrote a concurring opinion in which he praised *Federal Baseball,* implicitly approving of the reserve clause, and said that "Baseball's welfare and future . . . should be for the voters through their elected representatives."

And so Flood's legal team approached the Supreme Court, where deliberations are complicated, convoluted, and, except for the very rare leak, secret. The justices hear oral arguments, of course, to which the public is invited, but their conferences as a group of nine and their informal meetings are strictly private, with no public record made. What we know about how the Court handled Flood's case comes from a series of revelations well after the fact.

On July 6, 1971, Flood's attorneys filed a petition with the Supreme Court for a *writ of certiorari*. In other words, they asked the justices to take the case, which they weren't required to do. The petition suggested *Federal Baseball* had produced a "bizarre result," that Organized Baseball should be subject to antitrust regulation, and that the Court should not wait for Congress to correct what had become an abusive system. The justices were not so sure. In fact, the Court at first declined to grant cert, as it is called. Only after a memo circulated in favor of hearing the case did Justice Byron "Whizzer" White, himself a former professional football player, change his mind. Had he not done so, the Court of Appeals' decision would have stood, and that would have been that.

Both sides submitted written briefs and prepared for oral argument on March 20, 1972. This was a historic day because rarely has a former justice argued a case before his former colleagues. Goldberg did so, but again, he botched the job. Flood himself was not present when Goldberg made what he later called "the worst argument I've ever made in my life." The Court listened with embarrassed patience and then heard Louis Hoynes deliver a much more polished presentation for the commissioner and the owners.

The Court took two months to announce its decision. Flood lost, 5–3, with one justice recusing himself because he owned stock in Anheuser-Busch. Justice Harry Blackmun wrote the much-criticized majority opinion. Basically, Blackmun defended the Court's reluctance to overturn *Federal Baseball* and *Toolson* as a matter of *stare decisis*, that is, respect for precedent. Although Blackmun admitted baseball was a business, he argued that "baseball's unique characteristics and needs" required continuing its special status unless Congress chose to intervene.

Even if Flood had won his case, his baseball career was over. He knew that. He sat out the 1970 season. He never reported to the Phillies. Had Flood won, he could not have returned to the Cardinals. They did not want him. In 1972, Flood negotiated a deal with Organized Baseball that allowed him to play without prejudicing the ongoing lawsuit. He signed with the Washington Senators but played only thirteen games. Flood's skills had eroded, and he left baseball a broken man with an uncertain future. His personal life was messy, too, and it remained so until his death in 1997.

As for the reserve clause, it still exists. Flood's loss refocused attention, as Miller had wanted, on collective bargaining and on the impartial arbitration process created in baseball's 1970 Basic Agreement. After pitchers Andy Messersmith and Dave McNally played the entire 1975 season without signing contracts, the Players Association filed a grievance arguing that the pair could not be reserved for 1976, and arbitrator Peter Seitz agreed. Chaos did not ensue. Rather, the owners and the players negotiated a system that, as later amended, allows a club to control a player for his minor league career and the first six years of his major league career before he becomes a free agent. When players reach that point, they often sign multiyear contracts for many millions of dollars. But how many remember Curt Flood and his lonely fight?

For Further Reading

Flood, Curt, with Richard Carter. *The Way It Is*. New York: Trident Press, 1971.

Halberstam, David. *October 1964*. New York: Villard, 1994.

Korr, Charles P. *The End of Baseball as We Knew It: The Players Union, 1969–81*. Urbana: University of Illinois Press, 2002.

Miller, Marvin. *A Whole Different Ball Game: The Sport and Business of Baseball*. New York: Birch Lane Press, 1991.

Snyder, Brad. *A Well-Paid Slave: Curt Flood's Fight for Free Agency in Professional Sports*. New York: Viking, 2006.

15

Dan Gable's Unbelievable Defeat

DAVID ZANG

For those who follow amateur wrestling, the legend of Dan Gable began germinating on the night in 1966 when his older sister was sexually assaulted and murdered in the family home, transforming an already ornery teenager into a crusading avenger. Undoubtedly, the legend was burnished in 1972 when Gable vanquished his Soviet foe in Munich, clinching Olympic gold after outscoring his world-class opponents by a collective 75–0. It became etched in stone when Gable won twenty-five consecutive Big Ten (and fifteen total national) titles as coach of the Iowa Hawkeyes. But the moment that alerted the wrestling world to his mythic status and built the platform for his ascension into the sporting heavens came on March 28, 1970, when Dan Gable suffered the only loss in a high school and college career that ended 181-1.

It was an outcome so unthinkable and stunning that the standing room crowd of 8,500 fans who saw it, some of whom had relished the possibility only as mean-spirited fantasy, immediately wished it had never happened. The match was not only the most thrilling and important eight minutes in the history of the sport, it also supplied Gable with the final element required of all mythic figures: the fall that makes possible redemption.

The salvation phase of the story began when Gable—atop the second step of the victory stand for the only time in his scholastic career—after a long interval of disbelief and quiet sobbing, slowly raised his head, an acknowledgment to the standing, cheering, and now sympathetic crowd that Act I had indeed come to its tragic close. Several decades later, when the resurgence had been fully realized, Gable would stand as the God of All Wrestling: the man who had singlehandedly saved his little-known sport from irrelevance in an era when television had begun feeding the public an addictive dose of spectacle that would lead to the eventual commodification and enervation of a great deal of American sport.

Gable, of course, never set out to save anything but himself. Raised in industrial Waterloo, Iowa, he found out early that sports—and particularly wrestling—provided a buffer against his demanding, and sometimes besotted, parents. Beginning in the 95-pound weight class, he ran off three undefeated state championship seasons in high school (finishing 64-0). Tales of his work ethic became the foundation of his reputation and an unspoken indictment of the idea that he—or any wrestler—might have real athletic talent. Though novelist John Irving later wrote in *Esquire* that "when Dan Gable lays his hands on you, you are in touch with grace," he also noted that Gable's unstinting work had turned his body into something "no more pretty than an axe head . . . no more elaborate than a hammer."

In other words, Gable shaped himself for success in a sport that is, as I've written elsewhere, "as old and merciless as the human race." Wrestling matches "feature barely dressed bodies entangled too intimately for some, and a pageant of disfigurement—crippled knees, crooked noses, and cauliflower ears—that mark it as coarse and vulgar to others." It is simply, according to *Sports Illustrated*'s Douglas Looney, the "cruelest mistress in the world." All of which made it a sport out of step with the nation's Vietnam-era youth.

Still, while wrestling's sense of gravity made Gable's quest antithetical to the surging fun crusades of the counterculture (a critic, writing for Portland's *Oregonian,* quipped that "Gable trains as if he's going to row stroke on a slave galley"), it endeared him to the nation's elders, who looked anxiously to the nation's athletes "for sober assurance that an entire generation had not been lost to hallucinogens, loud music, and an Asian jungle."

Not that Gable was paying attention to such matters. His days began and ended in the wrestling room, leaving him, in the words of former Wisconsin coach Russ Hellickson, "socially retarded." He had enjoyed baseball in his formative years, but with his early success on the high school mats and the trauma of his sister's death stripping away any urges toward mere pleasure, Gable became an early symbol of the post-'50s sports specialist. As with the twelve Greek gods, each of whom had just one special power to share with a world in need of it, Gable's singular gift to a nation humiliated in Vietnam was the ability to win: any time, every time. More victorious than Wooden, Lombardi, or the Celtics, his unceasing string of wins made following his career as mesmerizing as watching a roller at the craps table whose luck will just not run out.

Gable's winning ways at Iowa State began with a national title in his unde-feated sophomore season. (Freshmen were not then eligible for varsity com-petition.) When he went on a rampage to begin his junior year (1968–1969), the press took notice. Oblivious as ever, Gable put on perhaps the most dominating show ever staged by one athlete. At the elite collegiate level, where pins are a rarity, Gable pinned twenty-six of thirty opponents. He won his second consecutive NCAA title by pinning all five of his tournament foes. By season's end, his fame had begun fanning outward, owing in part to Herman Weiskopf's March 1969 depiction of him in *Sports Illustrated* as "Superwres-tler." In wrestling-mad Iowa, finding someone unfamiliar with Gable would have been like finding a Yankee fan who had never heard of Babe Ruth. The article noted, of course, the three thousand hours Gable had spent training in the previous thirty-two months. Contradicting John Updike's contention that "gods don't answer letters," Gable told Weiskopf that he was responding to as many as twenty of them a week. His status among wrestlers had become so unquestionable that a girl asked Gable to write her boyfriend to let him

Dan Gable. (NWHOF Dan Gable Museum.)

know she loved him. She was certain that the object of her affections—a high school state champion—would never doubt the word of Gable.

The 1969–1970 season, Gable's last, began, then, with unmatched expectations. No one doubted that he would win again, every match from November through the NCAA tourney. Most opponents in his 142-pound class would wrestle with unusual caution (some chose not to wrestle him at all, opting to go up a weight or go through the ordeal of shedding pounds to escape him at a lower weight), ceding preordained victory in the hope they would not get pinned. It was a failed strategy. At the season's start, Gable ran the pinning streak he'd begun the previous year to twenty-four in a row. He finished the year with thirty pins in thirty-four matches.

As he approached the NCAA tournament at Northwestern University's McGaw Hall in Evanston, Illinois, Gable's final title was as predictable as the scheduled coronation of a monarch. He had already been voted wrestling's Man of the Year. Further, ABC Sports, which would present a taped version of the championships on its *Wide World of Sports,* had inveigled a reluctant Gable to film a promo spot with this cursed line: "Come watch me next week as I finish my college career one eighty-two and oh."

Enter Goliath's twentieth-century David, Larry Owings from the University of Washington. A once-pudgy youth, Owings had grown taller and slimmer during his high school days in Oregon, and by 1968, his senior year in high school, he was confident enough in his abilities to travel to Ames, home to Iowa State, for the Olympic trials, where Dan Gable beat him 13–4 in the first round. He returned to the Northwest and won the PAC-8 championship at 158 pounds in his sophomore year. The following year, though he occasionally competed as high as 167 pounds, Owings dropped to the 142-pound class for the NCAA tournament. As he told noted wrestling writer Nolan Zavoral, 142 was not only his best weight, it was where he knew he would find Gable, explaining that "I always wanted to come back and beat people who'd beaten me."

Owings, matching Gable, pinned his first four tournament opponents and entered the championship match with a record of 30-1, having lost during the season only to a two-time national champion in the heavier 150-pound class. Even so, no one gave him a chance against Gable except, possibly, Gable. The champ had seen a newspaper the day of the match quoting Owings as saying, "I'm not going to this tournament to be a national champion. I'm coming here to beat Gable." Much has been made in the last forty years of that assertion's impact on Gable's state of mind. Assistant Iowa State coach Les Anderson has said flatly that Gable was "psyched out." Gable admitted that he had seen enough of Owings to instill in him a fear of falling victim to a cradle, a pinning move in which a wrestler clamps an opponent's leg and head together and rolls him to his back. "When we started," Gable said, "all I was thinking was, 'God, don't get caught in his cradle.'"

Dressed in the villain's black, Owings began the match by going right after Gable, but the defending champion, in Iowa State's gaudy red-and-gold singlet-and-tights combo, countered and took Owings down for the match's first two points and—this is important—while riding on top, then caught Owings with his back exposed to the mat for an elapsed moment of 1.7 seconds. One shoulder was momentarily down, the distance of the other from the mat too difficult to judge from video replay. The rule book stated that if a wrestler "has control of his opponent in a pinning position," and "both shoulders of the defensive wrestler are held *momentarily* within *approximately* [italics mine] four inches of the mat or less," a two-point predicament shall be scored. At the sport's highest level, however, referees were reluctant to award the points if a defensive wrestler's aggression had contributed to his position of jeopardy and if it did not appear that the top wrestler had any real chance of maintaining the hold for a pin (or fall). Veteran referee Pascal Perri never gave a moment's thought to awarding the points to Gable. With both wrestlers working furiously and with scant caution (a rare occurrence in college wrestling), the match swung Owings's way at the end of the first of three periods when he escaped from Gable and then took him down for a 3–2 lead.

The fast pace continued in the second period and, though Gable controlled Owings from the top position, he began to look listless. ABC's Frank Gifford noted the condition, and Gable confessed later that "I'd never been that tired before." After Owings escaped again and took Gable down with a fireman's carry, the lead grew to 6–2. Gable worked his way back to an 8–6 deficit as the period ended, but it had taken great effort to keep up with the relentless movement of Owings, so much effort that Gable had done the unthinkable. Unable to battle his way from underneath, he had forced a restart by crawling from the mat's center to out-of-bounds. Iowa State fans had never seen it before, and the fans in the hall showered Gable with boos as Perri awarded a penalty point to Owings.

Some spectators began to smell blood, and the noise level rose to a steady rumble, but Gable's teammates were unmoved, certain that he would take control in the final period. Indeed, Gable squirmed out of Owings's grasp quickly, then gained control of him for a two-point reversal. With the match tied, 8–8, Gable put in his signature arm bar and cranked it hard, trying to turn Owings to his back. Instead, Owings slipped out for a one-point escape to go back on top, 9–8. With one minute remaining and the crowd now bellowing, Owings secured one of Gable's legs and, driving him backward, secured a takedown for two points while also pushing Gable's shoulders within a hand's width of the mat for 1.5 seconds. This time, Perri signaled the extra two points for the predicament (also commonly termed "back points"), and suddenly the score was 13–8 with time running out. As Gable glanced at the scoreboard, he was visibly shocked to see the additional two points had been awarded against him. After escaping to trail 13–9, he wrestled the final seconds in a bewildered fog. When the match ended, Gable was awarded two points he'd earned for time spent "riding" atop Owings, bringing the final score to 13–11. As Perri brought the two men together in the center of the mat, Gable briefly touched hands with the new champion without looking at him, then stumbled in a daze from the mat.

He reappeared some minutes later to take his place on the medals podium. With his chin sunken into his chest, the heartbroken and grieving Gable shielded his crying eyes from view while Owings clapped respectfully. Eyewitnesses, overwhelmed with emotion, have estimated that Gable's head hung for anywhere from thirty seconds to five minutes. Regardless of the elapsed time, all agree that he appeared as uncomprehending as any distant god to the mortal event that had befallen him. The *Des Moines Register* had

Larry Owings and Dan Gable in front of referee Pascal Perri. (NWHOF Dan Gable Museum.)

the same reaction, offering the cruelest headline I've ever seen in sport: TITLE TO CYCLONES—GABLE FAILS!

The rest, as they say, is history. According to a teammate, after about a month Gable's mother lost patience with her son's sulking, slapped him in the face, and told him to grow up. Gable remembers only that she angrily told him to "put your ballet slippers on." Fueled by seething anger, he never lost again. Though Owings displaced Gable on the NCAA's wrestling guide cover the next year, he could not repeat his win. Gable beat him at the next Olympic trials before breezing to his gold medal, televised—for the first time ever—in prime time. In doing so, he became the most famous man his sport had ever seen. In the immediate wake of his ascendancy came an expansion of college wrestling, the sport even reaching into the previously uninterested Southeastern Conference for a time.

Both Gable and Owings submit courteously (though in Gable's case, still painfully) to periodic interviews that replay the match and search for new evaluations and insights. Never have I heard either wrestler question the competent Perri's decision to award Owings two points and deprive Gable of two in a similar situation. That may be a product of a time before instant replay and multiple camera angles and networks needing to fill twenty-four hours with programming turned officiating into a minefield of public opinion. It was simply a decent accommodation to human judgment.

No one, of course, can say whether or not Gable, without the loss, would have been as deeply driven to the manic training that brought him Olympic gold and his sport some measure of public respect that has allowed it to hobble along in spite of many challenges. Perhaps in some ways it is because the loss—in its stark contrast to unending and ceaseless victory—previewed the future of American sport, anticipating the 1996 Nike ad campaign that declared contemptuously: "You Don't Win Silver; You Lose Gold."

Gable himself may agree with that sentiment. I don't know. I never asked him. But when I interviewed him some years ago he told me this: "America needs wrestling to survive. . . . I mean work ethic. We're taking some very important values and letting them slide." He was referring not just to the days before Title IX made grapplers out of teenage girls and television made commodities out of all elite athletes; he was referring to a far more ancient past. As former Iowa State coach Bobby Douglas once told me, "There is a kind of cosmic connection between wrestling and life. You wrestle out of the womb, you struggle when you're dying. Every day is somewhat of a wrestling match in one way or another." For the million or more undervalued but rabid wrestling fans still left in this country, Gable's career—the wins *and* most assuredly the loss—recapitulates the struggles of a long-forgotten past, one in which men did not reach for legal resolutions in a complex world but for their own resolve—physical, emotional, primal—to make sense of a world that was ruled by gods who looked just like themselves.

For Further Reading

Gable, Dan, and Scott Schulte. *A Wrestling Life: The Inspiring Stories of Dan Gable*. Iowa City: University of Iowa Press, 2015.

Zavoral, Nolan. *A Season on the Mat: Dan Gable and the Pursuit of Perfection*. New York: Simon and Schuster, 2007.

16

The 1972 U.S.–U.S.S.R. Olympic Basketball Final

KEVIN WITHERSPOON

Of the many riveting images drawn from the final moments of the U.S.–U.S.S.R. 1972 Olympic gold medal basketball game, perhaps the most gripping was that of Doug Collins, pencil-thin and drenched in sweat, a welt rising under his right eye, standing at the free throw line preparing to attempt two shots with three seconds remaining. Moments earlier, he had lain unconscious on the end line, the victim of a hard foul by Zurab Sakandelidze, who was determined not to allow Collins to make the winning layup. Regaining consciousness, but still not entirely sure of his surroundings, Collins had the benefit of a timeout to get his bearings. His coach, Hank Iba, gave him a vote of confidence, saying, "If Collins can walk, he'll shoot," meaning that Collins now had to attempt two of the most pressure-packed free throws in basketball history while still not entirely coherent. Perhaps it was better that his mind was fuzzy, as it saved him from dwelling on the pressure upon him. America's sixty-three-game winning streak in the Olympics, seven consecutive gold medals, and the intense rivalry with the Soviet Union were all far from his mind at that moment. His body entered its pre-shot routine at the line as if on auto-pilot. Three confident dribbles, a bend of the knees, a spin of the ball, and release. The first free throw left his hand, arced perfectly through the air, and swished through the basket. The game was now tied, 49–49. Collins went through his routine again: another swish. The United States now led, 50–49, with only three ticks on the clock.

Had the most controversial three seconds in Olympic basketball history not immediately followed those free throws, Doug Collins would likely be known as one of America's great Olympic heroes. We might list his name along with

Bruce Jenner and Mike Eruzione, who had stared down the Soviets at the height of the Cold War and delivered the death blow. Instead, those clutch free throws provided the United States what proved to be a fleeting lead. After an unbelievable—and, from a rules perspective, very complex—sequence lasting five minutes in real time but only three seconds on the game clock, the Soviets converted a game-winning shot, dashing American hopes for the gold medal. Collins and the other members of the American squad, not only shocked at the defeat but also convinced they had been cheated, refused to accept their silver medals, which even today remain locked in a vault at the International Olympic Committee headquarters in Lausanne, Switzerland.

The 1972 Olympic basketball final remains one of the most notorious games in Olympic history. Along with the 1980 U.S.–U.S.S.R. hockey game, it ranks among the most memorable Olympic events of the Cold War era, the two events etched in the minds of American sports fans, but for opposite reasons. The game was saturated with Cold War overtones, as victory in such contests had come to symbolize broader cultural and social superiority. Global politics lent further meaning to the event, with America's reputation in the world waning as the conflict in Vietnam approached its awful, surreal climax. And only days earlier, the Olympic community, along with the world, suffered the shock of the terrorist attack that left eleven Israeli athletes dead, leaving many to wonder whether the games should even continue.

This basketball game has been the subject of much scrutiny from historians, analysts, fans, and commentators for more than four decades, and it remains a source of debate today. Though the initial pain of defeat eased with the passage of time, the American players, along with many of their supporters, remain convinced they were cheated. Historians and documentarians have dissected the final moments of the game, still leaving some questions unanswered and reaching no consensus regarding the outcome. Were those final seconds officiated correctly? Was the appeal on behalf of the team biased by Cold War politics? Could the United States have fielded a better team and played a better game, avoiding the narrow outcome altogether? These and other questions continue to swirl around a game now more than forty years behind us but yet still alive.

The sequence following Collins's two free throws is strange, convoluted, and—had it not unfolded before the eyes of millions—almost beyond belief. First, just before the second free throw left Collins's hands, the officials' horn sounded, indicating a stoppage of play. Despite the horn, Collins shot, and Soviet player Alshan Sharmukhamedov took the ball out-of-bounds and hurried to throw it in. The clock ticked down to one second as his teammate struggled to advance the ball to half court. However, even as this action unfolded, Brazilian referee Renato Righetto called for the ball to be returned and for the Soviets to inbound the ball again. Why? The Soviet coach, Vladimir Kondrashin, had attempted to call a timeout, which was the reason for the horn. The ball should never have been inbounded in the first place. Instead, the referees honored the Soviets' request for a timeout.

Kondrashin later claimed he had attempted to call a timeout using the electronic buzzer provided to both coaches, but that officials misunderstood his intentions. He said he pressed the buzzer prior to Collins's first free throw but wanted the timeout between shots. As Collins took his second free throw, Kondrashin and several Soviet players erupted in protest that the timeout had not been granted. If Kondrashin had in fact called for a timeout to follow Collins's first free throw, then the ultimate call was correct, or at least within the spirit of fair play. However, it was the *way* in which Righetto made the call that launched a protest from the Americans. In an attempt to restore order, R. William Jones, secretary-general of FIBA, international basketball's governing body, came down from the stands to the officials' table and ordered three seconds put back on the clock. Americans have insisted that Jones, who was British, was on record as opposing American dominance in the sport and thus arranged the Soviet victory. Even those not convinced by this conspiracy theory argue that it was a breach of the rules for Jones to interfere. That Jones's intervention—acting as something like a replay official before there were replay officials—led to the correct call was an irrelevant coincidence to the Americans arguing their case.

Following this first delay, game officials put three seconds back on the clock, and the ball was again given to a Soviet player to inbound, leading to a desperate full-court shot that deflected off the backboard and rim. As time expired, the American players erupted in jubilation. In the midst of this chaos, though, the officials convened once again. They told the American players, now dismayed and confused, to take the court again. The clock had not, in fact, been reset to :03, but rather it had stuck on :50. Officials took several minutes to remedy the situation before allowing the Soviets to inbound the ball for a third time.

On this final attempt, Bulgarian referee Artenik Arabadjian, who spoke no English, gestured to American center Tom McMillen, who was guarding the Soviet inbounder. The referee appeared to be pointing to the end line, and indicating that McMillen should not step over it. McMillen, not understanding clearly, began to drop back, leaving a clear line for the Soviet passer, Ivan Edeshenko, to heave a pass the length of the court to the far free throw line. There, leaping free of two American defenders, Soviet center Alexander Belov caught the pass. With an American player at his feet and a clear line to the rim, Belov laid in the winning basket. Their dreams of victory shattered, the Americans had been beaten, 51–50. Or so it seemed.

That night, the United States filed a protest, and a five-member jury denied it. In the aftermath, many complained that the jury was fixed as well, because three members represented the Soviet bloc and two represented the West. Further examination revealed, however, that the chairman of the committee, Hungarian Ferenc Hepp—whom many assumed supported the Soviet case out of nothing more than Cold War loyalty—had in fact been educated in the United States and shared no love for the Soviet Union. His vote against the Americans was based not on fealty to the Soviets but rather his interpretation of the facts. A final American appeal to the International Olympic Committee, some six months later, was also denied.

The American protest and the appeal focused on the handling of the final few seconds and, most important, on Jones's intervention. However, there were several other irregularities that American authorities also questioned. Clock issues notwithstanding, the final play itself was illegal, they argued. The Soviet passer, Edeshenko, had stepped on the line while making his pass. Belov, who received the pass, had committed a foul as he pushed away the American player attempting to guard him. Belov then traveled with the ball before putting up the final layup. Each of these complaints is, at best, subject to debate. Close review of the replay of that final sequence shows that the passer did not step on the line. Though there was contact on the final play, officials routinely allow a bit of jostling, especially in international play. Similarly, if Belov traveled with the ball, it was close enough to be deemed a judgment call for the official. Had any of these calls been made the other way, the Soviets would likely have had an equally valid complaint.

At other times, American players and officials complained about the generally rough play of the Soviets and one incident in particular. With just over twelve minutes remaining, Soviet player Mikhail Korkia became entangled with the leading American scorer and rebounder, Dwight Jones. Jones retaliated with a modest push of his own, and both players were ejected. Jones and other American players assert that Korkia, the "last man on the bench," as he has been called, was put in the game specifically to goad Jones into a fight. In fact, Korkia was an important cog on the Soviet team and had played significant minutes in the game. A review of the game tape shows no conclusive evidence of malicious intent by the Soviet player. On the ensuing jump ball, American Jim Brewer took an elbow to the head and was lost for the rest of the game, another incident that some have claimed was intentional. As one writer later suggested, "The Americans thought at every turn they had been cheated, when they probably hadn't been."

Though the appeal to the IOC officially ended the story of the 1972 Olympic team, debate continues. Those studying the game eventually shifted their thinking, focusing not on the decisions made by the officials in the final moments, but on the players, coaching, and play of the game itself. Many—including some of the players—have claimed that coach Hank Iba cost the team the victory. Iba, at the end of a long and much-decorated career, was sixty-eight years old and two years removed from his last coaching experience at the University of Maryland. Insisting on a slow, defense-oriented game, Iba ignored trends leading the sport in a more dynamic, offensive direction, stifling what was a potentially explosive team. Only after throwing off Iba's restraints in a desperate attempt to come back late in the game did the American offense hit its stride. Many believe that playing a similar style over the entire game would have made the U.S. team unbeatable.

Others direct the blame even higher, at the organizers of the American team and even American amateur sport itself. The superiority of the American national team was, by 1972, largely a mirage. Media members citing the Olympic unbeaten streak failed to take note of defeats in other events, including a disappointing fifth-place finish at the 1970 FIBA World Championships and a dismal showing during a nine-game exhibition series against the Soviet national team in 1971. Both signaled deepening cracks in the team's foundation. The 1972 team was further depleted by a number of factors. These included the continued rise of the ABA, which had poached top NCAA players, sometimes even in the midst of the NCAA season. This tactic forced NBA teams, which in the past had agreed to allow top college players to compete in the Olympics before signing them, to abandon the practice and sign players before the ABA could get them. Top NCAA seniors intending to play in the pros, in short, were ineligible for the Olympics. Other top players missed the Olympics because of injury. Several either were not invited to try out or dropped out in the midst of Hank Iba's boot-camp style training camp. Bill Walton—the most obvious absence—opted against playing because of nagging knee injuries, though his aversion to militaristic coaching was also a factor. The U.S. team that took the court in Munich, while athletic and talented compared to most other teams in the world, was the youngest and perhaps least talented U.S. Olympic team up to that point.

With the outcome settled and all avenues for protest exhausted, the American team and its supporters had little recourse but to simmer in frustration. The old wounds continued to fester, in part because there was no Olympic rematch in the offing. The Soviets failed to advance past the semifinals in 1976, leaving the United States less than satisfied with its victory over Yugoslavia in the gold-medal game. And, the two sides avoided each other in 1980 and

1984 by virtue of the infamous "dueling boycotts." The United States, denied an opportunity to avenge the defeat, took small solace in victories over the Soviets in lesser competitions and exhibition matches. Only an Olympic rematch would satiate American calls for vengeance. All the more bitter, then, was the final U.S.–U.S.S.R. game of the Cold War era, another win for the Soviets, this time an 82–76 victory in the semifinal game of the 1988 Seoul Olympics. The United States settled for the bronze and, soon after, realized there would be no redemption over the Soviets.

Still unsatisfied twenty years after the defeat, American attention was drawn once again to the 1972 team in the midst of its obsession with a rejuvenated Olympic squad, the 1992 "Dream Team." That team, made up of eleven future Hall of Famers and the best college player of the era, Christian Laettner, laid to rest any pipe dream that other nations could defeat a team of America's best players. Teams like the 1972 Soviet squad might have eked out a controversial win over a bunch of college kids and amateurs. But what if Bill Walton had played on that 1972 team? Kareem Abdul-Jabbar? Oscar Robertson, Walt Frazier, Jerry West, Wilt Chamberlain, or any one of dozens of America's greats? Such a "dream team" would surely have destroyed the Soviets. America's gold-medal-winning squad in Barcelona represented its best opportunity to avenge the 1972 defeat. Racking up victories by an average of more than forty-three points, the team proved beyond dispute that the United States was the dominant basketball nation in the world.

With American dominance on the court reestablished, the former Soviet Union dismantled, and the remaining Russian team only a shell of its former self, interpretation of the 1972 game entered a period of reconsideration, which peaked around the thirtieth anniversary of the game in 2002. Journalists, perhaps no longer feeling pressure to "defeat" the Soviets in print, adopted a more objective tone in dissecting the game. And scholars, less interested in taking sides than in uncovering the facts, began to participate in the discussion as well. During this period, a number of the best studies of the game were produced: a fine HBO documentary, :03 Seconds from Glory; an ESPN SportsCentury documentary and the re-airing of the game; a 2004 doctoral dissertation written by Chris Elzey at Purdue University; and Carson Cunningham's outstanding study of the history of the U.S. men's national team, American Hoops. Each of these works, more than any produced previously, examined the many controversial elements of the game from every angle. Breaking down game footage, researching previously uncited archival documents, and interviewing central figures from both sides (along with many neutral observers), these studies arrived at a more nuanced and objective interpretation of the game.

2002 was the right time for revisionism. With the turn of the millennium, scholars and journalists across a host of fields engaged in studying key events of the previous century. The 1972 basketball final was but one event that invited reconsideration. The field of Cold War studies more broadly entered a revisionist period, as the fall of the Soviet Union led to the release of many previously unseen documents, paving the way for a view of the Cold War in which blame for the animosity was shared more equally between the two superpowers, rather than directed solely at the Soviets. This way of thinking spilled over into interpretation of the 1972 basketball final, as more voices began to argue that the final officiating decisions represented not a conspiracy, but either simply incompetence or—more radically—the *correct* calls. Russia, in this era, also came to be viewed in the United States not as a hated rival, but a fallen power to be pitied. Events such as the Chernobyl nuclear disaster in 1986 and the collapse of the Russian economy demonstrated that Russia was no longer a frightening and intimidating superpower, but rather a sadly eroding nation. Finally, the global atmosphere after the terrorist attacks of September 11, 2001, had shifted decidedly. The world was more unified in its support of the United States than it had been in decades. For a time, rivals and former enemies came together not only to comfort and support one another, but also to assist in the growing "war on terror." Russia became a friend and ally. The rapprochement seems to have affected even those studying the 1972 basketball game. At last, historians, taking a measured approach, seemed to have calmed the controversy.

And yet, on its fortieth anniversary in 2012, the game returned to prominence once again, accompanied by a long-awaited reunion of the twelve men who had made up the American team. A new wave of articles, documentaries, and interviews—not to mention blogs, tweets, and other digital phenomena—flooded the public consciousness. Despite the advances in understanding achieved by the studies of the previous decade, the tone of most of these new works was, once-again, decidedly pro-American and anti-Soviet. The old refrain, "We were cheated!" was revived. The title of the most prominent book on the topic in this period provides an apt summary: *Stolen Glory: The U.S., the Soviet Union, and the Olympic Basketball Game That Never Ended*. Similarly, the ESPN documentary *Silver Reunion*, while providing a forum for the members of the U.S. team to get together for the first time in forty years, was far from even-handed in its depiction of the various controversies.

What might explain this renewal of hyper-patriotism? A number of factors had changed since the "era of understanding" of the early 2000s. Most important, there was growing talk of a "new Cold War" with Russia. Russian president Vladimir Putin, physically robust and athletic in his own right, was a product of the Cold War, a former KGB officer, a throwback to Khrushchev and his confrontational tactics. Diplomatic clashes over a host of issues, such as Russian incursions into Chechnya and Lithuania, unrest in many of the former Soviet satellite states, and wavering support for America's war on terror, further evoked memories of the Cold War rivalry. In the minds of many Americans, Russia was no longer a close ally to be trusted and aided, but rather was once again a rival to be put down.

Adding to the climate was the charged atmosphere surrounding public discourse in the United States, reflected in everything from the ugly 2012 presidential campaign, to boisterous spectators shouting comments during political speeches, to the often noisy and provocative outbursts of sports media. Increasingly, headlines were dominated by exhibitionism and wild behavior, with one outrageous act following the last. While acts such as school shootings and terrorism fill the front pages, the sports pages recount shocking infractions like those of Harvey Updyke, the University of Alabama fan who poisoned the trees at Auburn's Toomer's Corner in 2010. Such an environment discourages calm, measured, objective commentary, and many writers, media members, and announcers find they have to shout to be heard above the din. Calmly suggesting that the controversial calls at the end of the 1972 game had probably been correct, or at least had been made in the spirit of fair play, is not the way to grab readers' attention. Shouting "We were robbed!" is more effective.

For sports enthusiasts interested in learning the real story of the 1972 Olympic basketball final, sifting through the miasma of articles and editorials, and discerning reliable sources from fraudulent ones, can be next to impossible. Thus, myths laid to rest a decade ago resurface, perhaps even stronger and more indelible than before. Endless controversy and circular debate notwithstanding, American sports fans are left with the painful and unpleasant reality of defeat.

For Further Reading

Cunningham, Carson. *American Hoops: U.S. Men's Olympic Basketball from Berlin to Beijing.* Lincoln: University of Nebraska Press, 2009.

Gallagher, Taps, and Mike Brewster. *Stolen Glory: The U.S., the Soviet Union, and the Olympic Basketball Game That Never Ended.* Beverly Hills, Calif.: GM Books, 2012.

17

Billie Jean King vs. Bobby Riggs, 1973

JAIME SCHULTZ

I was one of the forty-eight million Americans stationed in front of a television set tuned to the American Broadcasting Company on the evening of September 19, 1973. I just don't remember it. At eighteen days old, I was warmly ensconced somewhere in the folds of my exhausted, overwhelmed, first-time parents. Through bleary eyes, they watched as Billie Jean King beat Bobby Riggs in three straight sets of tennis. It would go down in history as the "Battle of the Sexes."

Where personal recollection fails me, cultural memories abound. The matchup earns habitual mention in popular and scholarly histories. Journalists frequently revisit the occasion on its anniversary, to mark milestones in the history of women's sport and American feminism, or to provide a cultural touchstone for any contest that pits men against women. The event has inspired several books, including *A Necessary Spectacle: Billie Jean King, Bobby Riggs, and the Tennis Match That Leveled the Game* (Roberts, 2005), *Pressure is a Privilege: Lessons I've Learned from Life and the Battle of the Sexes* (King and Brennan, 2008), and *Game, Set, Match: Billie Jean King and the Revolution in Women's Sports* (Ware, 2011). There have been television features, such as ABC's *When Billie Beat Bobby* (2001) and the BBC's *The Legend of Billie Jean King: Battle of the Sexes* (2013), along with HBO and PBS documentaries about King that treat the showdown with Riggs as if it were the crowning achievement in her biography. At the time of this writing, three different studios reportedly have feature films in various stages of production, including Fox Searchlight's 2017 *Battle of the Sexes,* starring Emma Stone and

Steve Carell. This is nothing short of astonishing, considering the appalling shortage of women athletes who grace the screens of sporting Hollywood.

Let's be honest. The match didn't showcase the best tennis of either competitor's career. And King's 6–4, 6–3, 6–3 victory didn't represent how utterly dominant she was over an opponent who was, as she pointed out, "old enough to be my father." (In fact, Riggs was the same age as King's father.) So why does it deserve such extensive memorialization, much less a place in this anthology? If we think about the various explanations as concentric circles, moving from inside to out with the match at the center, three seem most plausible: the match was less sporting event than it was a spectacle of the absurd; Riggs billed himself as the quintessential male chauvinist pig while King bore aloft the feminist baton; together they represented the larger women's movement and the backlash against it. In retrospect, it was one of those moments perfectly situated within its historical context, an episode in and of its time. Then again, retrospect has a remarkable ability to make the pieces fit together.

She should have beaten him, really. At twenty-nine years old, Billie Jean Moffitt King, ranked second in women's tennis, was at the top of her game, well on her way to collecting her lifetime total of thirty-nine Grand Slam titles. At fifty-five, Robert Larimore Riggs was decades past his prime. He'd taken Wimbledon's triple crown in 1939, winning the singles, doubles, and mixed doubles competitions. After his victory at the U.S. Championships that same year, Riggs stood as the top-ranked amateur player in the world. He won again at Forest Hills in 1941, turned pro, served three years in the navy, and subsequently won three championships (1946, 1947, and 1949) on the professional tennis circuit.

For the next two decades Riggs virtually dropped out of the spotlight. He started edging his way back in during the early 1970s after joining the senior tennis circuit (for players over the age of forty-five). Luring him back to the court was the 1968 onset of the sport's Open Era, which allowed both amateurs and professionals to compete at major tournaments, but it wasn't his tennis that earned him the attention he so desperately craved. It was his escalating habit of spewing outrageously sexist commentary, particularly directed against women's tennis, that drew notice.

The Open Era was a cause King threw herself behind in the late 1960s. But while it increased the sport's popularity, it also brought into sharp relief the growing inequalities between men's tennis and women's tennis. The United States Lawn Tennis Association (USLTA) offered far fewer competitions and egregiously smaller purses for its distaff players. At major tournaments, men typically earned two-and-a-half times more than women. At lesser events, the disparities increased by five-, eight-, even twelve-fold.

The 1970 Pacific Southwest Open was the final straw. When King and her compatriots learned that the men's winner would earn $12,500 while the women's champion would take home just $1,500, they turned to Gladys Heldman, a former player and the founder, publisher, and editor of the magazine *World Tennis*. With financial backing from the Philip Morris tobacco company, Heldman arranged the Houston Virginia Slims invitational to compete with the USLTA's Pacific Southwest Open. King and eight others (Rosie Casals, Nancy Richey, Val Ziegenfuss, Kristy Pigeon, Peaches Bartkowicz, Kerry Melville, Judy Tegart Dalton, and Heldman's daughter, Julie) defected to the Slims-sponsored event. As the "Original Nine" faced suspension from the USLTA, Gladys Heldman forged ahead to establish an autonomous tour, which began in earnest in January 1971. Likening their cause to "women's lib," Heldman called the venture "women's lob."

It was risky to defy the USLTA, but the women, their numbers growing, worked tirelessly to promote the endeavor. They not only played good tennis, they put on a good show. By 1972, there were sixty women on the Slims tour, where prize money outweighed what the USLTA offered its remaining female luminaries. In 1973, players on the Slims tour unionized to form the Women's Tennis Association (WTA); King served as the first president. In a matter of months the USLTA capitulated, and the two women's tours merged.

Later that year, under threat of a boycott from women players, the 1973 U.S. Open became the first Grand Slam tournament to offer equal prize money to men and women. (Wimbledon was the last, holding out until 2007.) King's position on the subject, as she explained in her 1974 autobiography, was not that men and women deserved equal purses because of their comparable athletic abilities, but rather because of their equivalent entertainment values. "The best men players were better than the best women, and I'd never said they weren't," she wrote, "but from a show-biz standpoint I felt we put on as good a performance as the men—sometimes better—and that that's what people paid to see."

Bobby Riggs vehemently disagreed. At least, that was his public posture. It was the men's senior players who deserved more recompense, he argued, not the women. Working from that position, he generated enough sexist zingers to make the media pay attention. "Women's tennis stinks," he declared on more than one occasion. "Women play about 25 per cent as good as men, so they should get about 25 per cent of the money men receive," he quipped to a *Time* reporter. "Even an old man like me, with one foot in the grave, could

beat any woman player." He challenged the era's top women tennis stars—
Margaret Court, Chris Evert, and especially Billie Jean King—to play him,
telling all who cared to listen that his victory would help "to keep our women
at home, taking care of the babies—where they belong." The antifeminist
caricature he cultivated in the early 1970s grabbed the public's attention. Set
against the burgeoning women's movement and women's push for equality
within the conservative tennis world, Riggs's self-professed "male chauvinist
pig" persona made for good copy.

King refused the gauntlet. There was nothing to be gained by indulging an
aging, loudmouthed ex-champ whose favorite T-shirt advertised his support
for WORMS: the World Organization for the Retention of Male Supremacy.
Yet, to King's dismay, Margaret Court, the top-ranked women's player in the
world, agreed to meet him on Sunday May 13, 1973—Mother's Day—for a
prize of $10,000.

Court and King were cut from different cloths. While the Original Nine
nurtured their fledgling circuit, Court remained loyal to the USLTA until
1973. And whereas King was "the pioneering spirit and leading player in the
'Women's Lob' movement," as *Newsweek* described her, Court dissented. "I
am not carrying the banner for women's lib," she remarked. "I've never said
we deserve prize money equal to the men."

At an isolated housing development in California's Cuyamaca Mountains,
in front of 3,200 onlookers and a television audience estimated at thirty million viewers, Margaret Court tanked. Whether it was the public pressure, the
circus-like atmosphere, Riggs's constant needling, or his on-court strategies,
she lost, 6–2, 6–1. Journalists called it the Mother's Day Massacre.

Riggs immediately reset his sights on King: "Now I want King bad. I'll play
her on clay, grass, wood, cement, marble, or roller skates. We got to keep this
sex thing going. I'm a woman specialist now." King had no choice. "Marge
blew it," she told reporters. "She set Women's Lib back and I'm going to put
Women's Lib where it should be."

Choreographing the event was promoter Jerry Perenchio, who in 1971 successfully pulled off "The Fight," a $5 million extravaganza between undefeated
heavyweight champions Muhammad Ali and Joe Frazier. King vs. Riggs
would be "The Match," a best-of-five sets (men's rules), $100,000 winner-
take-all spectacular, and it would all go down in the Houston Astrodome, a
preposterous venue for the usually refined game of tennis, but "The Match"
was in a different orbit. Just a few months earlier, NBC paid $50,000 to air
the prestigious Wimbledon tournament. ABC ponied up $750,000 for the
exclusive broadcast of the clash at the Astrodome. The company sold ad-

vertising at $50,000 a minute. It was no longer just a tennis match. It was a happening. It was a spectacle. It was a cultural phenomenon.

King prepared by calibrating her diet, perfecting her overhead smash, and ultimately retreating to South Carolina's Hilton Head Island for a little tranquility in the sea of hype that was rapidly raging out of control. Riggs, in contrast, didn't seem to take the whole thing seriously. He had trained hard for Margaret Court but did relatively little to ready himself for King. Instead, he waged a one-man publicity tour, made his rounds on the talk show circuit, chatted up reporters, and promoted everything from sporting goods to Hai Karate aftershave. As he purportedly downed a mindboggling 415 vitamins a day (another promotion) to put him in the peak of fitness for the match, he simultaneously reveled in the lifestyle that accompanied his newfound acclaim, enjoying all too well the vices of sex, alcohol, late nights, and wild parties.

Riggs also indulged in his favorite pastime: wagering. He was the consummate hustler (though he preferred the term "bettor"), who gambled on everything from tennis and golf to cards and backgammon. As he told *60 Minutes'* Mike Wallace, "If I can't play for big money, I play for little money. And if I can't play for a little money, I stay in bed that day." This was not a new development. He reportedly won £21,600 (the equivalent of $108,000 then or more than $1.7 million in today's dollars) by placing a £100-bet on himself to win the 1939 Wimbledon trifecta. He'd take on all comers, offering to play them while carrying a bucket of water, holding a dog on a leash, or chained to an elephant, and he almost always emerged the victor. He even took King's husband for $300 the day before the main event. Despite multiple handicaps (he wore galoshes, littered his side of the court with folding chairs, and spotted Larry King a 4–0 lead), Riggs won in six straight games.

The atmosphere in the Astrodome bordered on chaos that night. At 30,472 people, it was the largest crowd ever to witness a tennis event. Celebrities and high rollers paid $100 for courtside seats. Above them, the hoi polloi shelled out $6 for a bird's-eye view of the makeshift court laid atop the Houston Astros' infield. Spectators sported T-shirts and campaign-style buttons declaring their allegiances. Pig mascots danced in the aisles; couples got married in the stands; men facetiously donned aprons; women held signs reading "Bobby Riggs, Bleagh!"

Ninety million people around the world tuned in to watch. The broadcast began with a male-female duet of "Anything You Can Do I Can Do Better." It set a particular tone. Everything about the match, including the "battle" metaphor, was meant to polarize men and women—as if the event was symbolic

Tennis's Battle of the Sexes. (Associated Press.)

of a societal winner-take-all, rather than women's desire for equality. Rosie Casals, King's longtime doubles partner, served as a commentator. She later confessed to journalist Selena Roberts that her acerbic anti-Riggs rhetoric was yet another part of this careful orchestration. "The producers told me exactly what to say. I think I was a sideshow. They wanted me to play a certain role."

Anchoring the commentary was venerable sportscaster Howard Cosell. He lent a certain something to the match, though it sure as hell wasn't gravitas. "Hello again, everyone," he greeted viewers. "We're delighted to be able to bring to you this very, very quaint, unique event." *Unique* makes sense, considering there had never been another sporting event quite like the Battle of the Sexes; but *quaint* seems an odd choice to describe the over-the-top carnival that unfolded before him. Nothing epitomized this better than the arrival of the two contestants. Perenchio had arranged for six toga-clad members of Rice University men's track team to carry King, Cleopatra-style, atop a litter decorated with gold lamé and plumes of feathers. Riggs arrived via the gilded wheels of a red rickshaw, surrounded by a phalanx of Bobby's Bosom Buddies (a name that speaks for itself). The two competitors exchanged gifts. To the woman he called "the biggest sucker in the world," Riggs presented an oversized Sugar Daddy candy (still another promotion). In turn, King presented Riggs with a brown piglet named Larimore Hustle. It was "Astrotennis," described journalist Grace Lichtenstein, "a space-age Hollywood version of the Christians versus the Lions."

Few thought King would win. Even her Slims comrades expressed their doubts. Almost every major news outlet picked Riggs as the favorite. Famed odds maker Jimmy "The Greek" Snyder gave Riggs the advantage at 5–2. "King money is scarce," Snyder reported from Las Vegas. "It's hard to find a bet on the girl."

It was an easy payday for those who picked the "libber" over the "lobber." As King stayed in the backcourt, prolonging the rallies to tire her opponent, Riggs's vitality seemed to visibly drain from his body. He sweated profusely, and made uncharacteristic errors, double faulting and padding back soft returns when he could return the ball at all. Before long, he had devolved into a pathetic shell of his once boisterous self. On his final return, Riggs netted a backhand volley. In a reversal of convention, he mustered the energy to hop the net and congratulate the winner. "I underestimated you," Riggs admitted to King. Cosell provided the closing voiceover: "It began to become a *cause célèbre*—equality for women." The broadcast ended early.

In the decades since, the symbolic importance of the Battle of the Sexes has continued to grow. Observers credit the match for saving Title IX, for pushing forward the Equal Rights Amendment, for encouraging women to ask their bosses for a raise, or leave their abusive husbands, or become professional athletes or WNBA coaches, or CEOs of major corporations. Maybe all that is true. Who's to say? Billie Jean King beat an opponent who shouldn't have mattered. But he did. With all she accomplished before and after that night in Houston, three sets of bad tennis shouldn't matter. But it does.

Where does cultural memory end and myth-making begin? Looking at the commentary from 1973, it doesn't seem as though contemporary observers gave the contest the same historical weight. "With the possible exception of a nude tag-team wrestling match pitting Burt Reynolds and Norman Mailer against Gloria Steinem and Germaine Greer," suggested *Time,* assessing the competition's feminist import, "it is scarcely conceivable that any other single athletic event could burlesque the issue so outrageously." The "basic appeal" of it all, argued the *New York Times'* Neil Amdur, was that it was "more fun and games than any serious philosophical inquiry into the question of whether women can really hold their own with men in sports." Even so, the match has become a fable with a moral as clear and instructive as any that Aesop might have spun: women are capable of great things when given the respect and the opportunities they deserve. The event made King a feminist folk hero, a slayer of patriarchy, a sweaty champion for womankind.

Over time, detractors have tried to demythologize the match: King wasn't the feminist she claimed to be; she should have disclosed her romantic involvement with Marilyn Barnett; Riggs wasn't the jackass he played for the media; he threw the match to pay off his gambling debts to the mob. Regardless of any merit these claims might hold, they ring of something close to blasphemy. Among American sports mythologies, the Battle of the Sexes is sacrosanct. There are too few women in our athletic lore.

I asked my parents if they remembered watching the match. They did, they said, and they were glad to have watched it with their first and only daughter. In his youth, my father excelled in multiple sports and went on to a brief stint in big-time college football. My mother would have been a great athlete. She should have been a great athlete, but it was a different time. She didn't have the opportunities I did—opportunities that came as a cultural byproduct of the Battle of the Sexes, as so many accounts would have us believe. My mom remembers swelling with pride when King beat Riggs, but it was a bittersweet moment. It came too late for her. It came too late for too many women. And so, when I look back at this historical event and notice that there are certain plot points in the narrative, certain symbolic implications that seem not only doubtful, but implausible, I cast aside my reservations. I choose to believe. King vs. Riggs changed the world.

For Further Reading

King, Billie Jean, and Christine Brennan. *Pressure is a Privilege: Lessons I've Learned from Life and the Battle of the Sexes.* New York: LifeTime Media, 2008.

Roberts, Selena. *A Necessary Spectacle: Billie Jean King, Bobby Riggs, and the Tennis Match That Leveled the Game.* New York: Crown, 2005.

Ware, Susan. *Game, Set, Match: Billie Jean King and the Revolution in Women's Sports.* Chapel Hill: University of North Carolina Press, 2011.

18

Ali–Foreman and the Myth
of the Rope-a-Dope

MICHAEL EZRA

Myth now dominates our misunderstanding of Muhammad Ali, who was once the most accessible celebrity in the world. His true history is nearly irretrievable, the result of a self-imposed, three-decade silence that his financial security depended upon for a long time. Our ability to learn anything new from Ali vanished years ago, even as the enterprises that capitalized on his deified status as an all-time great man hit full stride. The myth of the rope-a-dope is perhaps the best example of a widely believed Ali story that misses the mark almost completely and obscures most of what's genuinely interesting about him as a fighter and cultural figure.

Ask people about Muhammad Ali's 1974 fight with George Foreman and you very well may hear that Ali scored a dramatic win by backing against the ropes, weathering a brutal battering, and then delivering a sudden knockout. They would be wrong if they said this, however, because what really happened is that Ali whipped Foreman comprehensively from start to finish. The whole fight, even in the rounds when he barely moved his feet, Ali landed more meaningful punches than he took. Whenever Foreman mounted an offensive, Ali jackknifed him by grabbing then pulling downward the back of his head and neck, an illegal tactic that went unpunished and gave Foreman almost no chance to win the bout at any time.

Although a blowout, the match remains etched in historical memory as a stunning trial-by-fire comeback embodying not only Ali's best as a fighter, but as someone whose determination and resolve made him into an icon. Only after the Foreman bout did a large chunk of the so-called American silent majority (perhaps represented by Gerald Ford, who invited the new champion to the White House, as every president has since and none had prior) afford him the respect that we now take for granted toward a living legend admired by millions of people around the world for decades. While other boxing matches provide better evidence of Ali's true supremacy as history's best heavyweight, the rope-a-dope endures as the pop culture repository where his ring greatness and cultural significance most keenly intersect, even if most of the meaning making has been wrong-headed.

Coming back from three-and-a-half years out of the ring, Ali retreated to the ropes in all of his toughest postexile fights. Skill, courage, and strategy—the heroic things people associate with the rope-a-dope—did not factor significantly into Ali's decision to employ it against Foreman. Ali went to the ropes simply because he had no choice. Foreman could either cut off the ring or use his prodigious arm strength to push Ali into corners. Ali was too old to dance for more than a round or two, and it was too hot and humid for that in Zaire, anyway. Rather than a master stroke, the rope-a-dope unfolded fortunately for a fighter who might otherwise have been in trouble had he not been facing someone whose skill set disappeared when tested by ring-savvy opponents such as Gregorio Peralta and Jimmy Young, much less the great Ali.

An Ali standard in those years, the rope-a-dope, when he leaned back against the ropes while covering up, usually didn't work because it needed

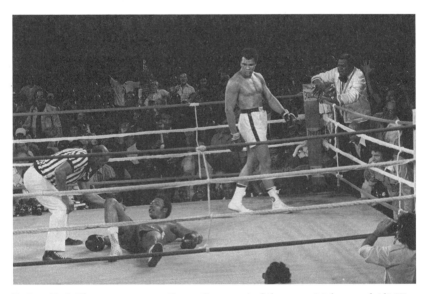

Referee Zack Clayton counts out George Foreman in fight versus Muhammad Ali, Kinshasa, Zaire. (Associated Press.)

a sucker, a literal dope, to be effective. Joe Frazier, no dope, hurt Ali when he used the tactic. Ron Lyle, no dope, waited at ring center and waved Ali forward whenever he retreated. Only Foreman fought dopily enough for it to work; unequipped to do anything noteworthy once he had his man in that compromised position, other than inflict blunt-force trauma to his arms, kidneys, and upper torso. This tactic was proven effective for certain fighters at certain times, battering opponents' defenses to open up clean head shots, but anyone who thinks that's what could have happened in Zaire doesn't understand the difference between Muhammad Ali and Roland LaStarza.

The wide power punches that pummeled Joe Frazier and Ken Norton did not work in the Rumble in the Jungle. Even though Frazier and Norton gave Ali fits in all six of their combined bouts against him, while Foreman crushed them both, Ali had no problem with Foreman. Time and again boxing fans forget that although paper beats rock and rock beats scissors, scissors still beats paper. Ali was a bad stylistic match for Foreman, as Foreman was for Norton and Frazier, as Norton and Frazier were for Ali. Norton lost to Foreman quickly and decisively, just as he fared against the other devastating sluggers he faced, Earnie Shavers and Gerry Cooney. Foreman's weak results against Young matched those versus Peralta and Ali. Even in his incredible third act, which culminated when he became the oldest heavyweight champion, Foreman ate jab after jab, stifled by the likes of Tommy Morrison, Axel Schulz, and even Michael Moorer before landing the historic victory punch. Neither man defied expectation in Zaire even if it seemed that both had. Hindsight also makes it easy to see that Frazier left something behind in the ring with Ali during their sublime first contest, truly the sport's greatest event of all time, when he fought as good a bout as anyone in his division's history, becoming an even easier target for Foreman two years later.

Explanations exist for the misinterpretation of the rope-a-dope, even though debunking the role it played in Ali–Foreman is now as simple as watching the bout in its entirety on YouTube. Although we may take for granted the fight's availability for viewing, for a long time few people had seen it more than once, if at all. A big closed-circuit television event, Ali–Foreman showed in a very healthy 450 U.S. locations, and then months later ABC rebroadcast it, years before many households had videocassette recorders. After that it went away and became something people either read about or saw excerpted on the occasional TV special. It is not far-fetched that more people have heard about the rope-a-dope version of the fight, backed by select clips indicating that Ali took a beating and then rallied, than have seen the whole bout. Those who actually witnessed the emotionally charged match in real time no doubt perceived Ali to be in much deeper trouble than he really was. This group includes the sportswriters who would accept uncritically Ali's version of what happened and even his name for it, the "rope-a-dope." All sorts of stories about the fight now exist to explain the result, from Angelo Dundee's loosening the ropes (or preventing them from being tightened, or even tightening them, depending on which version of the story you read) to Foreman's bizarre supposition—in an otherwise bland autobiography—that someone slipped him a mickey.

Many such mythical moments sprinkle Muhammad Ali's boxing career when invented *post-facto* explanations justify (often ridiculously) unforeseen ring turns. More people accept the silly story that Ali felled Sonny Liston in their rematch using Jack Johnson's "anchor punch" taught to him by Stepin Fetchit than the more likely one that the iron-chinned Liston, whose death five years later still lingers mysteriously, took a dive in fear of some perceived external threat. There was no long break between rounds after Henry Cooper dropped Cassius Clay in their first bout. What happened is that Clay recovered in the standard amount of time and then returned to thumping Cooper. *When We Were Kings,* the 1996 film that won the Academy Award for best documentary despite its fundamentally dishonest approach to the rope-a-dope, now informs the public's sense of Ali–Foreman more than any source. It suggests that Ali rather than Foreman began the fight in deep water, and that the winner's extraordinary character rather than Foreman's poor performance kept him afloat.

Typically hagiographic in its representation of Ali's boxing abilities and cultural significance, *When We Were Kings* premiered to critical acclaim, with the rope-a-dope at the center, as Roger Ebert's review makes clear: "History records Ali's famous strategy, the 'Rope-a-Dope' defense, in which he simply outwaited Foreman, absorbing incalculable punishment. . . . *When We Were Kings* gives the impression that Ali got nowhere in the first round and adopted the Rope-a-Dope almost by default." The rope-a-dope, however, was neither genius premeditated strategy nor brilliant athletic improvisation. It was not a default, either, but something Ali actively developed in training. He knew he would have to go to the ropes like he did in every hard fight following his exile, so he sparred accordingly, because he would have to be good at it to survive. Ali had no second option beyond the rope-a-dope given the circumstances, which luckily for him wound up posing fewer obstacles than anticipated to his formidable, if faded, brilliance.

When We Were Kings, after lying cold on the cutting room floor for two decades, got made at a time when Ali had rebounded into the major media spotlight through books, television, and Hollywood after a postretirement dry spell. The Ali renaissance started with the heavily publicized authorized biography *Muhammad Ali: His Life and Times* by Thomas Hauser in 1991, which takes readers little closer to knowing what makes Ali tick; its myriad interviews obscure but cannot hide its lack of insight into his character. Other books followed, including a 1998 bestseller by *New Yorker* editor David Remnick. Ali provided the shining moment that climaxed the made-for-television lighting of the Olympic torch in 1996. The Hollywood biopic *Ali,* starring Will Smith, came in 2001. None of these works capture Ali's character in original and exciting ways like those written many years ago by Claude Lewis, Jack Olsen, and Wilfrid Sheed, all of whose studies make better quality meaning of Ali's life than any of the above-mentioned, more-recent texts. For at least forty years Muhammad Ali has eluded our grasp as the subject of satisfying biographical inquiries that take the measure of his existence. *When We Were Kings* fits the time period well; when it comes to Ali, it is quintessentially nineties, almost all hero worship and no critical substance.

Myth penetrates Ali's story because the fighter (or someone close to him), to explain unforeseen out-of-the-ring events, time and again spun ridiculous *post-facto* yarns in high-profile sites that then become stuck in popular memory, like the one about why he didn't possess the gold medal he won at the 1960 Olympics. If you believe the tale as told in Ali's 1975 autobiography, *The Greatest: My Own Story*—a book spurred by his dramatic win in Zaire—then you, too, might have fallen for the rope-a-dope. The book claims that racist bikers pursued Ali and a friend on a no-way-out, high-speed, movie-grade motorcycle chase through the streets of Louisville and then to a bridge spanning the Ohio River. Expert riding and self-defensive martial artistry by Ali and friend forced the rednecks to crash and retreat. That night Ali chucked the medal off the bridge in protest—the whole episode started because he, an Olympic hero in his hometown, merely asked to be served in a local restaurant.

Even as a black power allegory, the tale represented Ali out of character; he never rode motorcycles proficiently or got into street fights. Come 1996, when Ali received an honorary replacement medal, NBC commentators informed audiences that the bridge story was not true and that he had simply lost the original; a more appropriate narrative for the Olympic moment, anyhow. The backing of *The Greatest* by a major publishing firm, Random House, with future Nobel Prize winner Toni Morrison as the book's in-house editor, and longtime journalist and *Muhammad Speaks* editor Richard Durham as its writer, complicates Ali's deniability as the main source of error in the on-the-record version of his life story. Why Ali lied about this in the first place and thereafter remains unanswered even though he had for many years been in a position to address it. Ali to his dying day remained the main barrier to our getting a truthful sense of his life.

Blaming Herbert Muhammad and the Nation of Islam for the autobiography's many inadequacies, as writers have, does not take into account Ali's long-term tendency to lie so often that he believed myths of his own creation. Ali only talked about the bridge incident when people inquired if it was true, according to his wife Lonnie, but when they did he either said yes or didn't answer. "He never says no," she reported. "I've never heard him say no." Everyone else knows, however, that Ali lost the medal, which is what Ali himself said, embarrassingly, during a press conference hyping his very own autobiography. Even the museum dedicated to chronicling him seems comfortable with this degree of interpretive flexibility. In calling the gold medal story "a legend," Muhammad Ali Center vice president for communications Jeanie Kahnke also notes that no one can say for certain whether it's true or untrue, which is how Ali liked it.

Although he was capable of resolving them, so many questions at the heart of his story still lie unexplained because Ali said almost nothing on his own behalf for his final three decades. He talked on camera after the events of 9/11, but that was the lone circumstance cataclysmic enough to bring him out of his shell. Ali's silence did not change the fact that in his later years, he could communicate with the world, and not just through the occasional tweet written by someone being paid to do so. Being older and sicker does not consign public figures to silence, and some like Ebert even grew in stature after losing their speaking voices. With modern technology, and Ali's access to the best care, his long insulation had been more self-imposed than the sad and inevitable result of Parkinson's disease. What should have been Ali's reflective years—the period when we were able to tap most deeply into his character, learn from his accrued wisdom, and best analyze the meaning of his life—instead brought forth no new understanding of him. Ali rested more unknowable than ever before; myth had become the legitimate substitute for the facts of his life. We should not have to guess about the nature of his relationship with the Nation of Islam, or Joe Frazier, or Malcolm X, or what happened in those two fights with Liston, and how did that story about the bridge get out, anyway? The baffling reality—the truly outrageous contradiction—is that there exists an entire Muhammad Ali Center dedicated to understanding a man who did not give a long interview or press conference in thirty years.

Prior to his renaissance, upon Ali's 1981 retirement and throughout the decade, Ali's life served as a cautionary tale of how not to do it, of a boxer who had everything—riches, good health, family—and lost his grasp on nearly all of it. Ali left boxing a broken man and tragic figure, a punch-drunk and pathetic laughingstock parodied mercilessly on TV shows like *Saturday Night Live* and *In Living Color* as an over-the-hill half-wit. He had little money and was in rapidly declining health, less relevant to the zeitgeist than ever before, reduced to appearing at boxing matches in exchange for walking-around money. Remarkably, Ali's recasting from tragic to triumphant figure occurred while he said virtually nothing on his own behalf. Silence and myth-making girded Ali's iconography far sturdier than anything he might have produced organically, and probably had for a very long time. The near-total lack of access to him didn't negate his greatness, of course, but rather made it harder to capture his value as a historical figure. How could he really represent all of things the Ali Center says he did if he couldn't even bring himself to speak honestly about his past, or at least to have opinions about more recent matters of importance, for all those years?

The rope-a-dope myth helps define Ali's public standing in significant ways, filling holes in his résumé as a boxer and cultural figure. The win over Foreman legitimated Ali's victories over Liston and is the major contributing factor to those two bouts undeservingly losing their stink. He courageously absorbed Foreman's assault and came back for the dramatic win. This true gut check legitimated for many skeptics Ali's draft resistance as no longer a cowardly excuse but instead a principled stand, when combined with the Supreme Court decision in his favor and his gutsy first fight with Frazier. Before he was champ, Ali's high voice, flamboyant personality, hairless body, calling himself pretty, and lack of interest in anything besides boxing combined with a less-than-rugged fighting style to produce whispers questioning his sexual orientation. Along somewhat similar lines, the taint of the Liston victories and especially his draft resistance, when combined with Ali's personal idiosyncrasies that did not always jibe with contemporary white masculine heterosexual standards, caused people including many of the era's most popular journalists and broadcasters to believe he lacked a certain crucial character trait known then as manhood. Ali never served his duty to his country nor to the ring, having failed to engage in bloody, to-the-death combat on either front. The Foreman fight satisfied those urges for many, and opened the floodgates for the mainstream political acceptance and corporate sponsorship that had for at least twenty-five years defined Ali's legacy. First President Ford, then the Olympic torch, then the Ali Center, which was made possible by a government land grant.

The Ali–Foreman fight hardly illustrates Ali's courage and resolve; better places exist for that. Instead, it shows our willingness to accept that lies about him are the best we can expect, even though he exists as a legend who conceivably could have been answering questions truthfully for three decades. Shutting up was good business for Ali; between the Ali Center's institutionalized version of his life and the commercial licensing of his image, critical inquiries were all but drowned out, and the days of learning anything more about him are done. At its heart, then, the rope-a-dope myth spotlights how little we have chosen to know about Ali, and how little he chose to reveal of himself, even as a revered world-historical figure all too often placed in the same company with the likes of King, Mandela, or Gandhi.

For Further Reading

Ezra, Michael. *Muhammad Ali: The Making of an Icon*. Philadelphia: Temple University Press, 2009.

Mailer, Norman. *The Fight*. Boston: Little, Brown, 1975.

Marqusee, Mike. *Redemption Song: Muhammad Ali and the Spirit of the Sixties*. New York: Verso Books, 1999.

19

Larry Bird vs. Magic Johnson, 1979

MURRY NELSON

In sports it is no surprise that myth outlives fact, story trumps data, and the embellishment of story makes it all that more attractive. The 1979 NCAA championship game, in which Michigan State defeated Indiana State, 75–64, has become laden with both myth and embellishment since the game was played in Salt Lake City. To appreciate what really happened and assess its impact fully, we should examine both the story and the data to gain a complete understanding of what the game meant in 1979 and beyond.

One of the first myths to explore is the greatness of the game itself. Certainly the lead actors, Larry Bird and Earvin "Magic" Johnson, have retained their mythological qualities over the years, not necessarily for this game, but rather for the excellence they demonstrated over their long careers as professional players. The NCAA championship contest pitted an undefeated Indiana State team (33-0) led by Bird against Michigan State, the preseason No. 1 team that had stumbled to five early season losses (three on last-second desperation shots) before a ten-game winning streak propelled them to a share of the Big Ten title, a 21-6 record, and a No. 3 national ranking.

The Michigan State roster had two other top players. Greg Kelser went on to a six-year NBA career with the Detroit Pistons, Seattle Supersonics, San Diego Clippers, and Indiana Pacers, and Jay Vincent had a nine-year NBA career with the Dallas Mavericks, Washington Bullets, Denver Nuggets, San Antonio Spurs, Philadelphia 76ers, and Los Angeles Lakers. Indiana State produced only one NBA player besides Bird. Carl Nicks played two full seasons with Denver and the Utah Jazz, plus nine games with the Cleveland Cavaliers in a third season before his career ended.

Michigan State's spot in the tournament was hardly a *fait accompli*, despite the team's high ranking in the polls. The Spartans tied for the Big Ten title with Purdue and Iowa, all going 10-4 in conference play, but until 1975, the NCAA tournament accepted only one team per conference. The Big Ten did not allow its members to accept NIT bids, so nine teams sat at home each year, no matter how good their records. Then, in 1975, the NCAA expanded its field from twenty-five to thirty-two and allowed two teams from a conference to accept bids for the tournament. In 1979, Michigan State and Iowa got in. Purdue did not.

Indiana State's invitation to the tournament was clear-cut. The Sycamores won the Missouri Valley Conference tournament, gaining an automatic bid. Indiana State had joined the Valley only in 1976, but the league had a rich history of success in the NCAA tournament, including four national champions—Oklahoma A&M (later Oklahoma State) twice and the University of Cincinnati twice. Both teams had since left the conference, but the notion that the Valley was an "upstart" league, one of the myths that embellished the 1979 game, was simply not so.

By contrast, the Big Ten was seen as a longtime power—it was—with far more success in the NCAA tournament, but this was not the case if one considers only championships. Big Ten schools had won just five NCAA titles—one by Ohio State, three by Indiana, and one by Wisconsin.

Despite this long, storied history, many still regarded the Big Ten as a football league. When Ohio State reached three consecutive NCAA basketball championship games from 1960 to 1962, the school didn't even bother to put out a press brochure. "The conference was too busy taking care of football," said former OSU coach Fred Taylor. Before the start of the 1977–1978 season, Michigan State coach Jud Heathcote complained, "I don't think our conference publicizes basketball the way it should. There's no highlight film, no publication, no booklet."

The 1979 Final Four was the last to be played on a college campus, at the University of Utah. Beginning in 1980, the Final Four moved to large off-campus arenas, and in 1982, as a direct result of the great demand for tickets and the television ratings of the 1979 game, the NCAA championship was played in an indoor football stadium, the New Orleans Superdome, with a capacity exceeding seventy-five thousand. "Smaller" venues have subsequently been utilized, but since 1996, Final Four venues have seated at least forty thousand and as many as a hundred thousand. This was a long-term result of the success of the 1979 championship game.

Magic Johnson and Larry Bird before the 1979 NCAA championship game. (Associated Press.)

Examining the rosters of the 1979 participants illustrates a pattern that had been largely true at most Division I schools until that time, that is, almost every player on each roster was either from the home state of the university or a contiguous state. Recruiting was simply much different in the 1970s. Many players went "unnoticed" because of minimal television coverage, the lack of the Internet and social media, and the low recruiting budgets of colleges. Bird was lightly recruited and ended up at Indiana, where Bobby Knight basically ignored him, and he left Bloomington after two weeks. Johnson was more widely pursued, but he would not leave the state of Michigan, and that left only Michigan and Michigan State as serious contenders for his talents.

The coaches also had their own stories. Jud Heathcote was seen as a veteran coach who badgered players and referees into submission. Many have viewed the Sycamores' Bill Hodges as a young coach in the right place at the right time. To a degree, both characterizations were true. Heathcote was a wily coach, but he was just fifty-two and had been a head coach for only eight years when he led the Spartans to the 1979 tournament. His snow-white hair may have belied his age and his experience (five years at the University of Montana and three at Michigan State after fourteen years of high school coaching and seven years as an assistant at Washington State, his alma mater). Heathcote remained at Michigan State for sixteen more years, retiring at sixty-eight, and that long tenure, in retrospect, may have altered the way he is viewed.

At the beginning of the season, Bill Hodges was thirty-five and had been an assistant coach for eight years at Tennessee Tech and Indiana State. The school named him interim head coach when head coach Bob King suffered a stroke as a result of a brain aneurysm and was forced to leave coaching. Hodges's low-key approach stood in marked contrast to Heathcote's, and his coaching style was more attuned to encouragement and making sure Larry Bird was involved in every offensive play. After Bird left Terre Haute, Indiana State was unable to recruit or perform nearly as well, and Hodges was fired after the 1982 season. He later became head coach at Georgia College (1986–1991) and Mercer University (1991–1997).

Some thought that the championship game was the first time Johnson and Bird had met, let alone seen one another play, but that, too, was not so. In 1978, both had been part of a team of college players who represented the United States in a series of games in Moscow. Joe B. Hall, coach of the NCAA champion Kentucky Wildcats, handled this team, and neither Bird nor Johnson made his starting five. They rode the bench much of the time as the Americans defeated all their opponents. Johnson and Bird got to observe each other at practice and, at times, to play together in their reserve roles.

Returning to the championship game itself, few observers described it as great. In later years, neither Bird nor Johnson spent a lot of time on it in their various autobiographies. Johnson was voted Most Outstanding Player of the tournament, and his line in the final game reflected that. He had a game-high twenty-four points, seven rebounds, and five assists. Bird, by contrast, had one of his worst games, despite scoring nineteen points. He shot only 7-of-21 from the field and 5-of-8 from the free-throw line and contributed but two assists. He also committed six of the Sycamores' turnovers. Bird noted that, "We played a bad game, but they were better. I think if we played them ten times, we might have beaten them twice." Larry Keith, writing in *Sports Illustrated* the next week, summarized Bird's woeful game in this manner, "Bird missed shots, committed turnovers and failed to find the open man."

Two rules not implemented at that time might have changed the nature of the game. There was no shot clock, which the NCAA did not introduce until 1986. The lack of a clock allowed the Spartans to hold the ball for more than a minute at a time near the end of the game when they had a seven- to eleven-point lead. There was also no three-point shot, which was not allowed in NCAA play until 1987. Bird made 40 percent of his three-pointers the next year (1979–1980) as a member of the Boston Celtics. He led the NBA in three-pointers in two different years and made more than fifty in eight of his thirteen years in the league. Including the three-point shot would have made a difference in the way the 1979 finals game played out, considering Michigan State played a zone for much of the game, but it may have had no effect on the outcome.

One legendary statistic, that the game was the highest-rated ever on television, is true. The game achieved a Nielsen rating of 24.1, as fans were eager not only to see the great match-up of Johnson vs. Bird, but simply to see them at all, especially Bird. College basketball was not nationally televised to a great degree at that time, and most viewers had not seen Indiana State.

Because Bird had appeared on television so few times, a considerable number of fans thought he was African American. Once it became widely known that Bird was white, a number of easy dichotomies appeared. There was the big, flagship, state university against the smaller, less-respected state school. There was the black-white difference, but, in a reversal of stereotype, there was also Bird, the boy raised by a single parent or grandmother, versus Johnson, from a stable family. Promoters played up the urban-rural contrast. Johnson was a city lad from Lansing while Bird hailed from French Lick, Indiana, and played basketball in jeans and tennis shoes for much of his youth (even wearing that outfit when he played on his recruiting visit to Terre Haute). Then there were their personalities, with the ebullient Johnson contrasted with the shy, introverted Bird. A corollary of this was Bird's refusal to engage with reporters, while Johnson was always ready to provide quotes or a publicity photo. After the game, it was no different, although the circumstances, that is, Johnson's team winning and Bird's losing, made this much more understandable.

For such a widely anticipated game, the contest was not a "back-and-forth" affair. The Spartans played a suffocating 2-3 zone, trying to deny Bird the ball and doubling him whenever he put it on the floor. ISU, by contrast, went with a man-to-man defense and, surprisingly, played Bird on Kelser, who was much quicker and scored on four of his team's first five possessions. Kelser, however, also got into foul trouble, picking up three in the first half.

The Sycamores led, 8–7, when Terry Donnelly sank a jumper for the Spartans, giving them a 9–8 lead; they never trailed again. Bird had trouble getting the ball and, when he did, the double-teaming made him indecisive or had him putting up shots with difficulty. He went 4-for-11 in the opening twenty minutes, and the Spartans put on a good run to end the half, leading 37–28.

In the second half, MSU kept it up and built a 42–28 lead with eighteen minutes left. Kelser picked up his fourth foul with 15:33 to go, and the Spartans slowed the pace to try to keep their lead. Instead, they lost their tempo, and Indiana State got as close as 52–46 with ten minutes to go. Magic then scored four quick points on a dunk and two free throws, and the lead went back to eleven. The rest of the game saw the Spartans march to the free throw line repeatedly as the clock ran down to 0:00.

Two big factors in the game were free-throw and field-goal percentage. ISU shot poorly from the line, just 10-for-22 (45 percent), while MSU was 23-for-33 (70 percent); from the floor, ISU shot 42 percent, while the Spartans hit a sparkling 61 percent. The teams each snared thirty-four rebounds, with Bird taking thirteen for game honors. He shot just 3-for-10 in the second half.

The game's greatest impact was probably its effect on television, not just the NCAA's airing of games, but also the NBA's television package. College broadcasting was limited in 1979; there were no conference packages. National coverage included only some Saturday games and the NCAA tournament on NBC. Surprisingly, that network lost the tournament after 1981 when new president Fred Silverman "poor mouthed" and lost exclusive rights to NCAA basketball and the tournament, despite having a window that gave it the exclusive option to negotiate. After NBC failed to take advantage of its window of opportunity, CBS swooped in and secured the rights to the next three years of the tournament for $48 million.

In September 1979 came the debut of the Entertainment and Sports Programming Network (ESPN). Initially ESPN accepted almost any programming it could get, including minor-league football and various sports competitions created for television. When regular-season college basketball rights became available for bid, ESPN jumped into the fray. In 1981–1982, NBC, CBS, and ESPN all broadcast college basketball. CBS had sixteen regular-season games and sixteen tournament games, NBC offered twenty-seven regular-season games, and ESPN aired ninety-one regular-season contests plus the first two rounds of the tournament. In the next bidding round, CBS retained the rights to the tournament for the next three years for $96 million and has kept those rights through 2024, at minimum.

Even more dramatic, however, was the effect the 1979 Bird–Johnson final had on the growth and telecasting of professional basketball. Bird and Johnson both entered the NBA the following season, and many fans wanted to follow their careers, as well as their rivalry, as they played in the pros. In 1979, CBS aired the NBA Finals between the Washington Bullets and the Seattle Supersonics in prime time, and the ratings were disastrous. CBS seemed to know what it had in the rookie duo. Bird and Johnson appeared on the cover of the 1979–1980 CBS media guide, the first time rookies had ever received that recognition. Nevertheless, CBS chose to show the 1980 Finals between Philadelphia and Los Angeles on a tape-delay basis. What that meant was that most basketball fans missed the fantastic final game when the Lakers, missing their star center, Kareem Abdul-Jabbar, who was out with a severe ankle sprain, defeated the 76ers. Magic Johnson scored forty-two points, many of them from the pivot position, where he was unstoppable. Only in Philadelphia and Los Angeles was the game picked up live; other affiliates showed it at 10:30 (Central/Midwest) or 11:30 (East and West), when the majority of fans knew the score and had already gone to sleep.

Magic Johnson's performance in that final game made basketball fans clamor for more exposure to NBA games, especially those with Magic or Bird and, more specifically, the NBA championship round. The next year, 1981, the old contracts remained in place, and CBS allowed affiliate stations to show the NBA Finals between the Houston Rockets and the Boston Celtics with Bird either live or on tape delay. Again, only in the two home cities were the games telecast live. Other major markets chose to air CBS's regular shows. The last game of the Finals came on a Thursday, the most popular night for network television, and CBS's line-up featured three shows that night, *The Waltons, Magnum, P.I.,* and *Knots Landing,* that were highly rated and won their time slots.

Beginning in 1982, CBS showed the NBA Finals live in prime time, perhaps because Magic Johnson and the Lakers were again in the Finals, facing, as in 1980, the 76ers and Julius Erving. Johnson and the Lakers won, and Magic was selected Most Valuable Player of the series. To accommodate CBS, the NBA season had started two weeks later so that the Finals would be played in late May or early June, after the networks' mid-May sweeps weeks. This was duplicated in 1983 when the same two teams met again, but this time, Philadelphia won.

In 1984, the Celtics and Lakers met in the NBA Finals, the first time Bird and Johnson faced each other for a championship since 1979. This was the most-watched series in NBA history, and Boston won, four games to three. The ratings rose again the next year when the same two teams and players met in the Finals, and the Lakers reversed the results. This upward trend continued over the next nine years, with one exception, 1992.

One more thing. NBA player endorsements grew decidedly after Bird and Johnson entered the NBA. Probably the most highly rated and remembered commercials on television during the 1990s and early 2000s were a series of

McDonald's commercials in which Bird and Michael Jordan played H-O-R-S-E, with the winner gaining a Big Mac sandwich. From his initial shy demeanor, Bird became a marketing monster, representing General Mills, Kellogg's, Heinz, Pepsi, and MCI, among others. Johnson had fewer endorsements (by choice), but these included Pepsi, KFC, Red Rooster, and Converse. He spent more time and energy on creating his own business empire, including various franchises such as Starbucks, Magic Johnson Theaters (a chain of movie theaters), Magic Johnson Entertainment (a movie studio), and Magic Johnson Productions (a promotional company that produces concerts, tours, and boxing events), not to mention his purchase (with partners) of the Los Angeles Dodgers.

These business developments set a tone and pattern for Michael Jordan's enterprises, beginning with Air Jordans for Nike, then Gatorade, Hanes, and the aforementioned McDonald's commercials, among others. The Dream Team of 1992 solidified the commercial endeavors of these three and set a standard other basketball players strive to emulate. Magic and Larry need no last names; they have become basketball and commercial icons. It all can be traced to the 1979 NCAA tournament.

For Further Reading

Bird, Larry, with Bob Ryan. *Drive: The Story of My Life*. New York: Doubleday, 1989.

Bird, Larry, and Earvin Magic Johnson, with Jackie MacMullan. *When the Game Was Ours*. New York: Houghton Mifflin Harcourt, 2009.

Davis, Seth. *When March Went Mad: The Game That Transformed Basketball*. New York: Times Books, 2009.

Einhorn, Eddie, and Ron Rapaport. *How March Became Madness: How the NCAA Tournament Became the Greatest Sporting Event in America*. Chicago: Triumph Books, 2006.

Johnson, Earvin "Magic," with William Novak. *My Life*. New York: Random House, 1992.

Shaw, Mark. *Larry Legend*. Chicago: Masters Press, 1998.

20

The Birth of ESPN,
A Sports Junkie's Nirvana

TRAVIS VOGAN

Six weeks prior to the cable sports television network ESPN's September 7, 1979, launch, *Sports Illustrated* media critic William O. Johnson speculated on the outlet's potential impact. "ESPN," he claimed, "may become the biggest thing in TV sports since *Monday Night Football* and night-time World Series games." ESPN—the self-dubbed "Worldwide Leader in Sports" that a 2012 *Forbes* report named the world's most valuable media property—has met and surpassed Johnson's prophecy. In fact, ESPN took over *Monday Night Football* from fellow Walt Disney Company property and former parent company ABC in 2006. What's more, its *Monday Night Football* broadcasts now typically yield larger audiences than the World Series games periodically scheduled against them on major networks.

In a 2014 *Sports Illustrated* special issue commemorating its sixtieth anniversary, the legacy magazine named ESPN's creation one of the signal events in sport that has occurred during its lifespan—no small compliment given ESPN's position as one of *Sports Illustrated*'s main competitors. ESPN, as *Sports Illustrated* rightly suggested, revolutionized how sport is packaged, delivered, and consumed. The cable channel turned multiplatform media empire created a seemingly unquenchable demand for instantaneous sports content—from game scores to trade updates to gossip. It also—for better or worse—expanded sports media's conventional boundaries by fashioning diverse brand extensions that include niche sport channels, magazines, documentary series, video games, and even licensed apparel.

But the genesis of ESPN's birth—like most creation myths—is typically oversimplified. Many cast the organization as the product of the plucky

Connecticut-based entrepreneur Bill Rasmussen's ingenious and unprecedented vision of sports television's relatively untapped potential. From the storybook accounts most chroniclers provide, one would think ESPN sprang from Rasmussen's rib. Though Rasmussen is undoubtedly central to ESPN's creation, the organization's story is far more complex. ESPN is the product of a vast combination of stakeholders operating within a specific set of cultural, historical, industrial, and technological circumstances that are often glossed over in favor of nestling the story within a familiar framework. ESPN's monumental importance to American sport history and popular culture can only be properly appreciated when we take these intersecting contexts into account. Doing so demonstrates that the story of ESPN's birth is not simply the tale of an inspired businessman, but a far more nuanced—and much more interesting—outgrowth of a sports media industry and a popular culture in flux.

Rasmussen was unexpectedly dismissed from his marketing and publicity position with the World Hockey Association's New England Whalers on Memorial Day weekend 1978. Just days later, the freshly unemployed businessman brought along his twenty-two-year-old son, Scott, to a meeting with insurance agent Ed Eagan and telecommunications contractor Bob Beyus, who had joined forces to produce a cable TV show on Connecticut-area sports. While chatting about Eagan and Beyus's program—which had thus far produced only an unpolished pilot episode—the notion of a subscription cable channel devoted entirely to Connecticut-area sports emerged. Though none of the meeting's attendees had experience in cable television, they considered it an idea worth investigating. For the interim, they settled on the name Entertainment and Sports Programming Network or ESP-TV.

Shortly after this rendezvous, the ambitious group hastily organized its thoughts, penned a press release, and staged a press conference. ESP would be a cable network, they announced, centered on University of Connecticut and other regional sports. It would cost subscribers $18 per year and run roughly five hours daily during the nine-month school year. Though they sent out thirty-five invitations, only four people attended their announcement. Beyus left the group shortly thereafter. "He thought we were crazy and left," Rasmussen chuckled thirty-five years later. Beyus, however, has asserted that Eagan and the Rasmussens exploited his financial and technological resources to get the nascent project off the ground.

Undeterred by the press conference's poor turnout and its interpersonal discord, the ESP group's remaining members decided to investigate satellite transmission—a new and potentially cheaper alternative to terrestrial cable that would allow ESP to expand its reach well beyond the Northeast. The speculators scheduled a meeting with RCA's Al Parinello, who sold transponder space on the company's SATCOM 1 satellite. After Parinello explained RCA's rates for ESP's desired five hours per evening, the group realized it would actually be less expensive to rent space around-the-clock. They couldn't afford either deal, recalls Scott Rasmussen, so the men reasoned that they might as well reserve space for twenty-four hours' worth of programming.

In his memoir, Bill Rasmussen suggested that purchasing the transponder rights initiated "a series of events that no scriptwriter worth his salt could concoct." The entrepreneur proffered a creation story that situated his colleagues and him as the lone visionaries who invented twenty-four-hour sports TV—a yarn most chroniclers have reproduced without scrutiny. Though certainly original, their idea was not as pioneering as Rasmussen indicated. By the late 1970s, sports television was more popular and pervasive than ever. The previous two decades saw ABC Sports remake sports TV's formal techniques and demographic range with the "up close and personal" approach producer Roone Arledge developed for its NCAA football telecasts, *Wide World of Sports,* the Olympics, and *Monday Night Football.* "Television," as a 1979 *New York Times* report put it, "became America's Big Daddy of sports during the 1970s." ESP grew in large part out of the abundant ground its broadcast forefathers nurtured.

Though ESP would become the first all-sports network, sports content had already found a welcome home in early cable. The Madison Square Garden Network, which launched in 1971 and became the USA Network in 1979, offered a schedule dominated by sports. Home Box Office (HBO), born in 1972, also employed sporting events to cull a national audience. Media mogul Ted Turner used the sports franchises he owned to fuel his superstation, WTCG (later renamed WTBS), which had been transmitting via satellite since 1976. A twenty-four-hour sports network still seemed peculiar; however, if a cable outlet was to devote itself entirely to a particular brand of TV, sport was certainly one of the best candidates.

Though the ESP group possessed a license for twenty-four hours' worth of satellite distribution, it remained unsure exactly how to use it. One thing had become apparent: programming that focused entirely on Connecticut sports would have no chance at attracting a national audience. The entrepreneurs consequently began to consider how to augment their regional sports with anything that might inexpensively attract advertisers and eyeballs. After briefly considering old movies and sitcom reruns, they recognized an opportunity in simply offering more sports. They realized only a small fraction of the hundreds of college football games played on autumn weekends were televised at the time, and that many less-prominent sports received hardly any exposure. The ESP group also shifted its original plan to operate as a subscription service to an advertiser-supported model that would capitalize on the adult male demographic sports content many companies coveted.

Confident with its plan, the group embarked on a hunt for investors. After several flat-out rejections and a handful of discouraging responses of the "don't call us, we'll call you" variety, ESPN drew interest from K.S. Sweet Associates, an investment firm that was actually more attracted to the value of the transponder space ESPN purchased than how the upstart would fill it. K.S. Sweet agreed to provide ESP $75,000 in seed money—a contribution that ultimately swelled to $275,000. The ESP group primarily used the capital to traverse the country in search of financial backing, cable operators willing to give them space, and content providers. They focused most of their attention on the NCAA, an organization with a rich, and largely untapped, bounty of sports ripe for televising.

Meanwhile, K.S. Sweet shopped the network to six potential buyers, with no luck. Its seventh meeting was with Getty Oil Company vice president of diversified operations Stuart Evey. The Los Angeles–based executive was a devoted sports fan who always wanted to be part of the comparatively glitzy entertainment industry. More important, Evey became convinced that ESP had the potential to serve as what the cable industry calls a "lift"—a popular channel whose inclusion in subscription packages provides operators greater potential to sell their more lucrative pay channels. Evey was further motivated by early interest Anheuser-Busch expressed in ESP. The brewing company rightly speculated that although ESP might not immediately attract large total audience numbers, those viewers who did tune in would probably fall within its target market of adult men. Given the combination of Evey's successful track record and Anheuser-Busch's interest, Getty's board approved the endeavor. The oil company's initial $10 million investment—a relative pittance to a company used to dealing in billions—gave it 85 percent ownership of ESP. Though the terms of the agreement weighed heavily in Getty's favor, ESP had no other options.

Once Getty came on board, the pieces began to fall into place. The oil company's high-profile support made the NCAA confident enough to sign a contract with ESP, and the NCAA's commitment was enough to convince Anheuser-Busch to ink a $1.38 million agreement, the largest ever in cable TV. With a marquee content provider, a deep-pocketed sponsor, and an expanding roster of cable operators in place, ESP bought a one-acre parcel of land in Bristol, Connecticut, and took to preparing for the network's ambitiously scheduled September 1979 launch. The company also changed its name to ESPN, or Entertainment and Sports Programming Network. Evey sought a staff with the industrial pull necessary to help ESPN secure TV rights, attract advertisers, and recruit other employees. His first major hire was NBC Sports' gentlemanly and recognizable senior sportscaster, Jim Simpson. He also looked to NBC to hire ESPN's first president, Chet Simmons, an industry giant who helped Roone Arledge develop *Wide World of Sports* before leaving ABC to join, and eventually preside over, NBC Sports.

Like most cable networks at the time, ESPN adopted a funding model inspired by broadcast networks' payment of affiliates for carriage. Simmons negotiated a combination of per-subscriber rates and advertising incentives with cable operators to get ESPN on the air. While he imitated the broadcast networks' funding model, Simmons billed ESPN's projected relationship with the networks as more harmonious than antagonistic. He claimed ESPN could augment, and even help to promote, the networks' mostly weekend broadcasts. Though it did not initially cast itself as a competitor to the networks, ESPN did work to place itself into association with them. In late 1979 the bold young outlet bid for the rights to televise the 1984 Summer Olympic Games in Los Angeles. ESPN management realized the company could never afford to purchase the rights. However, they paid the $750,000 deposit required to place a bid for the publicity it generated.

In a *Sports Illustrated* article published less than two months before ESPN's launch, Scott Rasmussen provided a comment that would become the budding channel's mission statement: "What we're creating here is a network for sports junkies. This is not programming for soft-core sports fans who like to watch an NFL game and then switch to the news." ESPN's first broadcast on September 7, 1979, underscored this sensibility. It opened with host Lee Leonard's voice along with stock footage of sports fans wildly cheering: "If you're a fan, *if you're a fan,* what you'll see in the next minutes, hours, and days that follow may convince you you've gone to sports heaven. Beyond that blue horizon," Leonard explained as the screen cuts to the sky, "is a limitless world of sport and right now you're standing on the edge of tomorrow with sports twenty-four-hours-a-day and seven-days-a-week with ESPN." The introduction then transitioned to a fast-paced montage of sports moments not unlike *Wide World of Sports*' iconic introductory package and an upbeat song that assures viewers ESPN is "the one worth watching."

A sign at 935 Middle Street in Bristol marks the construction of ESPN's first building, the Broadcast Center, also known as Building 1. (Bill Rasmussen/ESPN Images.)

Leonard reemerged after the introductory montage to explain the largely unfamiliar technological means by which ESPN planned to create this sports nirvana. "And note the stars of the show," he stated as the network's two satellite dishes appear. "These H. G. Wells invaders of the quiet countryside . . . are a pair of eyes peering up at RCA SATCOM 1, 22,300 miles up in the sky near the equator south of Hawaii. ESPN extends from New York to Los Angeles, from Miami to Point Barrow [Alaska], and from New England to Texas," he proclaimed with the aid of a crude diagram of the satellite transmission process.

The segment then unveiled the *SportsCenter* desk, where Leonard's younger counterpart, George Grande, outlined the show's purpose. "It goes without saying that we'll be bringing you highlights of the action. But we'll go beyond the highlights; we'll go beyond the scores." To deliver on this promise, Grande offered an update of a Billie Jean King and Chris Evert tennis match that Evert dominated. With harsh candor, he suggested King should retire rather than continue to humiliate herself. Grande's remarks combined with

Leonard's introductory comments to bill ESPN as an innovative media outlet that pulled no editorial punches.

Though the introduction established a clear vision for ESPN, the network's opening hours were rife with hitches. Its first event footage presented a softball game that featured the Milwaukee Schlitzes—a team sponsored by an Anheuser-Busch competitor. Not long afterward, it presented a live interview with University of Colorado football coach Chuck Fairbanks without sound. Though these bugs appalled ESPN's new staff, the network's administrators shrugged them off. "We told them not to worry," Scott Rasmussen snickered. "Nobody was watching anyhow."

ESPN originally ran from 3:00 P.M. to about 4:00 A.M., Monday afternoon through Thursday morning, and around-the-clock from Friday afternoon through early Monday morning. It showed a wheel of promotional messages and its daily schedule after signoff until transitioning entirely to a twenty-four-hour format on September 1, 1980. The network's earliest programming notoriously featured obscure sports to which it could secure inexpensive rights, such as hurling, darts, and table tennis. It also took great advantage of its agreement with the NCAA by using the organization to fill some 65 percent of the network's footage during its first years—from volleyball games to instructional programs. The few prominent college contests it did showcase were typically limited to tape-delayed presentations. Other productions would be postponed or cancelled altogether based on when tapes arrived at the network's headquarters. When content was thin, some programs ran multiple times.

Critics responded to ESPN's emergence with a combination of enthusiasm and dystopian skepticism. The *Sporting News,* for instance, named the network's development "the biggest [sports] story of the year." Striking a different tone, the *New York Times*'s iconic sportswriter, Red Smith, drolly warned that the cable TV experiment might "represent the ghastliest threat to the social fabric of America since the invention of the automobile." One thing was clear: the young network had made an impression within and beyond the realm of sports media.

As ESPN struggled to find its stride, tensions flared among its leaders. Evey forced Scott Rasmussen to resign days after the network's launch. Bill followed in December 1980. While its administrators battled it out behind the scenes, ESPN was cultivating engaging new personalities on screen. Aside from polished and conventional anchors like Simpson, Leonard, and Grande, it hired fresh faces such as Chris Berman, Greg Gumbel, Bob Ley, and Dick

Vitale. Berman's habit of giving players nicknames and Vitale's raspy effusiveness established a popular sports vernacular organized around ESPN that *SportsCenter* anchors like Keith Olbermann, Dan Patrick, and Stuart Scott pushed to irony-laden new heights in the 1990s.

ESPN continued to lose money despite its modest successes. Between its production costs and the fees it paid cable operators for carriage, the network was spending roughly 1.5 million of Getty Oil's dollars a month. These economic constraints compelled ESPN to create new events from sports happenings that cost little to license. Several of these became popular sports media traditions. Most notably, its telecasts of the early rounds of the NCAA men's basketball tournament games paved the way for "March Madness," and its NFL draft coverage precipitated year-round commentary on the event.

Simmons suggested ESPN's vast tracts of programming real estate and total commitment to sports enabled it to offer more detailed and comprehensive coverage than its competitors. In 1982, for instance, it showcased a six-and-a-half-hour Davis Cup tennis match between John McEnroe and Mats Wilanders, which was then the longest-ever continuous sports telecast. Some critics, however, pointed out that ESPN's commitment to quantity came at the cost of quality. While it had yet to secure contracts with major sports leagues or carry marquee events, ESPN slowly raised its profile. For instance, when Simmons left in early 1982 to become commissioner of the United States Football League (USFL) he immediately negotiated a deal with his successor, Bill Grimes, wherein ESPN would share with ABC rights to the league's games. The two-year contract was ESPN's first foray into carrying professional football games, and its initial USFL telecasts shattered the network's previous viewing records.

With the help of its USFL contract and expanding menu of content, ESPN surpassed TBS as the United States' most popular cable TV service by 1983. Cable operators could no longer sell their packages without including the self-proclaimed "Total Sports Network." The advertiser-supported network, however, continued to hemorrhage capital. ESPN boldly decided to leverage its popularity by demanding that cable operators pay it ten cents per subscriber. The new model inverted ESPN's original relationship with cable providers to give it another revenue stream and cut costs. The arrangement, which ESPN chroniclers James A. Miller and Tom Shales compare to "selling cake and getting paid to eat it," has become standard practice throughout the cable TV industry.

After investing a total of $67 million in the cable venture without a profit, Getty sold ABC a 15 percent stake in ESPN in January 1984. Texaco purchased

Getty the following month for $10 billion. Texaco compensated for the cost of its mammoth acquisition by selling to ABC—an already sports-heavy network that was just beginning to explore the cable market—ESPN's remaining 85 percent for $227 million. To offset its substantial investment in ESPN, along with the debt it incurred after purchasing the rights to televise the 1984 Olympics, ABC sold 20 percent of the cable outlet to RJR Nabisco for $60 million. ESPN maintained its separate brand after the purchase and continued to use less expensive, nonunion labor—a practice it has continued ever since. Though its institutional practices and personnel differed from ABC's, ESPN integrated into its new parent's programming and promotional activities by airing material ABC did not have room to include on its schedule.

The 1984 Cable Communications Act, which allowed cable operators to set rates and let the market decide their feasibility, aided ABC's purchase, along with Capital Cities Communications' acquisition of ABC the following year. ABC, and then Capital Cities, took advantage of this legislation by increasing ESPN's per-subscriber fee from ten to thirteen cents in 1984, and again raising it to nineteen cents in 1985. Because of ESPN's growing popularity, cable operators were forced to acquiesce and, as they are wont to do, simply passed along the costs to their customers. Not coincidentally, ESPN turned a profit for the first time in 1985. That same year it officially changed its name from Entertainment and Sports Programming Network to ESPN—a decision that confirmed the clunky acronym's status as an identifiable signification of cable sports television.

ESPN expanded unceasingly since becoming a part of ABC. In 1987, it secured its first contract with the National Football League—a development Chris Berman named ESPN's biggest accomplishment since its launch. ESPN capitalized further on its popularity by developing sister channels designed for more specific groups of sports fans, such as ESPN2 (1993), ESPNews (1995), and ESPN Classic (1997), ESPN Deportes (2004), and ESPNU (2005). The bulging network's immense popularity, in fact, triggered the Walt Disney Company's 1996 decision to purchase Capital Cities Communications, the second-largest corporate takeover ever. Disney CEO Michael Eisner even called ESPN the "crown jewel" of Capital Cities. By the century's end, ESPN was Disney's most valuable property.

Two years after Disney acquired it, ESPN changed its motto from "The Total Sports Network" to the "Worldwide Leader in Sports." Its prominence eventually compelled Disney to move ABC's *Monday Night Football* to ESPN in 2006 and, more dramatically, to rebrand all of ABC Sports' content as "ESPN on ABC." The rebranding marked ESPN's transformation from a cable

TV curiosity into a sports media titan that had effectively eclipsed what was sports television's most influential organization. In the process, it made the media outlet's self-given status as the "Worldwide Leader" seem less like a provocative marketing chip than a statement of the obvious.

"We believe," Bill Rasmussen announced while promoting ESPN prior to its launch, "that the appetite for sports in this country is insatiable." There is little evidence in media culture since ESPN's emergence to suggest otherwise. ESPN helped to create this appetite and now drives an industry that incessantly stokes it. The network spearheaded the creation of a product consumers did not yet know they wanted, but now seemingly cannot live without. To understand ESPN's meteoric, and somewhat unlikely, rise, it is necessary to consider its emergence through the intersecting contexts that shaped it.

For Further Reading

Miller, James Andrew, and Tom Shales. *Those Guys Have All the Fun: Inside the World of ESPN*. New York: Back Bay Books, 2011.

Vogan, Travis. *ESPN: The Making of a Sports Media Empire*. Urbana: University of Illinois Press, 2015.

21

Remembering and Forgetting America's Hockey Miracles

STEPHEN HARDY

It's a scene for the ages. In the Olympic ice hockey medal round, the United States leads the Soviet Union by one goal as a huge arena crowd and a national television audience anticipates a momentous upset that will lead to the gold medal. The announcer counts down the final seconds. "10, 9, 8. . . ." Everyone watching at home can sense a punch line, something to be remembered for all time. Sound familiar? Of course, except in 1960, CBS's Bud Palmer simply said, "And the game is over, the United States wins." Twenty years later, ABC's Al Michaels sent his game into history with "Do you believe in miracles? Yes!"

Two Olympics, with very similar results and very different legacies. Most sports fans have never heard of the 1960 miracle, while 1980 has been the subject of numerous books, articles, Web sites, an HBO documentary, and a Disney feature film. The 1980 "Miracle on Ice" has been justly celebrated. Its real significance, however, may be better appreciated if we examine both its similarities and contrasts to 1960: in team performance, in political context, and most importantly, in the shape and scope of sport as an industry.

Few people remember the 1960 CBS telecasts from Squaw Valley, California. Most contained only highlights hosted by news anchor Walter Cronkite. After the U.S. victory over Canada, however, CBS sensed a big story brewing. With the gold medal on the line, the games against the Soviets and the Czechs were broadcast live in their entirety on Saturday and Sunday afternoon—an Olympic first for Americans. The production values were solid because the network had been doing NHL games for three years.

By contrast, ABC came to Lake Placid in 1980 with limited hockey experience. Al Michaels had worked hockey for NBC at the 1972 Sapporo Games, but largely as an assistant to the network's number-one announcer, Curt Gowdy. In 1980, ABC telecast every American game, but Michaels's famous words were *not* carried live. The development of international satellite transmissions complicated everything. Time slots for the medal round competition had been set long before the Americans made their run. The Soviets (who had veto power) refused to move the faceoff from 5:00 P.M., Eastern time, because they wanted *their* home audience to see a live broadcast no later than midnight, Moscow time. ABC thus elected to show the game to its American audience on tape-delay at 8:30 P.M. More than thirty-five million watched, a number of whom surely knew the outcome.

Both United States head coaches represented the core components of an American hockey system that emerged between 1920 and 1960, a system dominated by high school, college, and senior amateur hockey in New England and Minnesota. Both coaches were selected by AHAUS (the Amateur Hockey Association of the United States), the forerunner of USA Hockey. Jack Riley (1960) was from the Boston area. He had played at Dartmouth and on several USA national teams. Herb Brooks (1980) hailed from the Twin Cities. He had played at the University of Minnesota and likewise had a long career on U.S. national teams. Riley was head coach at West Point; Brooks at his alma mater. In their roster management, both skillfully negotiated the Boston–Minnesota tension that had existed since the 1920s. Both stressed

Team USA celebrates after defeating Team USSR, 4–3. (Associated Press.)

conditioning as a key to any chance of victory. Both made difficult cuts on the tournament's eve. Neither cared about popularity. As Riley recalled, "I made those bastards work. I knew that was the only way we could win." Twenty years later, Brooks adopted approaches to discipline, conditioning, and puck control preached by Anatoli Tarasov, the Soviet national coach from 1958 to 1972. As the author of a *New York Times* profile said in December 1979, Brooks's "skaters, spectacularly swift, will crisscross over the ice, as the Russians do."

Few observers expected either American squad to do much. A *Sports Illustrated* preview in February 1960 noted that "most experts feel the U.S. will have to scramble to stay out of fourth place," although Riley insisted "we will be up among the top three." Most pundits felt the key 1960 battle would be between Canada and the Soviets, who had shaken the hockey world by winning gold in their first appearance at the International Ice Hockey Federation (IIHF) world championship in 1954 and the gold medal at the 1956 Winter Olympics. By 1980, Canada's amateurs were a second-rate team run by an organization that had boycotted IIHF and Olympic tournaments from 1970 to 1977 to protest the hypocrisy of the Soviets' state-sponsored "amateurism." At Lake Placid, all eyes were on the Russians, as they were often called, a team that had regrouped after 1960 to win the next four Olympics. Even Brooks acknowledged the difficulty his team would face. In a promotional *TV Viewer's Guide*, he said, "We're going to send a bunch of 22-year-old college kids up against this well-oiled machine."

These two American miracle teams share much in their histories; that is, up to the point of receiving their gold medals. *Sports Illustrated* celebrated 1960's triumph with a low-key article entitled "Our Never-Say-Die Hockeymen." Author William Leggett's most effusive commentary was simply that the team arrived "unheralded and unsung," but "they left national heroes." This hero-worshipping, however, did not amount to much. Minnesotan John Mayasich, who played center on the 1960 team and later became a broadcasting executive, recalled that the gold medal ceremony was on a Sunday afternoon, and "Monday morning I was working in Green Bay, so there wasn't the hoopla that you see today." A March 1960 Associated Press story noted that players from Boston returned to "the airs of a brass band," and "the sirens of fire engines," directed at team captain Jack Kirrane, who was a firefighter; in other words, a small parade. National media attention focused on goalie Jack McCartan's call up to the New York Rangers. It was newsworthy because the NHL had few Americans on its rosters. When McCartan soon faded, so did the gold medal memories.

In 1980, by contrast, as the *New York Times* explained, "The switchboards of newspapers and television studios lit up with avalanches of calls from people bursting with pride, not merely in the team's victory over a seemingly invincible foe, but in a kind of national vindication after years of tensions with the Soviet Union and adversity in Afghanistan, Iran, the Middle East and other world arenas." The celebration continued at a White House reception, where President Jimmy Carter—who needed good news—claimed the win as "one of the most breathtaking upsets, not only in Olympic history but in the entire history of sports." Team captain Mike Eruzione spoke a week later of the team's symbolic importance. "We typify the American public in how we feel about the Russian situation," he said. "The only difference is that we can do something about it on the ice."

In fact, a Gallup poll in late January suggested that Americans were primed for the victory that no one anticipated. Respondents overwhelmingly had a negative opinion of the Soviet Union, ranking that feared nation behind only Iran and Cuba. At the same time, the public was turning on President Carter, giving him negative reviews for not being tough enough in his dealings with the Soviets.

In some ways, however, the 1960 Squaw Valley Games occurred during a more intense phase of the Cold War. The world was rigidly aligned into two great blocs, American and Soviet, with terror and tempers flaring after various incidents, such as Britain's ill-fated 1956 Suez Canal invasion, the Soviets' 1956 assault on Hungary, NATO and American bomber deployments, and the 1957 launching of the Soviet satellite, Sputnik. West Berlin was under continuous threat. In 1957, the United States, Canada, Switzerland, and other nations boycotted the IIHF world championship in Moscow to protest the USSR's invasion of Hungary. Democrats started talking of a "missile gap," and a Gallup poll in February 1960 found that significantly more Americans (47 percent to 33 percent) felt that Russia beat America as the country "farther ahead in the field of long range missiles and rockets." Thus, as the Squaw Valley Games opened, a lot more than athletic competition seemed to be on the line.

But history is quirky. For a few months on either side of the 1960 Olympics, there was a bit of a thaw in the Cold War. Soviet Premier Nikita Khrushchev brought a human face to communism during his thirteen-day visit to America in September 1959. As historian James MacGregor Burns wrote, Khrushchev "made the most" of his visit, "all the while wisecracking, praising, arguing, criticizing, and complaining." He seemed "more conciliatory about Berlin," and he agreed "tentatively" to an August summit meeting in

Paris. Three months *after* Squaw Valley, all this changed when the Soviets shot down an American U-2 spy plane, and Khrushchev made President Dwight Eisenhower twist in a bitter wind of public humiliation. Just ninety miles south of the United States, Cuban dictator Fidel Castro fully exposed his "commie" intentions with his June 1960 nationalization of some $850 million in American-owned property and businesses. Perhaps Squaw Valley would have produced a more lasting miracle if it had hosted the 1956 games, or if the Hungarian crisis and Sputnik had happened in January 1960. But that was not the case.

Symbolic victories have importance, but they should be kept in perspective. When *Sports Illustrated* announced its "Sportsmen of the Year" for 1980, Eruzione admitted that winning the gold medal didn't solve the Iranian crisis or the Afghanistan war, even if "people felt better." Brooks concluded that the real story was about developing a team. In his words, "That was the end of the story for me." Their reflections nicely resonate with a position—seldom quoted—that forward Mark Pavelich took at the same time: "If people want to think that performance was for our country, that's fine. But the truth of the matter is, it was just a hockey game. There was enough to worry about without worrying about Afghanistan or winning it for the pride and glory of the United States. We wanted to win it for ourselves."

The players on the 1980 team represented themselves very well. They also represented some striking changes in the hockey industry. The 1980 team was—and still is—described as a bunch of "young college kids," in neat contrast to the grizzled veterans who filled the Soviet roster. True enough. But this fact glosses over how much American hockey had changed since 1960. For starters, in 1969, the IIHF fundamentally changed the amateur game by allowing body checking all over the ice. In 1972, the NCAA did the same. The NHL had lobbied both governing bodies hard to make the change. Some college coaches lamented the move, fearing a rise in on-ice violence, but most fans agreed with Boston State coach Eddie Barry, who stated flatly, "We'll be giving our kids a better chance to make pro hockey. With all the new pro teams being formed, there has to be plenty of openings and the college kid will be sought after even more now." Barry was referring to the general expansion of pro hockey franchises in the late 1960s and early 1970s, including expansion in the NHL, the birth of the World Hockey Association, and the growth of minor leagues. In 1960, few American boys had considered careers in professional hockey, and most Canadian scouts, coaches, and general managers viewed American talent—groomed under rules with limited checking—as subpar. American stars like forward Bill Cleary (Harvard) or

Mayasich (Minnesota) would have suffered financial hardship by quitting their jobs in insurance or radio sales to play professional hockey. That had changed dramatically by 1980. American-born players were not only signing lucrative pro contracts, some were leaving school early to sign, and growing numbers were skipping college altogether to play in the Canadian Junior A leagues.

Amateur rules loosened, in part so the West could compete against world powers like the Soviets and the Czechs. Mayasich recalled that he could not afford to leave his job in Green Bay to attend the American training camp in December 1959. Things were different two decades later. One of the first books on 1980's "young college kids" detailed their full-time national team schedule in the six months prior to Lake Placid, including sixty-one games against a range of college, minor league, and amateur clubs and other national teams. In addition, AHAUS paid each of them "a salary of at least $7200 for six-months, plus expenses . . . better than, or on par with, minor league clubs."

As a sport, hockey had also grown a much broader media market, some of it linked to professional league expansion, some of it linked to international exhibitions pitting Soviet national and top club teams against North American professionals—events branded with titles like "Summit Series" (1972, 1974), "Super Series" (1975–1976, 1978, 1979), and "Canada Cup" (1976). Established and *ad hoc* television networks beamed images across continents and oceans via technologies unrolled since 1960: satellite transponders, antenna and dish receivers, microwave boosters, coaxial cable, slow-motion replay. New networks like Home Box Office (HBO) and ESPN competed with the old to sell sports, including hockey.

Television both transmitted and triggered industry changes, including rival professional leagues competing for players, at ever higher salaries, building demand for a category of professional rarely seen in team sports before the 1960s—the player representative. Most of the 1980 team was represented by one of hockey's first super-agents, Arthur Kaminsky, a graduate of Cornell and Yale Law School. After negotiating goalie Ken Dryden's first contract with the Montréal Canadiens, he was soon representing a dozen Canadiens and then players from other teams. As American university programs began turning out more recognizable professional hockey talent, Kaminsky engaged in conduct fraught with conflict of interest. While in law school, he had written about college hockey for the *Yale Daily News* and the *New York Times*. And so, even after becoming an agent, he was able to enter college arenas and locker rooms with press pass in hand. It was only a matter of time before players he wrote about ended up leaving school to sign pro contracts he negotiated. A number of college coaches, including Brooks, objected. Brooks, in fact, had Kaminsky ejected from the Minnesota locker room.

By 1980, however, coach and agent had patched things up. In the run up to Lake Placid, Kaminsky and his associate, Bob Murray, skillfully counseled their players to remain Olympic "amateurs" and keep their eyes on a bigger payday. The strategy worked well for many of the players, who signed pro contracts immediately after the Games. The bigger story, though, was Brooks himself. He had left Minnesota and was now a "free agent" coach, represented by none other than Arthur Kaminsky. The Rangers were interested, and so were the Colorado Rockies. In the end, Brooks took a job in Switzerland, only to return home a year later to coach the Rangers. Such a scenario—players and coaches represented by an agent who negotiated their professional contracts—would have been unthinkable in 1960, not just in hockey, but in virtually all sports.

The American Olympic team boycotted the 1980 Summer Games in Moscow. That may have made it easier for *Sports Illustrated* to select the Miracle boys as "Sportsmen of the Year." (By contrast, Arnold Palmer took the laurels in 1960.) Similar honors came from the Associated Press and ABC's *Wide World of Sports*. For his part, Al Michaels was named "Sportscaster of the Year." It was a general triumph. But we tend to forget that it, too, faded over time. Within a decade, the Mujahideen (with the help of American Stinger missiles) humbled the Red Army in Afghanistan. The Iron Curtain crumbled. The Soviet Union itself was "restructuring," a collapse that triggered the ultimate ruination of the Big Red Hockey Machine. Americans had little need to celebrate athletic victories when they seemed to have won the actual war.

For all the talk about Cold War drama, it is also interesting to note that the 1980 gold medal mustered no immediate cinematic interest beyond the mercifully forgotten 1981 made-for-TV *Miracle on Ice,* staring Karl Malden as Brooks. Hollywood had earlier produced a long string of Cold War tales, both direct (Dana Andrews as a Soviet defector in *Iron Curtain* in 1948) and metaphorical (*Invaders from Mars* in 1953). But when the big screen embraced a sports movie with 1980's Cold War flavor, it was *Rocky IV* (1985) in which pugilists, not pucksters, represented the death match between rival political and social systems. In this movie, a Soviet apparatchik bragged that Ivan Drago, who had already killed the Ali-like American Apollo Creed, was "a look at the future" whose destruction of Rocky Balboa would "be a perfect example of how pathetically weak your society has become." Drago was the prototype of state socialism and the command economy, while Rocky was the up-from-the-bootstraps American individualist. In those years, it would have been difficult for Hollywood to pump up a hockey film in which the American coach deliberately adopted the Soviet style of training and playing!

Perhaps the Lake Placid miracle also ran a normal half-life in collective memory. Fans tend to move on, to find and celebrate other symbolic heroes, unless something thrusts up memory. As sports historian Daniel Nathan observed, events are remembered or forgotten in line with a form of "narrative physics" or inertia: "An untold story tends to stay untold, whereas an often-told story tends to be repeated." The 1919 Black Sox, for instance, are resurrected with every subsequent gambling scandal. The miracles on ice seemed to lack such thrusters through the 1980s and into the 1990s. Then came the end of the century and the millennium. It was a time for summation, for scorekeeping, and for lists, made even more popular by the still-young Internet and its infant forms of what became known as "social media." While Jackie Robinson's reintegration of major league baseball was often pegged as a top story, the "Miracle on Ice" was always ranked highly. *Sports Illustrated* ranked Lake Placid as the greatest sports "moment" of the twentieth century. ESPN's *SportsCentury* had the 1980 Miracle as the fourth greatest game played in any sport.

With new traction from these millennial rankings, it made sense for HBO to produce *Do You Believe in Miracles?* (2001), a documentary that inflated the political importance of 1980. Three years later, Disney's feature, *Miracle,* starring Kurt Russell, wisely focused on Brooks's masterful job of team development. By 2004, in the glow of global capitalism, it was okay to celebrate his adoption of Soviet methods. Russian players had been starring in the NHL since the early 1990s. The next step cinematically was to get the Soviet players' version of events. Their recollections in several documentaries mix frustration and anger with nostalgia for the greatness of their national team.

Psychologists sometimes study something called "flashbulb" memory, that is, recalling where you were when you heard about or watched a major event. On the Lake Placid Miracle's twenty-fifth anniversary, Mike Eruzione told a wire service writer that his most amazing experience was learning how much the win had affected younger generations. Men would often approach him after one of his motivational speeches and "describe how they sat with their dads and watched a hockey game become a fairy tale." As Eruzione described it, people would remember that "I was fifteen years old and my dad sat in the chair and he was crying and crying . . . and I couldn't figure what it was all about, but now I realize it."

Both gold medal teams were honored when the IIHF compiled its hundredth anniversary lists of the "Top 100" stories in hockey. 1980 was ranked

No. 1 and 1960 as No. 16. In the IIHF's estimation, 1980 was a double miracle, the upset of the Soviets and the "greater miracle" of transforming "a nation with nothing more than a mild interest in the game . . . into a world power-house. . . ." But the IIHF also stressed that 1960 "was a much greater miracle" because the Squaw Valley team "had to defeat the top four teams in the world to win gold." In the end, however, the IIHF did not hedge. In their words "there is only one game, one team, one moment, that can truly be called a miracle." And in the end, the 1980 Miracle sparked many more flashbulbs.

For Further Reading

BOOKS

Gilbert, John. *Herb Brooks: The Inside Story of a Hockey Mastermind*. Minneapolis: Voyageur Press, 2008.

O'Coughlin, Seamus. *Squaw Valley Gold: American Hockey's Olympic Odyssey*. San Jose, Calif.: Writer's Showcase, 2001.

Wendel, Tim. *Going for the Gold: How the U.S. Won at Lake Placid*. Westport, Conn.: Lawrence Hill, 1980.

DOCUMENTARIES

Do You Believe in Miracles: The Story of the 1980 U.S. Olympic Team. HBO Home Video, 2001.

Forgotten Miracle: The Story of the 1960 Gold Medal Team. Golden Puck Pictures and Northland Films in Association with USA Hockey, 2009.

Jonathan Hock. "Of Miracles and Men," ESPN *30 for 30*, 2015.

22

Remembering and Reliving "The Drive" in Cleveland and Denver

ANDREW D. LINDEN

> "Jan. 11, 1987, turned out to be so many things besides just the American Football Conference championship game."
>
> —Jim Saccomano, V.P. of Public Relations, Denver Broncos

With 5:32 remaining in the fourth quarter of the 1986 AFC championship game, Denver Broncos quarterback John Elway took to the field against the Cleveland Browns. The home team had just taken the lead over Denver, 20–13, on a dramatic touchdown. With only minutes remaining, the Browns believed they had secured a Super Bowl berth—the first in the club's storied history. On the ensuing kickoff, Gene Lang, the Broncos' kick returner, erroneously fell on the ball near the goal line. Lang's panic forced the Broncos to start the following offensive series at their own two-yard line. "We got 'em right where we want 'em!" one Bronco offensive lineman reportedly quipped as Elway and the other ten Broncos entered the huddle.

With the quarterback's feet in the end zone, the Broncos began with a quick five-yard pass to running back Sammy Winder, giving the team some room to operate. Two short runs by Winder edged Denver close to a first down. Browns player Hanford Dixon excitedly motioned to the sidelines that the defense had indeed stopped the Broncos. The referees dragged the chains onto the gridiron to measure. Dixon was wrong by the length of a football. First down, Denver.

4:11 on the clock

After the Browns' linebackers stuffed another Winder run up the middle, Elway dropped back, scanned the Cleveland defense and took off running, diving forward to end an eleven-yard scamper. With the Broncos' momentum building, Elway rocketed a spiral on the next play to wide receiver Steve Sewell down the middle of the field, picking up twenty-two precious yards. The Broncos' march had begun to materialize. On first down, receiver Steve Watson ran down the right sideline and caught a twelve-yard pass from Elway. At the two-minute warning, Denver was in Cleveland territory. The Browns' victory, seemingly inevitable a few minutes before, now looked uncertain.

For the Browns, a collapse would be devastating. For the team's fans, it could be even worse. A breakdown would be just one more episode in a sad tale of losing and negativity that, at that time, had haunted the city on the shores of Lake Erie for years. Indeed, this football game meant more to both Cleveland and Denver than just a ticket to the Super Bowl.

From "The City of Champions" to "The Mistake on the Lake"

Sport in Cleveland and the city itself grew along parallel lines throughout the twentieth century. In the early 1900s, the city boomed. It was once the fifth-largest city in the country, and a number of large industries called it home. People moved to Cleveland for work. The auto industry helped the city become one of the leading assembly and parts-manufacturing centers in the country, and Cleveland was second (only to Detroit) for the highest percentage of industrial workers. Furthermore, for a brief period at the beginning of the century, Cleveland was the largest oil-refining city in the world. All things considered, Cleveland represented the industrial boom of the turn-of-the-twentieth-century United States.

Sports teams in Cleveland also thrived. The city boasted "major league" status since the late nineteenth century—having professional baseball during the late 1800s—and the city's club won the World Series in 1920 and 1948. Moreover, when professional football caught popular wind at midcentury, the Browns became one of the most dominant teams, first in the All-America Football Conference in the late 1940s and then in the National Football

League (NFL) during the 1950s and early 1960s. Even the Cleveland Barons—an ice hockey team playing in the American Hockey League—became one of the most dominant clubs in the country. All of this economic and athletic success led the local press to declare triumphantly that Cleveland was "The City of Champions."

Yet, things quickly changed. The label did not resonate with sports fans in the late twentieth century except as a distant memory.

Soon after World War II, large cities in the midwestern United States began to experience urban decline. Cleveland was no exception. Much of the city's industry moved to warmer climates or to the suburbs. Factories sat empty. A polluted (and sometimes burning) river became a national storyline. Cleveland lost nearly 130,000 jobs from the late 1950s through the 1970s. And demographic changes led to social angst and violent racism. No longer a thriving industrial metropolis, Cleveland now represented the growing midwestern Rust Belt.

The fortunes of the sports teams also plummeted. After the Browns hoisted the NFL championship trophy in 1964, none of the other major sports teams in Cleveland won a title for fifty-two years, until the Cavaliers won the 2016 National Basketball Association (NBA) championship. The baseball team became a joke, ridiculed in the 1980s motion picture, *Major League*. The at-the-time upstart Cavaliers won only one playoff series during the 1970s. The Barons folded, and the city could never keep a National Hockey League team in town. Instead of the press's late 1940s decree, the city now held claim to the negative moniker coined by *Tonight Show* host Johnny Carson: "The Mistake on the Lake."

Memories of this history swirled through Cleveland Municipal Stadium as John Elway and the Broncos retook the field after the two-minute warning to continue their march against Cleveland's defense.

1:59 on the clock
Elway took a shot. He lofted a pass down the right sideline into the end zone, missing his target, wide receiver Vance Johnson. On the next play, Cleveland's nose tackle Dave Puzzuoli ripped through the Broncos' offensive line, sacked Elway, and drove the Broncos back to their own 49-yard line. Cleveland, again, seemed to have reclaimed the momentum.

After a timeout, Elway walked to the line of scrimmage facing third down and eighteen yards to go. A palpable anxiety overtook the field and grandstands. The next play could make or break the game.

On the snap, the ball accidently hit receiver Steve Watson, who was in motion behind the line of scrimmage. But chaos turned to fortune for the orange and blue as the ball miraculously bounced into Elway's hands. He quickly forced a pass to receiver Mark Jackson, who picked up twenty yards. First down. What could have been a disaster now had the Broncos deep in Cleveland territory.

Elway and company could taste the end zone. Coming this far and not finishing with a game-tying touchdown would seem an unusual ending for a team and a city that had experienced such hope, prosperity, and growth in the years and decades leading to this moment.

Birth of the "Mile High City"

Colorado's leading city, Denver, grew throughout the twentieth century. "Located at the intersection of the plains and the mountains," wrote the authors of the standard state history, "its people and institutions have tied together the sections of the state at the same time that they have filtered contacts with the outside world." Indeed, over the course of the century, Denver was transformed into a mega-metropolis, earning the positive label, "Mile High City."

Yet, for a lot of its history, Denver felt an inferiority complex. The city had once been a small western town, a stop high in the Rockies between major cities in the Midwest and the West Coast, really only important as a mining town and a haven for traveling forty-niners during the gold rush. Industrial growth and population increases made the city not just a pit stop, but a landmark in the large region between Chicago and the Pacific Coast. The U.S. Treasury built its second mint in Denver in 1906. In 1911, the Mountain States Telephone and Telegraph Company opened and helped the city become a leader in telecommunications. The Gates Corporation began producing automobile parts in the 1910s, and soon Denver was the largest producer of those parts in the world. By midcentury, the city clearly had long since rebounded from the collapse of the late-nineteenth-century gold rush.

In the post–World War II era, Denver boomed. As many cities in the Midwest (like Cleveland) declined, the expansion of new industries, especially energy, allowed cities like Denver to explode. New skyscrapers rising and flourishing affluent suburbs represented Denver's present success and future potential. By 1980, more than a half-million people called the Mile High City home.

Slowly, Denver also became "major league." For years, the city—like many other urban areas outside the eastern and midwestern United States—had a hard time competing culturally with the rest of the nation because of a lack of major professional sports teams. But following World War II, professional sports began to bring Denver brighter lights.

Beginning play in 1960, the Broncos sputtered in their first decade, but the 1970s (specifically 1977, when the city was gripped by "Broncomania") brought a sports fervor to Denver that became part of its civic identity. In the 1960s, the Denver Rockets of the American Basketball Association emerged and became the current-day Nuggets in the 1970s, joining the NBA. In the 1980s, the city began a push for a major league baseball team and welcomed the Rockies in 1993. When the Broncos secured quarterback John Elway in 1983—the phenom from Stanford and the first overall pick in the NFL draft— Denver the city and Denver the sports town began to dream of prominence. While Elway and the Broncos did not reach gridiron greatness the first few years, by 1986–1987, on the muddy grass of Cleveland Municipal Stadium, the stars began to align. And Denver seemed to be within arm's reach of making a substantial mark on the landscape of major American professional sports.

1:24 on the clock

Although the Elway-to-Jackson pass seemed to turn the tide in the Broncos' favor, Denver still had work to do. Running up to the line of scrimmage, the Broncos rushed to snap the ball. Elway tried to hit Watson again, but the pass fell incomplete. On the following play, Elway dumped a short pass off to Steve Sewell, who found open space down the left side of the field for fourteen yards, giving Denver another fresh set of downs.

On the next play, with less than a minute on the clock, Elway let go of a pass aimed for Watson in the end zone. But he overthrew it, pulling the receiver out of bounds. On the next snap, Elway dropped back, looked downfield, and then took off running. Directing his blockers, he slid hard into the dirt near the right sideline, stopping the clock at 0:42 while a Cleveland defender pummeled his mud-soaked body.

While this game would ultimately end in despair for Cleveland and jubilation for Denver, people in both cities continue to relive the moment.

Reliving the Game in Cleveland and Denver

Ever since that day in January 1987, whenever a Cleveland professional sports team nears a potential championship, people recall this game. Every time the city makes a positive public relations splash, the Browns' collapse appears in headlines, reminding readers of all the negatives in recent Cleveland history. It's as if Cleveland has been trying to heal the wound of Elway's dagger ever since that winter day. It's as if the AFC Championship game against the Broncos represents all the negative aspects of the city on the shores of Lake Erie over the past half-century. A Cleveland team came excruciatingly close to reaching Super Bowl glory—only to come up short. When Clevelanders recall that game, they rarely remember the triumphs of the rest of the season, and they do not recall that the Browns were one of the best teams in the NFL. Instead, they connect it to the ongoing ineptitudes of a city that had for decades attempted to revitalize a lampooned image in popular culture. When remembering the game, for example, former player (and current Baltimore Ravens general manager) Ozzie Newsome reminisced: "The city at that point was the butt of a lot of jokes around the country. Defaulting, the river burning, just a lot of negative things being joked about." This football contest thus remains in the back of the minds of Clevelanders whenever other hardships appear.

Much of this rhetoric derives from the context of Cleveland's collapse. The city seemed to be undergoing revitalization—both economically and in sports. Certainly, in the last few decades of the twentieth century and the first few years of the twenty-first, Cleveland attempted to reinvent itself. While the city experienced economic decline and social tensions throughout the postwar era, in the 1980s, the press believed Cleveland became a "comeback city." It came out of economic default, construction on Key Tower (now the largest building in the city's skyline) began, and numerous efforts to clean up pollution and crime, and improve civic infrastructure took place.

But, sports were also supposed to be part of this comeback.

In the 1980s, Cleveland teams came agonizingly close to reaching championships. In 1980, the Browns needed only a field goal to secure a playoff victory against the Oakland Raiders, but quarterback Brian Sipe instead threw an interception in the end zone. Ted Stepien purchased the Cavaliers in 1980 hoping to reinvigorate the basketball franchise, but he made so many poor trades that the NBA created the Stepien rule, preventing teams from trading consecutive first round picks. In 1987, *Sports Illustrated* picked Cleveland to win baseball's World Series; the team instead lost 101 games. Cleveland sports, it seemed, was cursed.

Slowly, things began to change. After Bernie Kosar, a talented quarter-back from the University of Miami, chose to be drafted during the NFL's supplemental draft (instead of the regular draft) in order to be taken by his hometown Browns, the team started to find success. During his second season, 1986, Kosar threw for more than 3,800 yards and seventeen touchdowns. In the playoffs, the team seemed to be one of destiny. In their playoff game against the New York Jets a week before the showdown with Denver, the Browns won a thrilling double-overtime game, even overcoming three missed field goals from their aging kicker, Mark Moseley. It seemed that, finally, Cleveland would not come up short.

The end of the game against Denver, however, proved otherwise. And misfortunes for Cleveland teams continued throughout the next few decades, providing ample opportunities for Clevelanders to relive the game. As former Browns executive Ernie Accorsi said in the recent ESPN *30 for 30*, "Believeland," "it's 30 years [later], and it's no different."

The following year, for instance, at the end of the 1987–1988 season, running back Earnest Byner fumbled near the goal line at the end of the conference championship, and another chance at the Super Bowl was lost (Cleveland would lose again to the Broncos, this time in lopsided fashion, in the 1989 AFC Championship match). Following the 1995 season, Browns owner Art Modell shocked the sports world when he moved his team to Baltimore. The baseball team lost twice in the World Series in the 1990s, coming within one inning of a championship in 1997 (these narratives reemerged again in 2016 when Cleveland lost the World Series to the Chicago Cubs after leading the series three games to one). Michael Jordan and the Chicago Bulls shocked the Cavs with "The Shot" in 1989, and the team remained mediocre throughout the 1990s. The Cavs found success with LeBron James as its star, but the dominant San Antonio Spurs quickly swept them when they reached the 2007 NBA Finals. Ultimately, as journalist Todd Leopold wrote when James decided to leave Cleveland in 2010 for the Miami Heat, "It never seems to end." The curse that for some recently ended with the Cavs' 2016 NBA Finals victory, continued to resonate in the city's sports world.

Of course, everything was different in the Mile High City.

The day after the game, the *Denver Post* boasted, calling Elway's march down the field a "Drive to destiny." The game is remembered as the moment when Elway became a hero in Denver. As David Ramsey of the *Colorado Gazette* recalled, "The Elway of the 1986 season was not yet the Elway who inspired men to name their sons and dogs after him." Yet, soon after the game, he became just that. *Sports Illustrated* writer S. L. Price called him a "comeback wizard." Elway took over the zeitgeist of a city that needed a symbol of hope and prosperity. According to the *Denver Post's* Irv Moss, "[T]he 1980s will forever be remembered in Denver as a time when Elwaymania pushed the Broncos to the forefront of the local sports scene."

However, in the late 1980s and early 1990s, Denver seemed to reach a plateau, both economically and in sports. The Broncos won the AFC title three times, but lost the Super Bowl in each instance, often in blowout fashion. Likewise, the Denver economy waned in the late 1980s, leading some to believe it would enter another depression, similar to the 1930s. Yet, in the 1990s, things began to change for the Rocky Mountain metropolis. The new Denver Airport allowed the city to compete with other western cities like Dallas. New opportunities for minorities made it a city comparable to the large urban metropolises on the East Coast, and new physical structures gave the city a needed image of renaissance. The Broncos also got over their Lombardi Trophy hump. In the late 1990s, Elway and the Broncos won two Super Bowls, securing the quarterback's place in football lore and his position as a Denver legend.

As Denver became one of the most economically and culturally successful cities in the United States, the 1986 AFC Championship game against the Browns therefore endures as an important moment of revelry, a symbol and turning point for the success of the Mile High City over the past quarter century. Denver's success made the memories of the battle against Cleveland crisper and more memorable. A year after the game, for example, as the two teams geared up to play again in the AFC Championship game, Elway had then simply told a reporter, "It was too long ago for me to remember." Twenty-five years later, Elway could now reminisce on the game, fondly remembering that Cleveland and Denver is "a great rivalry and has been for a long time."

Looking back at the game does not elicit negative reactions for Denverites as it does for the Cleveland faithful. Rather, the ending of this game illuminates nostalgic visions of Denver's progressive past.

0:42 on the clock

Facing third down-and-one, Elway dropped back yet again with a defender closing in on him. Rocketing a pass into the middle of the end zone, a few inches above the grasp of a Browns defensive lineman, Elway connected with Jackson, who slid into painted grass as he held on to the ball.

Touchdown. Game tied, 20–20.

In overtime, the Broncos forced the Browns to punt on their first possession. Elway then led Denver sixty yards to set up a field goal attempt. Rich Karlis's thirty-three-yard kick barely made it inside the left upright, but the field goal was good. The Broncos had won.

Karlis's kick sent the team to the Super Bowl in Southern California and catapulted Elway to football legend. The Browns trudged off the field. What looked like a triumph and a shot at the Lombardi Trophy ended in despair. Instead of lining up in Pasadena's sunny Rose Bowl stadium, the Browns spent the United States's unofficial winter holiday in front of their television sets.

The scoring series—those "fifteen dramatic plays" as commentator Dick Enberg immediately dubbed them during the NBC postgame broadcast—lasted just under five minutes. Yet, people in both cities have continued to relive those moments that say so much about the past, present, and future of both metropolises. Whether good or bad, joyful or painful, this short series of football plays will forever be known in Cleveland and Denver, simply, as "The Drive."

For Further Reading

Abbott, Carl, Stephen J. Leonard, and Thomas J. Noel. *Colorado: A History of the Centennial State*. 5th ed. Boulder: University Press of Colorado, 2013.

Henkel, Frank M. *Cleveland Browns History*. Charleston, S.C.: Arcadia Publishing, 2005.

Huler, Scott. *On Being Brown: What It Means to be a Cleveland Browns Fan*. Cleveland: Gray and Company, 1999.

Martin, Russell. *The Color Orange: A Super Bowl Season With the Denver Broncos*. New York: Henry Holt, 1987.

Miller, Carol Poh, and Robert A. Wheeler. *Cleveland: A Concise History, 1796–1996*. 2nd ed. Bloomington: Indiana University Press, 1997.

23

The Rise and Fall of
The National Sports Daily

DENNIS GILDEA

The National Sports Daily was less than six weeks old in March 1990 when a letter crossed the desk of editor-in-chief Frank Deford. It came from the Beverly Hills law firm of Weinstein and Hart, and in it Jerome E. Weinstein informed Deford that his publication was in violation of Section 990 of the California Civil Code and that the newspaper must "cease and desist forthwith" from displaying drawings of Abbott and Costello as art for its "Playground" page. Weinstein and Hart, it turned out, represented the heirs of the comedy duo. "Abbott and Costello Enterprises," the letter said, "own and control all right, title, and interest in and to the likenesses of the late Abbott and Costello." Hence, Deford's publication was ordered to "cease and desist forthwith in your utilization . . . of Abbott and Costello."

Deford had elected to use line drawings of Abbott and Costello as a tribute to their legendary "Who's On First" baseball comedy routine and as a sign that sports and the writing of sports should be fun. "All stats and standings make Jack a dull boy," Deford wrote. "And so . . . we put together a silly little section with good old Joe Palooka and puzzles and tidbits and other nonsense. And one day in a moment of terribly minor inspiration, I thought we'll honor Abbott and Costello by putting them at the top of the page." Minor inspiration, though, led to the threat of impending litigation; regardless, Deford once again could not resist the impulse to have fun. "L.A. Law lives!" he wrote in a column headlined "Abbott & Costello, you're not funny anymore. Cease and desist forthwith. Forthwith! And people in other countries (like Japan where there are virtually no lawyers) wonder why we make jokes comparing lawyers to laboratory rats."

Using the Abbott and Costello images typified one aspect of how Deford thought his newspaper should cover sports. Another especially noteworthy aspect of the paper's coverage was the excellence of its writing and reporting. Alex French and Howie Kahn wrote the best review of what *The National* tried to accomplish. Their "The Greatest Paper That Ever Died" appeared in www .grantland.com. "Radically brilliant. Absurdly ahead of its time," they wrote. Significantly, the letter from the Beverly Hills law firm proved more consistent with the cultural trends of the late-twentieth century United States than did the attempt to launch a thoroughly literate daily all-sports newspaper. On June 13, 1991, Deford and his staff of talented writers and editors were forced to "cease and desist forthwith" from publishing. *The National Sports Daily,* the latest and perhaps the last noble experiment in literate daily print journalism in the nation, succumbed to financial exigencies and the lamentable fact "that Americans read less, younger Americans least of all." In an unsigned editorial in the last issue, a piece that smacks stylistically of Deford's touch, he offered this observation, "It is cold comfort, but at least we can take satisfaction that, as Anita Loos wrote of Lorelie Lee, 'She always believed in the old adage— Leave them while you're looking good.'" It risks stating the obvious to note that few, if any, sports sections anywhere quoted Anita Loos.

But necessary exposition before further elegy. *The National*'s home office was located at 666 Fifth Avenue in New York City, a Manhattan tower that came complete with architectural excesses that included a $52,000 brass eagle in the lobby. The foreboding symbolism of the street number—666—was not lost on the staff. News editor Nathan Atsales called it "the devil office." The paper also had branch offices in major sports cities throughout the United States. *The National* was a tabloid-sized newspaper that came out five days a week from January 31, 1990 until June 13, 1991. "I don't remember it at all," a responder to a Web site wrote in 2014. "Did you have to subscribe to it, or could you purchase it anywhere?" Ah, there was the rub. The paper sold at newsstands for fifty cents and before long for seventy-five cents. But unreliable distribution contributed mightily to its demise. Associate editor Vince Doria remembered, "There was a recession going on. Advertising wasn't in great supply. The ability to distribute the paper, printing and distributing, was a mess. Our writers in the field were saying, 'The same paper's been in the box [sales boxes on city streets] for five straight days.'"

While the business side of *The National* was falling miserably short of turning a profit, the editorial side was a glittering success. The paper tried to cover sports in ways that no other American publication ever had. The idea for the paper as well as the money backing it came from Emilio Azcarraga, a prominent Mexican businessman with a net worth generally thought to

Front page of the final edition of *The National*. (Courtesy of Frank Deford.)

make him the richest man in his country. Launching and trying to sustain *The National*, however, would deplete even his bank account. Before the journalistic experiment went under, Azcarraga lost approximately 150 million dollars.

Ironically Azcarraga, who died in 1997, had no professional background in print journalism. Most of his fortune was derived from a television empire, *Tele-*

visa, which specialized in producing Mexican *novelas*, relatively short narrative dramas similar to the soaps popular in the United States, that were translated into any number of different languages and distributed by satellite to viewers in countries throughout the world. Nevertheless, Azcarraga desperately wanted to break into the North American print journalism market, and the vehicle to do so, he reasoned, would be an all-sports daily. "Why is it that the most developed country in the world doesn't have a daily sports newspaper?" he asked Peter Price, the paper's future publisher, by way of a tactic to convince Price that the time was ripe for such a paper in the United States. "We've got one in Mexico. The Italians have two. The Brits have tabloid sports papers. *L'equipe* in France is reigning strong, and Japan has a sports paper." Price, at the time publisher of the *New York Post*, was persuaded to take the same position on Azcarraga's sports start-up, and he soon lured his Princeton classmate, Deford, from *Sports Illustrated* to become *The National*'s editor.

Understandably impressed by *El Tigre*'s, as Azcarraga liked to be known, determination, and bankroll, Deford assembled an impressive collection of sportswriters plucked from the staffs of major American newspapers. Included in that number were football writer Chris Mortensen and auto-racing specialist Ed Hinton from the *Atlanta Journal-Constitution;* John Feinstein, Tony Kornheiser, and Dave Kindred from the *Washington Post;* Mike Lupica from the *New York Daily News;* and Leigh Montville and Charles Pierce from the *Boston Globe,* to name just a few. "A lot of people signed on right away," Deford noted. "So much of it was the money. You had to have more money to make people take the risk" of leaving a secure position. But for almost all of the writers who came aboard, money may have been secondary to the chance to be part of sports journalism history. "Here was this great adventure and chance to invent something new," Rob Fleder said. "This was as close to a frontier as we had."

For his part, Deford was aware of being a major figure in a pioneering effort, but he also had a historical perspective on *The National*'s place in American sports journalism. Deford christened the paper, somewhat prosaically, *The National Sports Daily,* but he admitted that his original idea was to name it *The Spirit,* an homage to William Trotter Porter's *Spirit of the Times,* a genuinely pioneering sports weekly that Porter began publishing in 1831. Like *The National*, the *Spirit of the Times* resulted from its founder's recognition of the importance of sports in American culture, as historian Norris W. Yates wrote in a biography of Porter. And like *The National*, Porter's paper eventually ceased publication because of financial difficulties.

During *The National*'s brief existence, though, the paper left its mark on sportswriting. When editors Glenn Stout and David Halberstam compiled and published *The Best American Sports Writing of 1991*, four pieces from *The National*, more than any other publication, made the list. Peter Richmond's "The Sports Fan," a profile of legendary Los Angeles sportswriter Jim Murray, was cited, as was Richmond's "Death of a Cowboy," a piece that displayed the writer's stylistic elegance as well as the paper's eagerness to go beyond the boundaries of traditional mainstream American sports. Richmond began his profile of cowboy Lane Frost, who was killed in a bull-riding incident in a Wyoming rodeo, this way, "Some don't join the diaspora to the cities, to fill up the buildings and prowl the gray streets. Some decide to stay behind and to work the land, and to work with the land—to live on it and play on it, dwarfed by its permanence, and secure in it." He continued, "Because there is always this about the land, about prairie, pond and mountain: they never go away. Beneath a roof of sky, yesterday and tomorrow always have a great deal in common. And to live here, planted on the planet's surface, so that you can sense the roll of the seasons, is, inevitably, to feel some of that same permanence for yourself." Richmond's lyrical treatment of the American West and the men who revere it was an example of the masterful long-form pieces published in a section known as "Main Event" writing, a regular feature of *The National*.

In addition to Richmond's two efforts, Charles Pierce's "Thieves of Time," a profile of Negro League baseball great Cool Papa Bell, and Johnette Howard's profile of Detroit Red Wings enforcer Joey Kocur, appeared in the collection of best sportswriting. Howard's article was one of just three pieces in the anthology written by women reporters. About her recruitment by Deford, Howard recalled, "I was twenty-eight when Frank called and said he wanted me to come to New York. I desperately wanted to do features. We went to lunch, talked for two-and-a-half hours and drank two bottles of wine."

While the four pieces included in the Halberstam and Stout anthology can be categorized as feature stories, similarly stylish writing appeared in *The National*'s next-day coverage of events. One of the biggest—and most surprising—stories of 1990 was Buster Douglas's knockout victory over the seemingly indestructible heavyweight champion, Mike Tyson. Unlike virtually every other media outlet, *The National* covered the prefight buildup not by recycling the conventional ring-insider narrative that gave Douglas little chance for a win. "As noon approaches on Sunday in Japan, a bell will clang like dawn breaking upon an execution, and slowly all the people will climb down from the ring to their seats leaving James Douglas there to fight the snorting Mike Tyson," Ian Thomsen wrote. "An execution!" Exactly what everyone expected. But Thomsen's lead paragraph continued, "For months the world has been teasing the challenger, laughing at all his hard work, telling him in the newspapers and public places how easily and badly he will lose the fight. But in this moment's eve, he might sense a sudden hush of respect. They may see him seriously for the first time, meaning to put down this bully."

Thomsen quoted Douglas as deriding the "non-believers," an exceedingly large group that included Douglas's wife, who walked out of his life a few months earlier. In the tenth round of the bout in Tokyo, Douglas converted the non-believers and shocked the few American reporters who were on hand to cover the event. *The National*'s Sam Donnellon was at ringside, and his report, "Countdown for Buster," ran on the day after the fight. It not only covered details of the bout but also analyzed the postfight claim by promoter Don King that Tyson was victimized by a long-count referee when Tyson floored Douglas in the eighth round. Donnellon led his story with this sentence: "It started like a disease, this idea that Mike Tyson had really won the heavyweight championship fight with James (Buster) Douglas Saturday night." In many ways, *The National*'s coverage of the fight was indicative of the way it approached sports reporting—the story was a veritable exclusive, and it came at great financial cost. Still, assistant managing editor Rick Jaffe said, "The Tyson-Buster Douglas story in February 1990 put us on the map."

Staff writer Tom Friend was the only reporter in the hospital with the family and friends of Hank Gathers as the Loyola Marymount basketball star was fighting for his life. Gathers had collapsed during a game earlier that March day in 1990. Friend noted later that he made it a point not to intrude on the family, but he described the scene when they got the news that Gathers had died. "Hospital priests entered, but there was relative calm. At about 7:10 P.M., the university physician, Dan Hyslop, mussed with sweat, approached them all; he was wearing a Nebraska Cornhuskers cap. He motioned the clan into a room, whereupon he delivered the grave news." Friend's re-creation of the scene was emotional, sensitive, and excellent spot reporting.

Even on the day in 1991 when the paper folded, it covered a major sports event with more style and depth than other publications. Ted Green was in Inglewood, California, when the Chicago Bulls and Michael Jordan clinched the NBA championship with a 105–101 win over the Los Angeles Lakers. Green wrote, "The city of Chicago had more than two decades of unfulfilled expectations in professional basketball lifted from its legendary broad shoulders Wednesday night when the Bulls won the first NBA title since joining the league in 1966."

When the end of the paper's run came, Dave Kindred was in Chaska, Minnesota, preparing to cover the United States Open golf tournament. Deford called to tell him that the grand experiment that was *The National* was over. "I'm here for the U.S. Open golf tournament and the summer sun is cooking the place," Kindred wrote in his column. "But as I write this, an hour after the news, I feel sorrow's chilling emptiness." It was a sensation shared by the entire staff, regardless of where they were when they got the news. Deford remembered the moment, "But one day, after only eighteen months of issues, I had to clamber up onto a desk in the newsroom and tell the men and women clustered around me that we were finished. The last great newspaper experiment in America had failed." The page-one headline read: "WE HAD A BALL: The fat lady sings our song."

The publication was a journalistic effort, Kindred contended, that "reached for the stars." That reach, however worthy and ambitious, proved too costly for even the deep-pocketed Azcarraga to continue to support. "We wanted to have fun, because the games are fun, and we wanted to take a stand, because the corroding effects of big-bucks sports are so seldom challenged," Kindred wrote. Everyone associated with *The National* was dedicated "to show how good a newspaper can be," a dedication to the pursuit of excellence that ran counter to "Wizard of Oz journalism: no heart, no brain, no courage."

Those qualities, so rarely found in the news business, were exhibited by another newspaper and its staff working more than a century earlier than the time when *The National* flickered on and off the journalism scene. Another editor attempted to do for news coverage what Deford and his staff attempted to do for sports coverage, both working "to show how good a newspaper can be." The parallels in these two journalistic ventures are striking. In 1881, E. L. Godkin assumed editorship of the *Nation,* a magazine, and its sister publication, the *New York Post,* a newspaper. What the United States needed, largely because nothing else like it existed, Godkin reasoned, was a "high-grade journal of opinion." Godkin attracted a literate, intelligent staff, and he had the good editorial sense to let them write. Historian Allan Nevins observed, "Godkin showed at once a distinctive style, a refreshing penetration, and a skill in ironic analysis never before equaled in American journalism." But even in a late-nineteenth-century America awash with newspapers that were turning a profit, the bottom line loomed large. Neither the *Nation* nor Godkin's *New York Post* flourished financially.

Make the transition in journalistic eras from the final decades of the nineteenth century to the final decade of the twentieth century, a time when commentators made similar glowing observations about Deford and his newspaper. The *New York Times'* story on the paper's demise paid tribute to the quality of the writing and also may have pointed out one of the key reasons for its failure. "But *The National*'s sophisticated writing talent was somewhat unsuited to its audience," an audience that the story characterized as composed of "rabid fans" who "spent much of their leisure time watching sports on television." So, the dilemma facing Godkin in the nineteenth century proved much the same as the dilemma facing Deford at the end of the twentieth century—the gap separating highbrow and lowbrow, sophisticated writers and the masses who never read much of anything. Or, as in the case of Godkin's journals, customers who preferred the popular yellow journalism of Joseph Pulitzer and William Randolph Hearst to sophisticated, analytical writing. For Deford and his writers, too many sports fans in the late twentieth century were getting their information from ESPN and radio talk shows.

Typically, the content of *The National* was so well written that it appealed primarily to other writers. Features editor David Granger lamented, "What Rob [Fleder] and I did was separate from the daily news operation. We were supposed to create five 4,000-word magazine stories every week." They were up to the challenge, but the combination of more traditional next-day game coverage with the "long form" feature pieces puzzled even those on the paper's staff. "Were we a paper or a magazine?" Nathan Atsales asked after the fact. The long-form writers, he recalled, questioned whether the publication needed next-day game coverage, while the staffers who came from a sports news background argued for the necessity of "the scores." It was a fascinating argument, one made moot by the financial drain that killed the paper. In sports, "the scores" tell the basic tale of who won and who lost. In the end, *The National* lost. So, too, for that matter, did American sports journalism. Abbott, Costello, and Deford did not get the last laugh.

For Further Reading

Deford, Frank. *Over Time: My Life as a Sportswriter*. New York: Atlantic Monthly Press, 2012.

Yates, Norris W. *William T. Porter and the Spirit of the Times*. Baton Rouge: Louisiana State University Press, 1957.

Afterword

The Future of Sports Memories

The authors of the essays in this book hope you have enjoyed reading their work. They are all experts, and they have gladly shared their views on some of the greatest events and personalities in the history of American sports. Realistically, they do not expect this book will end any debates or bring discussions of these provocative topics to an end. The collective memories covered here are robust. They are mythic, and regardless of how well academic historians dissect them, they will endure. Nevertheless, it might be worthwhile to speculate about the future of American sports memories.

Nearly every event covered in this book occurred before the advent of what most of us call "cable television." Sports fans experienced these events in a variety of ways: some few in person, others by reading newspapers, magazines, or books, others by listening to the radio, and later, by watching local or national telecasts. No wonder our memories differ! Yet, today, it is no stretch to say that the majority of us experience current sporting events in the same way: through access provided by a small number of television networks coming into our homes—or onto our devices—via cable or satellite. Given this aggregate approach, given the way we all see the same things together, doesn't it make sense to suggest that the truth will win out and that myth may very well disappear? Television is a powerful medium that necessarily conveys certitude and dispels ambiguity. With slow motion, stop action, and instant replay available from multiple angles, is not the goal to determine what really happened and peremptorily end debate?

Maybe, and yet television's power is so immense that sometimes an attempt to dispel a myth might actually distort the truth and serve to create and enshrine a new myth in its place. Consider this unusual example. In the spring of 2016, PBS broadcast *Jackie Robinson*, a two-part, four-hour documentary co-produced and co-directed by the eminent Ken Burns. Overall an excellent piece of work, the film spent considerable time addressing one of the hallowed chapters in the story of baseball's great experiment, namely, that at some point early in Robinson's career, Brooklyn Dodgers shortstop Pee Wee Reese showed support for his pioneering teammate by walking across the field and putting his arm around him.

Reese was a southerner from Louisville. Moreover, he played the same position Robinson had played in the Negro Leagues before his one year in the minors with the Montreal Royals. Thus, for both personal and professional reasons, Reese could have opposed Branch Rickey's plan to integrate baseball. But he did not. The evidence on this point is beyond dispute, but what is less than certain is whether Reese embraced Robinson on the field. A nice story, some have said, an act of gentlemanly courage if it occurred, but show me the proof.

After the Burns broadcast, attorney and historian Brad Snyder analyzed the case pro and con. In Peter Golenbock's *Bums*, an oral history of the Dodgers published in 1984, pitcher Rex Barney recalled that Reese put his arm around Robinson in 1947, his rookie season, perhaps in Philadelphia, where racism was pervasive, or in Cincinnati, the National League city closest to Reese's home. What reason would Barney have to gild the lily? Robinson himself recalled the incident, too, but he placed it in Boston in 1948, and he testified to its veracity several times: in a 1952 interview in a magazine called *Focus*; in an article in *Look* magazine in 1955; in a talk to the Connecticut Sports Writers' Alliance in 1959; and in his autobiography, *I Never Had It Made*, published in 1972.

The trouble is, say the doubters, that no daily newspaper in any of these major-league cities made mention of such a newsworthy gesture by Reese. Nor did Robinson mention the deed in *Jackie Robinson: My Own Story*, published in May 1948. Dodgers center fielder Duke Snider also was bewildered. "I was there," he told Snyder in 2006, "but I don't remember the incident. I thought it was in Cincinnati. That's what I read."

Given this ambiguity, perhaps it would have been best for Burns to leave this story just where it was, a myth whose exactitude has been lost in the mists of history. But no. Burns sought to be definitive, and he used Jonathan Eig, author of *Opening Day*, to remove all doubt. "Today it's remembered in statues, in children's books, but I don't think it happened," Eig said on camera. "The myth serves a really nice purpose. Unfortunately, it is a myth."

That Eig later tempered his denial in his blog hardly mattered. It is the Burns documentary, with its enormous viewership and impact, that framed the new narrative. Burns later doubled down, telling ESPN categorically that it "never happened."

Thus, we have a peculiar situation. Modern research, we hope, should be able to explore a complex situation and, if uncertainty deserves to remain in place, to leave it there. Burns, on the other hand, did the past a disservice. He found ambiguity and wrangled from it an unwarranted certainty, in the process creating a new sports myth. In the future, given Burns's gravitas and the import of his work, we can expect our collective memory to recall that Pee Wee Reese categorically did not put his arm around Jackie Robinson. That would be a shame.

Television and the sports networks that dominate the market pack considerable wallop. But power does not always lead to clarity. Sports myths will continue to exist and, over time, their numbers may increase, not decrease.

Contributors

THOMAS L. ALTHERR is emeritus professor of history at Metropolitan State University of Denver, where he has taught an American baseball history course since 1991. He has published several articles on early baseball history, two of which earned SABR/McFarland Publishers Research Awards in 2001 and 2012. He also co-wrote Charlie Metro's 2002 baseball autobiography, *Safe by a Mile*, and continues to research a book about pre-1845 North American ball games.

CHAD CARLSON is an assistant professor in the Kinesiology Department at Hope College in Holland, Michigan. He is also the men's junior varsity basketball coach. His research centers on the sociocultural aspects of sport and focuses on the philosophy of play and games, sports ethics, and the history of basketball. His book, *Making March Madness*, will be published in 2017.

RICHARD C. CREPEAU is professor of history at the University of Central Florida. He is the author of *Baseball: America's Diamond Mind* and numerous academic articles on the history of sport. He has written a column of sport commentary for the Sport Literature Association for nearly twenty years.

MARK DYRESON is professor of kinesiology, affiliate professor of history, and director of research and educational programs for the Center for the Study of Sports in Society at Penn State University, where he teaches undergraduate and graduate courses in the history of sport. He has published numerous articles and books on the history of sport, including *Making the American Team: Sport, Culture and the Olympic Experience* and *Crafting Patriotism for Global Dominance: America at the Olympics*. He has won several awards for his writing, including the 2006 Webb-Smith Essay Contest in American history, the 2001 best article award from the *International Journal of the History of Sport*, the 1994 best article award for social sciences from the Utah Academy of Arts, Sciences, and Letters, the 1993 best article award from the Missouri Conference on History, and the 1989 graduate student essay contest from the North American Society for Sport History Graduate Student Essay Contest, 1989.

MICHAEL EZRA is professor of American multicultural studies at Sonoma State University. He is the author of *Muhammad Ali: The Making of an Icon* and *Civil Rights Movement: People and Perspectives* and editor of *The Economic Civil Rights Movement: African Americans and the Struggle for Economic Power*. He is the founding editor of the *Journal of Civil and Human Rights*, published by the University of Illinois Press. His next book, co-edited with Carlo Rotella, is titled *The Bittersweet Science: Fifteen Writers in the Ring, the Gym, and at Ringside*.

LARRY R. GERLACH, former president of the Society for American Baseball Research, has retired as professor of history at the University of Utah, where he taught courses on the history of sport in America and on the Olympics, ancient to modern. His writings include *The Men in Blue: Conversations With Umpires*.

STEVEN GIETSCHIER is associate professor of history at Lindenwood University, St. Charles, Missouri. Formerly the research director at *The Sporting News*, he has written widely on various topics in twentieth-century American sports history.

DENNIS GILDEA, a former sportswriter and news reporter, is a professor of communications at Springfield College, where he teaches courses in sport literature, media history, and sport and American culture. He is the author of *Hoop Crazy: The Lives of Clair Bee and Chip Hilton*, as well as essays on sport history and the history of sports writing.

STEPHEN HARDY retired from the University of New Hampshire in 2014. His publications include *How Boston Played* and *Sport Marketing* (with Bernie

Mullin and Bill Sutton), which has been translated into eight languages. He is a founder of the Charles Holt Archives of American Hockey, which are located at UNH's Dimond Library. He is working (with Andrew Holman) on a book entitled *Coolest Game: A Global History of Ice Hockey*.

LESLIE HEAPHY is associate professor of history at Kent State University at Stark. She has written or edited four books on the Negro Leagues and women's baseball and one on the 1986 New York Mets. Heaphy also serves as the editor of the peer-reviewed national journal *Black Ball*, published by McFarland Publishing. She is also a member of the Board of Directors for the Society of American Baseball Research and the committee chair for the annual Jerry Malloy Negro League Conference.

ANDREW D. LINDEN is an assistant professor of sport management at Adrian College in Adrian, Michigan. His research on sport, politics, and historiography appears in several journals.

DANIEL A. NATHAN is professor of American studies at Skidmore College, the author of the award-winning *Saying It's So: A Cultural History of the Black Sox Scandal*, and the editor of *Rooting For the Home Team: Sport, Community and Identity*. Past president of the North American Society for Sport History, Nathan has served as the film, media, and museum reviews editor for the *Journal of Sport History* and on several editorial boards.

MURRY NELSON is professor emeritus of education and American studies at Penn State University and a former Fulbright Scholar at the University of Iceland, the Norwegian Ministry of Education and Church, and the University of Debrecen in Hungary, where he held the Lazlo Orszagh Chair in American Studies. He is the author of several works on the history of basketball, most recently *Big Ten Basketball, 1943–1972*.

LINDSAY PARKS PIEPER is assistant professor of sport management at Lynchburg College in Lynchburg, Virginia. Her book, *Sex Testing: Gender Policing in Women's Sports*, examines the history of sex testing in elite sport.

SAMUEL O. REGALADO is professor of history at California State University, Stanislaus. He is the author of *Viva Baseball! Latin Major Leaguers and Their Special Hunger* and *Nikkei Baseball: Japanese American Players from Immigration and Internment to the Major Leagues*. He also co-authored *Latinos* *in U.S. Sport: A History of Isolation, Cultural Identity, and Acceptance,* and co-edited *Mexican Americans and Sports: A Reader on Athletics and Barrio Life* and *Sport and the Law: Historical and Cultural Intersections.* Regalado was a 1994 Smithsonian Fellow and 1998 Davies Fellow at the University of San Francisco.

JAIME SCHULTZ is an associate professor in the Department of Kinesiology at Pennsylvania State University. In addition to multiple journal articles and book chapters, she is the author or editor of several books, including *Qualifying Times: Points of Change in US Women's Sport* (University of Illinois Press, 2014) and *Moments of Impact: Injury, Racialized Memory, and Reconciliation in College Football* (University of Nebraska Press, 2016).

MAUREEN SMITH is a professor in the Department of Kinesiology and Health Science at California State University, Sacramento, where she teaches courses in sport history and sport sociology. Her research interests cover a range of topics, including African American sport after World War II, the Olympic Games, and material culture in sport, specifically sport statues. She is the co-author (with Rita Liberti) of *(Re)Presenting Wilma Rudolph* (Syracuse University Press, 2015).

RONALD A. SMITH is professor emeritus at Penn State University, having been affiliated with the university since 1968. His research has focused on the study of intercollegiate athletics. *Play for Pay: A History of Big-Time College Athletic Reform* emphasizes the role of students, faculty, coaches and athletic directors, presidents, and boards of trustees in reform movements. His recent book on the Jerry Sandusky scandal is *Wounded Lions: Joe Paterno, Jerry Sandusky and the Crises in Penn State Athletics,* published by the University of Illinois Press in 2016.

ROBERT TRUMPBOUR is an associate professor of communications at Penn State Altoona. He is author and editor of three recent texts, *The New Cathedrals: Politics and Media in the History of Stadium Construction; Cathedrals of Sport: The Rise of Stadiums in the Modern United States;* and *The Eighth Wonder of the World: The Life of Houston's Iconic Astrodome.*

TRAVIS VOGAN is assistant professor in the School of Journalism and Mass Communication and the Department of American Studies at the University of Iowa. He is the author of *Keepers of the Flame: NFL Films and the Rise of Sports Media* and *ESPN: The Making of a Sports Media Empire.*

DAVID K. WIGGINS is a professor in the School of Recreation, Health, and Tourism at George Mason University in Manassas, Virginia. He has published extensively on the history of African American participation in sport and physical activity. Among his books are *Glory Bound: Black Athletes in a White America*; *The Unlevel Playing Field: A Documentary History of the African American Experience in Sport*; *Out of the Shadows: A Biographical History of African American Athletes*; and *Rivals: Legendary Matchups that Made Sport History*.

KEVIN WITHERSPOON is professor of history and chair of the Department of History and Philosophy at Lander University in Greenwood, South Carolina. In 2014 he was recognized with Lander's Distinguished Faculty award. His book, *Before the Eyes of the World: Mexico and the 1968 Olympics* won the 2009 North American Society for Sport History (NASSH) Annual Book Award. He has published a number of articles related to sports during the Cold War and is currently researching the United States cultural/athletic exchange programs of the Cold War.

DAVID ZANG, a professor in Towson University's Department of Kinesiology, is a social historian whose work has explored race, the 1960s, sports, and pop music. His 1995 biography, *Fleet Walker's Divided Heart,* won the inaugural Seymour Medal for Outstanding History from the Society for American Baseball Research. In 1999 his article on America's 1972 Olympic wrestlers was honored as Notable Sports Writing by Houghton-Mifflin's annual *The Best American Sports Writing.* He is also the author of *SportsWar: Athletes in the Age of Aquarius* (2002) and *I Wore Babe Ruth's Hat: Field Notes from a Life in Sports* (2015).

Index

The University of Illinois Press
is a founding member of the
Association of American University Presses.

Composed in 10.5/13 Minion Pro
with Frutiger LT Std display
by Lisa Connery
at the University of Illinois Press
Manufactured by Cushing-Malloy, Inc.

University of Illinois Press
1325 South Oak Street
Champaign, IL 61820-6903
www.press.uillinois.edu